THE GOLDEN NUGGETS FOR SUCCESS AND HAPPINESS

DR. M. SREE PRATHAP

ISBN
Paperback 979-8-89744-616-2
Hardcase 979-8-89929-686-4

Dear Readers,

I am a voracious reader and have read numerous books throughout my life. I used to share insightful observations and valid points on social media, and one day, I decided to publish them in a book so more people could benefit from them.

A golden nugget is a beautiful, naturally occurring piece of original gold! The golden nuggets we explore in this book symbolise valuable advice, insightful words of wisdom, and delightful food for thought. While placer mining helps recover those shiny natural gold nuggets, the fantastic concepts of golden nuggets in this book are revealed by diving deeper into its enriching contents. As the Dalai Lama says, **"The purpose of our lives is to be happy."** When we are happy, we can more effectively address our challenges and problems. Happiness also enhances productivity. According to research from the Harvard Business Review, people experience a 31 per cent increase in productivity and overall performance when they are happy compared to when they are unhappy. In this book, I aim to consolidate my knowledge and share my thoughts concisely so that others can understand. As a doctor, I have provided scientific explanations; as a psychiatrist, I have articulated psychological concepts. Additionally, I have shared my experiences as a successful entrepreneur, running a hospital service in India and a teaching business in the UK. I have contemplated several questions raised by audiences during my seminars on managing stress and maintaining wellness, providing answers and explanations in this book.

"Success is getting what you want; happiness is wanting what you get." – W. P. Kinsella, Canadian novelist. This highlights the distinction between success and happiness, encouraging a balanced approach to life. Success is pursued by achieving goals and reaching external benchmarks. In contrast, happiness relates to one's internal state and perspective, cultivated through a sincere appreciation of the present moment. Happiness resides in our minds; it is a choice. Success requires discipline, consistency, a positive mindset, and smart work. Have faith in your hard work; don't rely on luck to accomplish everything for you. Cultivate patience and learn to make sacrifices while maintaining discipline; you must give up many things to achieve your goals. Consistency transforms the ordinary into excellence.

Motivation drives you forward, but discipline ensures continuous growth. Perseverance and resilience yield rewards; learn to be adaptable and flexible in the face of change. Manage your body, mind, environment, and time effectively. This app roach will help you lead a more successful and fulfilling life. People want to know how to achieve it all, and this book will guide you on that journey.

Read each chapter twice to understand and apply the concepts in your practical life. **'Knowing something without using it is like not knowing it at all.'** After reading, try to implement what you've learned. It is challenging to walk the talk, but I practice what I preach. I follow the concepts outlined in this book, which have helped me achieve success and happiness. If I can do it, then you can too.

I truly hope you enjoy reading this book.

Dr. M. Sree Prathap, MBBS, MRCPsych.

Dedicated to my beloved grandfather, Gnanaoli Mr. Mahalingam Pillai, who provided me with a strong knowledge base, and my dear parents, Mrs. M. Kosalai Ammal and my father, Mr. Mohana Murthy, who gave me a good education, as well as to the Great Thiruvalluvar ("Author of the famous book 'The Thirukural, திருக்குறள்''), who imparted all the wisdom.

கற்க கசடறக் கற்பவை கற்றபின்
நிற்க அதற்குத் தக

– திருக்குறள்

*A special thanks to my beloved wife, Dr. Mythili Prathap,
my beautiful daughter, Shakthi Prathap, and my charming son,
Adithya Prathap, for all their love and support.*

Contents

Problems are a Part of Life; Let's Embrace and Resolve Them

All human beings alive in this world experience problems in one way or another; only a deceased person is free from challenges. Therefore, when you are alive—regardless of background or circumstances—you will encounter difficulties and face these problems, as you have no choice. **'This is the universal truth'.**

Many people express frustration over their problems and often say they are tired of them. I frequently challenge them to name a single person who claims to be problem-free. Most are unable to provide an answer. This question helps them realise that **'problems are inevitable and an inherent part of our daily lives'**. We all encounter challenges, and acknowledging this reality can assist us in 'shifting our perspective and better navigating our struggles'. By encouraging this shift in perspective, we empower individuals to view their problems as part of a **'shared human experience'** rather than burdens they alone must carry. It is a powerful way to help people realise they are not alone in their challenges, and it is a universal experience.

However, it is important to remember that **'where there is a problem, there is also a solution.'** No matter how difficult your problems may be, remember that there is always a way to fix them. Problems should be viewed as opportunities for growth and invitations to become even more creative. They are stepping stones; therefore, let's embrace the learning process.

Let's consider the following analogy, which effectively conveys the message about facing and overcoming difficulties in life: As a child, around seven or eight, my mum took me to the beach, and I was eager to jump into the water! However, the waves were challenging—scary yet exhilarating! My mother advised me to face the waves and enjoy the experience. Instead of running back to shore, she encouraged me to float and let them pass. This taught me to confront my fears while enjoying the moment. Whenever waves approached, I floated rather than fled. Through practice, I mastered navigating the waves and happily played in the water. Regardless of the wave size or tide strength, the thrill of the beach was immense. Ultimately, I found joy in facing waves with confidence, floating, and swimming freely in the sea. I learned that we should face our problems with courage instead of avoiding them. Difficulties keep us alert, and we should strive to overcome them, much like managing waves. Running away from waves is not viable, just as avoiding life's problems is not. We must learn strategies to tackle challenges rather than evade them.

'Problems are like waves. You cannot stop them, but learn how to handle them.'

Consider life's challenges as waves; each offers a chance for growth and joy. Just as mastering waves enhances our beach experience, confronting challenges reveals new strengths and pleasures. Obstacles are a natural part of our journey, so let's face them with courage and ride the tide confidently!

I remember a touching story about a determined donkey that fell into a well. The donkey's owner, a hardworking farmer from the village, tried his best to pull him out, but despite his efforts, he could not. Feeling that the donkey was getting on in years and the well was dry, he called on some kind friends and neighbours to help him close the well and sadly bury it inside. But then something unexpected happened as they started shovelling dirt—mud, rocks, sand, and all sorts of debris—into the well. With each shovelful of dirt that landed on him, the donkey shook it off and stepped up on the growing pile. Bit by bit, he rose higher, and before long, with a burst of determination, he jumped out of the well! This beautiful story reminds us that life can throw all sorts of challenges our way. It is so important to shake off those difficulties and keep moving forward. Like the brave donkey, if we don't give up, we can 'triumph over the most significant hurdles and rise above our deepest problems'.

Life presents many challenges, but the great news is that these **'challenges are temporary and can be worked through'**. Embrace your problems with a strong sense of confidence and remember to savour the joys of life! In my workshops, I love to ask everyone to raise their hands if they don't have any problems—and you know what? Not a single hand goes up! It is essential to recognise that challenges will always be a part of our journey, so let's focus less on bemoaning them and more on finding the silver linings!

Let's discuss who can help us solve our problems moving forward!

Resolving your problems lies solely with you; you alone hold the key to addressing your challenges. Once we gain insight and acceptance that problems are a part of life, we should strive to resolve our issues without expecting others to do it for us. It is up to you to resolve your issues, and it rests entirely on your shoulders. "True resolution comes from within, and you must learn to address your problems. No one else can address your problems, and it's a journey you can only undertake." Taking charge of addressing our challenges is essential! You hold the key to finding solutions for any dilemmas you face. Imagine swimming against the tide at the beach; just like that, we each have the power to tackle and navigate our challenges successfully. It is truly empowering to realise that addressing our problems is something we can all do ourselves. Remember, behind every difficulty lies a great opportunity! So, let's embrace these challenges and learn from them, as they can spark our creativity and help us grow instead of shying away from our problems.

> **'It takes half your life before you discover**
> **life is a do- it-yourself project'**
> – American Self-help author Napoleon Hill

When viewing life as a vehicle, we must recognise that we are not just passengers. We are the drivers, gripping the steering wheel and charting our course. Rather than being passive observers, we actively engage with our lives. Just like drivers who choose routes, speeds, and stops, we make decisions that influence our experiences and shape our outcomes as we navigate the ups and downs of life's journey. Keep in mind that no one is coming to rescue you. Your life is entirely your responsibility. The choices you make, your decisions, and your actions are the fundamental elements of your destiny. No one else can construct your life for you. You must build it with happiness, success, and resilience against challenges. Embrace ownership of your life and forge the masterpiece that is uniquely yours.

Some people don't recognise what their real problem is when encountering difficulties. It is crucial to **'identify the issue and clearly define the problem accurately'**. This process is akin to making a diagnosis in the medical field. It is often said that making an accurate diagnosis when seeing patients addresses half of the illness. This medical principle applies to everyday problems, so learning how to diagnose our issues accurately is essential. A clear understanding of the issue allows for better decision-making and targeted solutions. This approach helps prevent rushing into actions that may not address the root cause. It is essential to grasp the nature of your challenges. By doing so, we open the door to discovering solutions together. As Infosys Founder Mr Narayana Moorthy wisely said, **"Understanding challenges is the first step toward finding a solution."**

Once a problem is diagnosed correctly, it is essential to 'determine whether it is within your area of control or beyond it'. This critical distinction promotes a realistic assessment of situations, helping individuals focus their energy on what they can change rather than wasting time on things beyond their control. However, most daily issues are within our control, so prompt and appropriate action is necessary. If you believe the problem is within your control, take action to address it. Timely intervention can often mitigate more significant issues before they escalate. If you feel the problem is beyond your control, don't waste time or energy discussing or ruminating about it and taking active interventions may not be fruitful. If they are beyond your area of control, then you must wait and watch. In such situations, you have two options- **'diverting your mind or staying detached'** from the unpleasant circumstances. These are the only options to cope with it.

'More is lost by indecision than wrong decision'
– Roman Scholar and philosopher Marcus Tullius Cicero

Problems can be addressed promptly, regardless of their size. Providing solutions and making immediate decisions can quickly resolve about 80% of issues. This proactive approach can prevent problems from escalating, which may eventually lead to crises if left unattended. When we don't take steps to resolve such concerns, our minds can feel paralysed. Remember, it is okay if things are not perfect; corrections can always be made later. This approach does not apply to all situations, as some complex issues may require a longer timeframe and involve intricate decision-making processes. Adopting a structured methodology and setting deadlines can help effectively manage these challenges, as decisions ultimately shape one's future. (We'll explore this further in the next chapter!

When encountering problems or difficulties, I typically ask myself these four essential questions to empower myself.

Qn no 1 - How does this issue rank in my life on a scale from one to ten? A one represents a minor problem, such as littering the house's front entrance with crumpled papers, while a ten signifies the most severe types of issues, like a long-term relationship breakdown or the death of a close family member.

Qn no 2 - How significant will this problem be in a year, and how much will it bother me then? It is essential to see the big picture and put things in perspective. In most situations, I realise that problems often are not significant enough to warrant excessive worry, and we tend to worry more than necessary. Frequently, I laugh about issues that seemed crucial to me at the time, wondering why I stressed over them. In many cases, I can't even recall specific problems entirely after a year. I often don't remember things that bothered me just a few months ago.

Qn no 3 - Should I react immediately, or can I address this problem later? While responding promptly is essential, there are instances where a mindful response can be more effective. "**Mindful responding means taking some time to think before acting**". Practice patience and use your reflective time effectively. A mindful response is more important than reacting impulsively to problems. Advocating for thoughtful responses rather than immediate reactions fosters emotional intelligence, leading to better outcomes.

Qn no 4 - What can I learn from this experience? We encounter both good and bad experiences every day. If we learn something from a problem, we can transform it into a positive one; however, it will remain negative if we don't learn the proper lessons from this experience. By learning from our life experiences, we can turn negative s ituations in to positive ones.

Taking responsibility can be quite a journey! Many people eagerly embrace accountability when things go well, but the picture changes when faced with challenging outcomes. 'Inherent risks usually accompany responsibility.' Some individuals are willing to assume responsibility for positive outcomes; however, when faced with negative consequences, they tend to evade accountability for the resulting difficulties. It is only natural for us to want to take credit when positive outcomes occur. However, '**embracing responsibility and accountability is just as important when things don't go as planned.**'

I want to share a perspective on this valid point. As a doctor, I will cite a medical example from the 17th and 18th centuries when many women died within 48 hours of childbirth due to childbed fever, an infection mainly spread through contact with physicians. Doctors did autopsies in the morning and assisted in deliveries in the afternoon, raising mortality rates without understanding the cause. In 1843, Dr. Oliver Wendell Holmes identified that many doctors weren't washing their hands after autopsies, introducing infections that led to maternal deaths. His findings faced resistance, with many doctors unwilling to accept their responsibility for the issue. Then, Dr. Ignaz Semmelweis in Vienna found that routine handwashing with disinfectant before deliveries significantly reduced post-childbirth mortality. It became clear that neglecting handwashing and failing to sterilise instruments caused unnecessary fatalities. This chapter in medical history reminds us to confront uncomfortable truths about our roles in problems. Focusing solely on successes while avoiding accountability stifles growth. Embracing responsibility and learning from mistakes fosters trust, encourages communication, and improves outcomes.

"Our problems are man-made, and therefore, they can be solved by man. And man can be as big as he wants. No problem of human destiny is beyond human beings"
– Ex- American President John F. Kennedy

Many of our challenges are created by humans, and people often overlook their significant part in their downfall. The issues stemming from human actions can be resolved with effort. The phrase, 'You must acknowledge the role you play in your downfall,' highlights the importance of personal accountability. This involves reflecting on previous choices and behaviours and understanding how one's decisions have shaped current situations. It prompts individuals to think about where things went wrong and how their actions led to those results. Self- reflection is essential for recognising one's involvement in negative scenarios. Individuals can take charge and implement positive changes by grasping their role rather than feeling helpless. Identifying the part one plays in one's downfall paves the way for personal development and empowerment, encouraging a proactive stance in dealing with life's challenges.

Life is full of challenges and obstacles, and that's completely normal! However, how we respond to these bumps shapes our journey. When we embrace personal responsibility, we realise that we can make a difference in our lives rather than wait for solutions to appear elsewhere. This shift in mindset helps us move from feeling like a victim to feeling empowered. It encourages us to take control of our lives and tackle our problems head- on! We must all remember that '**we are the architects of our lives**', and that responsibility lies in our hands. Don't let others do it for you. Remember, no one is coming to save you, and your life is entirely your responsibility.

Let's dive into exploring how we can tackle problems together in the next chapter!

Golden Nuggets

- Problems are inevitable – they are an inherent part of our daily lives.

- No one is immune – Every person faces life's problems and challenges.

- All problems have solutions – Seek out these solutions and find the courage to tackle whatever comes our way to face the difficulties.

- Problems are not always just problems; they can also present opportunities.

- Challenges and difficulties are fleeting and can be overcome.

- You must resolve your problems, as nobody else can solve them.

- Identify the problem accurately. Ensure that you diagnose your issues before taking any action.

- Problems can be addressed promptly, regardless of their size.

- Most problems can be resolved quickly by providing immediate solutions and acting promptly to prevent them from escalating into crises. Making decisions and acting on them is far better than being stuck in a cycle of indecision!

- Mindful responding means taking some time to think before acting. It necessitates taking a moment and reflecting before responding, which is a more effective strategy than reacting impulsively to problems.

- Embracing responsibility and accountability is crucial, notably when outcomes differ from our expectations and things don't unfold as we hoped.

How to Tackle the Challenges Head-On

There is a famous quote: **'Success can also be defined as the ability to solve problems.'**

'Crack the challenges head-on' means **facing difficulties or problems directly instead of turning away from them or sidestepping them**. It involves taking a proactive and assertive approach to problem-solving. This approach encourages us to confront issues with courage and determination, following a structured path to overcome obstacles effectively.

Problem-solving is an excellent skill that can lead to success and happiness in life. When we succeed, we often feel happier and more fulfilled. That's why embracing challenges and working toward solutions in our everyday lives is so important! Problem-solving is a fundamental skill. Acquiring problem- solving skills from a young age is essential. Human beings possess large cerebral hemispheres, (the two main halves of the brain) and the frontal region of the cerebral cortex, known as the prefrontal cortex, is particularly well-developed. This area is crucial for problem-solving, which enables humans to resolve issues more effectively than other living beings on this planet. By developing the neural circuits in the brain involved in problem-solving and activating the areas responsible for decision-making and execution, this process can become significantly easier. However, successful problem- solving requires a thoughtful and systematic approach, and humans should develop and adapt these behaviours and elevate them to the next level.

Problem-solving abilities are not exclusive to humans and Homo sapiens; they are also observed in primates such as chimpanzees. For instance, when faced with reaching bananas hanging from the ceiling, chimpanzees used stacking boxes to climb up and demonstrated their use of tools to solve this problem. In another scenario, when chimpanzees were placed in a cage with a banana just outside but beyond their ability to reach, they thought about it, took a stick, and used it to pull the banana towards them. All these examples indicate that simple problem-solving skills exist even in chimpanzees.

During problem-solving, take a structured and thoughtful approach. The useful steps are given below:

STEP 1: **The first and foremost step is to articulate the problem clearly and 'write it down'** in one concise sentence. Most people I speak with often complain about various issues, but they struggle to define the exact problem. We all possess strong problem-solving abilities, but we must first take the time to identify the problems clearly and take the appropriate steps to resolve them. 'If you define the problem correctly, you almost have the solution' - Apple founder Steve Jobs.

Most importantly, please address one problem at a time to avoid confusion, and this will allow you to resolve each issue more effectively. People often try to tackle multiple problems simultaneously, leading to improper resolution. Don't try to hit many mangoes with a shot of an arrow. Focus on one issue before moving on to the next. Taking things one step at a time is much safer than attempting to take three or four steps at once and risking setbacks.

STEP 2: Once the problem is clearly defined, the next important step is **'brainstorming'**, which involves generating as many possible solutions as possible. The range of solutions can vary widely, so write down every possible solution that comes to mind, even if it appears silly.

STEP 3: After brainstorming, you should **'assess the pros and cons of each solution'**, identifying the advantages and disadvantages to select the best possible approach. Writing down these points will help you determine which solutions are realistically achievable. Once you have evaluated the pros and cons, choose the solution you believe is the most effective.

STEP 4: The next step is to '**outline the specific actions you need to take**' to implement this solution. Consider the following questions:

A. What will be done?

B. How will it be done?

C. When will it be done?

D. Who is involved?

E. Where will it take place?

After selecting a solution, move forward and make progress. Be mindful of potential obstacles and consider how to overcome them. Consider which actions you can take to address these hurdles and then implement them to resolve the issue.

STEP 5: Once a solution is implemented, '**it must be reviewed and monitored regularly**'. Remember that challenges and setbacks are common, so don't give up.

If the initial solution doesn't work, review the situation and try the next solution on your list. If nothing seems to work, take a break and revisit the situation in a few weeks or months; you may have gained new perspectives and potential solutions by then.

It is essential to recognise that setbacks are common; thus,

persistence is crucial.

If you are worried about challenges and risks and feel stuck, try asking yourself this simple yet powerful question: What is the worst that can happen? By reflecting on this question and exploring the answer, you might uncover a little spark of confidence to help you face whatever comes your way!

Following the above-mentioned steps will better equip individuals to tackle challenges, achieve their goals, and overcome obstacles. For example, my client wanted to spend more time with her son, so she decided to change her job from full-time to part-time—a decision she had contemplated for a long time. Her main priority was to be present for her son, so her job was deprioritised. By making this change, she could focus on her priorities and find more satisfaction and joy in her life.

How did she resolve it? We discussed this in our session and took the steps below.

STEP 1: **Problem Statement**: 'I want to reduce my work hours from 8 to 6 per day to spend more time with my son while maintaining my job'.

STEP 2: **Generate Potential Solutions**

Option 1: Request a Part-Time Shift: Consider asking for a shorter, 6-hour workday. This will show them you are committed to staying productive and meeting all deadlines!

Option 2: Propose Flexible Hours: If part-time work is not an option, you might suggest some flexible hours! For instance, you could work longer hours on certain days and take shorter shifts on others to balance your schedule.

Option 3: Explore Remote Work: Consider the benefits of working from home! It could help you save commute time and offer more flexibility in juggling work and personal life.

STEP 3: **Evaluate Solutions**- Pros and Cons Analysis: Part-Time Shift:

Pros: Enjoying more time with your son and creating clear boundaries between work and personal life can be fulfilling.

Cons: There might be a reduction in income and some adjustments needed for your workload.

Flexible Hours:

Pros:

Negotiating with your employer while keeping your full salary can make things much more manageable.

Cons:

However, it might lead to longer workdays overall.

Remote Work:

Pros:

This option can boost your time efficiency while allowing you to maintain your full pay.

Cons:

Remember that depending on your job might blur the lines between your work and family time.

STEP 4: Action - **Request a Meeting**

Arrange a formal meeting with your supervisor and HR on a specific date, time, and location to discuss your proposal for a part-time position with 6-hour shifts that help you balance work and personal life. Present how you will smoothly manage the transition to part-time work. Prepare your argument and gather evidence demonstrating how you consistently surpass performance targets, which can support your case that you will remain effective with reduced hours. Illustrate the benefits to the employer, emphasising how fewer hours can enhance your focus and decrease burnout. Be ready to negotiate: if a direct reduction to 6 hours is not feasible, consider suggesting fewer working days or adjusting your start and end times.

STEP 5: **Review and Monitoring**: Suggest a trial period, such as 6 hours daily for 3 months, so you and your employer can assess the impact. Be open to reviewing the arrangement after the trial.

Seek Feedback: After the trial period, ask your employer for feedback and make any necessary changes to your workflow to ensure both sides are satisfied.

Summary of the Steps

1. **Problem**: You want more time for your son but must continue working.

2. **Solution Generation**: To better balance work and family, propose a six-hour part-time shift, suggest flexible working hours, or recommend working remotely two days a week.

3. **Evaluation**: The best option is to request the 6-hour shift, with the remote work option as a backup. You have determined that working 6 hours daily will still allow you to meet your responsibilities, but your salary will decrease by 20%.

4. **Action and Implementation**: Schedule a meeting with your supervisor, present a well-prepared case for part- time work, and suggest a trial period.

5. **Monitor**: After three months, the new arrangement works well for you, and your supervisor agrees that your productivity remains high.

People and organisations often value individuals who 'effectively solve problems.' These individuals gain recognition and pave the way to more success and happiness. Organisations and employers appreciate the experience and ability to excel in problem-solving. Excuses should be minimised. Research suggests that individuals with strong problem-solving skills and traits are more likely to succeed in all life aspects.

After reading this chapter and reviewing the example, **I invite you to try using a similar structured approach** for the challenges you face in your life—whether they relate to relationships, finances, your career, or business. Embracing a thoughtful method with a clear action plan can really boost your confidence and help you overcome any hurdles you encounter!

Golden Nuggets

- Problem-solving is a fundamental skill. Learning problem-solving skills from an early age is essential.

- Achieving effective problem-solving necessitates the adoption of a systematic approach.

- Concentrating on one problem at a time is essential to prevent confusion.

- Please write down your problems and articulate them with clarity.

- Engage in brainstorming to develop a comprehensive list of potential solutions, analysing the advantages and disadvantages of each. Subsequently, select the most suitable solution.

- Once decided, specific actions should be undertaken to implement the chosen solution.

- Periodically review and monitor the situation to see if it works for you.

- It is important to remember that setbacks are common occurrences; therefore, persistence is key.

Happiness is a Free App Readily Available in Our Minds

"Happiness is like a free application (app within our minds, readily accessible. All we need to do is download, install, and utilise it."

Instead of seeking happiness in the external world, try to find it within yourself. Just as a free app can be accessed anytime, happiness is similarly accessible within our minds. Throughout history, we have been subtly conditioned to view happiness as an external pursuit. This leads to a deeply rooted belief that true happiness, contentment, and joy lie outside us. This ingrained notion significantly influences our lives, fostering a firm conviction that we must seek happiness in money, wealth, power, fame, status, and recognition. However, such endless quests do not lead to genuine fulfilment. Ultimately, your happiness depends on you and your mindset, so refrain from hunting for it externally.

"Happiness depends upon ourselves."
– stated the Greek philosopher Aristotle

Happiness is an **'internal state of mind'**. It all rests upon you, and we must try to find it; no one else can do it. **Your happiness will not come to you; it must come from within.**

A student asked his teacher where he could find happiness and what methods he could use to search for it. The teacher responded without comments, and after a few minutes, they both left the house. However, the teacher was seen searching for something outside his home. The student returned and inquired about what the teacher was looking for. The teacher replied that he was searching for the key to his house. The student asked, "Sir, did you lose your keys?" The teacher explained that he remembered losing them inside. Perplexed, the student wondered why the teacher searched outside when he thought the keys were inside. The teacher responded, "Because there is light outside, I thought it would be easier to look there." The student argued, "That doesn't make sense. Why search outside when the keys are inside?" At that moment, the teacher intervened, saying, "In the same way, the key to happiness lies within you. You must search for it inside, not outside." The student realised that happiness must be found within oneself rather than in the external world. Just as the keys to the teacher's door were already in the house, the key to happiness is also within our minds. He learned this valuable lesson and was extremely happy to grasp the message finally.

There is a famous saying: **"Happiness is a choice, not a result."**

Happiness begins with your choice. Remember, it is not about relying on others to bring you joy; instead, **embracing happiness is a personal decision you make for yourself**. Many people do not realise that the state of happiness is already within them and often fail to perceive it. **'Happiness will never come to those who do not appreciate what they already have.'** Another poignant story illustrates this lesson beautifully: a small fish named Jade was swimming happily in the ocean, yet she asked other fish where to find the sea. She would not be convinced if other fish in the sea tried to persuade her. Despite being surrounded by it, she remained doubtful. One day, her grandmother fish, Jana, took her to the seashore and temporarily threw her out of the water onto the land. Jade panicked and became breathless, struggling for life until her grandmother returned her to safety by taking her back into the sea. Confused and shaken, Jade questioned her grandmother's actions. Jana explained that the momentary struggle was meant to demonstrate that she was safe and secure in the ocean; **she just needed to look and perceive it. Like the ocean, true happiness is right before our eyes; we need only to explore it within ourselves.** By ceasing the external search for joy and turning our contemplation inward, we can choose to embrace the essence of happiness. Jade learned this vital lesson; we all have much to gain from the story. (Ref Anthony de Mello's book, The Song of Bird)

Two thousand years ago, the Ancient Greek philosopher Democritus proclaimed that **"happiness does not reside in possessions or gold but rather in the soul."** Many religions and philosophies echo this sentiment. For instance, the Hindu sacred book, Bhagavad Gita, teaches that **"Happiness lies within us,"** while the Bible states that **"The kingdom of heaven is found within."** Happiness resides in our minds, and this realisation is crucial.

I recently stumbled upon a fascinating concept about happiness in Mr Jay Shetty's book and podcast. Through a monk, he discusses the idea of a **"theatre of happiness."** He describes this theatre as having infinite seats, unlike a traditional one with limited capacity. In this theatre of joy, each person has a designated spot. There is no cost to enter the theatre of happiness; everyone already has their place. However, you must try to enter the theatre and find your seat of happiness. No one can take away your seat, and there is no competition for these seats. The only requirement is a sincere effort to step inside and locate your designated spot. Once you find your seat, sit down and enjoy the happy movie of life. Ultimately, it is up to you to seek it out. This powerful concept provides valuable life lessons, emphasising that **happiness is accessible if we take the initiative to find it, and you alone can discover it**. True happiness is a journey of fully immersing ourselves in the present moment, enjoying each experience, and expressing love and gratitude for what we already have.

The seed of happiness must be planted in your mind. However, your responsibility extends beyond that. You must nurture this seed with the right amount of water, sunlight, and all other essential elements to flourish. You can keep it as a seed in your mind with a minimal state of happiness, let it grow into a small plant with a moderate state of joy, or cultivate it into a big tree bearing the abundant fruits of happiness and providing the soothing shade of peace. Happiness and success are not limited at all.

There is a famous quote that "**Happiness is not a destination to be reached but a journey to be embraced.**"

Let's **not postpone joyful moments**; if we do, we might miss those precious times that make life special! Imagine a master and his student standing by the riverbank, eager to cross to the other side. The master notices the beautiful, lush green forest and encourages his student to take a moment to appreciate nature before they continue their journey. While the master plans to stay by the riverbank, the student hesitates to enjoy the lush forest, believing he shouldn't have any fun until completing his year-long apprenticeship. Even when the master encourages him, he declines the opportunity to enjoy himself. After a while, the student, curious about the master's stillness, asks why he has not crossed yet. The master replies that he is waiting for the entire river to flow before stepping in. Surprised, the student exclaims, "Sir, please forgive me. You'll never cross the river if you wait for all the water to flow, as that won't happen!" The master smiles gently and shares, "You have made the same mistake. When I suggested you enjoy the moment, you postponed happiness, potentially missing out altogether. People often think they'll embrace joy only after completing their essential tasks; yet, like the river that keeps flowing, life's responsibilities will never pause. This mindset can lead to missing out on delightful moments. It is crucial to find happiness in the little things without delay! Instead of waiting for everything else to be done, let's seek joyful moments amid our duties.

Making excuses to delay happiness is not wise! Instead, let's seize opportunities for joy and cherish life's small moments whenever they come. Don't leave anything for later, including the joyful moments when you can. For instance, some folks might want to go for a picnic with friends but wait until after their college exams at the year's end. Others dream of a beach getaway but hold off until they receive a job promotion in a few years. Don't delay your happy moments; embrace every joyful experience while you can! Time flies: before you know it, your coffee is cold, life passes by, and those beautiful moments may slip away. Later, you might regret not embracing happiness. So, let's not postpone anything.

Enjoying small moments of happiness rather than focusing solely on big wins is vital for emotional well-being. Embracing these smaller joys provides a more relaxed and enjoyable approach to life. "Small moments of joy and minor achievements can occur regularly, offering frequent boosts to your mood." Please incorporate this practice every day. You can strive to accomplish one area of achievement daily, enhancing your confidence and self-esteem. Achievements don't have to involve winning a gold medal; even the most minor daily accomplishments can bring happiness. For example, tidying your room, cooking a small meal for your family, completing some repair work you have been postponing, or finally taking a driving lesson on hold for a long time can all contribute to your daily sense of accomplishment. When you accomplish these small tasks regularly, you can learn to enjoy those moments of happiness instead of waiting for grand achievements to arrive. So don't stop at just achieving them; try to relish your accomplishments consistently and embrace the joy they bring.

Instead of waiting for a major accomplishment, which may take a long time to realise, you can **"experience happiness regularly, leading to a more sustained positive emotional state."** By focusing on small achievements rather than big wins, you "alleviate the pressure on yourself." The expectation of monumental accomplishments can lead to stress and disappointment. Finding joy in small things "fosters a sense of gratitude." When you recognise and celebrate little victories or small achievements, you cultivate a positive mindset and enhance your overall life satisfaction. Additionally, sharing small joys with friends and family can "strengthen relationships." Celebrating these minor achievements can keep you "inspired and motivated" on your journey.

Many people struggle to perceive happiness in their lives. The truth is that happiness and joyful experiences occur frequently in our daily lives. However, due to the hustle and bustle of everyday life, we often fail to slow down and appreciate these moments. When we pause, we can better acknowledge those happy moments in our minds. One effective strategy for enhancing our sense of happiness is to **take a moment to slow down, reflect on these experiences, and mentally revisit them several times**, allowing them to be firmly embedded in our memory. This practice can significantly increase our feelings of positivity and happiness. For instance, when my one year-old son smiles and giggles at me, those moments are incredibly precious. Instead of immediately shifting my focus to another task, such as answering a phone call or leaving the room, I take a few extra minutes to immerse myself in that experience. By taking a slight pause and revisiting this joyful moment in my mind, I ensure it is strongly registered in my brain, providing me with a more profound sense of satisfaction and happiness. I often record videos and audio of these interactions, which have helped reinforce those joyful feelings and generate even more positivity. The more we allow these feelings to be registered, the more positive we generally feel. Conversely, if we don't try to acknowledge these moments, they may fade away, leaving us feeling unfulfilled and disconnected from the joy in our lives. Therefore, taking pauses throughout our busy lives is crucial to reflect on and adequately register these joyful small moments. If we remain in "busy mode," constantly rushing about, we risk missing the small moments that can bring us genuine happiness.

Discussions about heaven and hell arise in various religious contexts. Specific geographic locations do not define these concepts; they do not refer to physical places that can be pinpointed. "A peaceful mind, filled with positive thoughts and capable of experiencing happiness, embodies heaven, whereas a lack of peace and the inability to feel joy symbolise hell".

'**You are the centre of your happiness. No one can take it from you, nor can anyone give it to you.** It is entirely up to you to feel and recognise your happiness. Not even your life partner, best friends, siblings, or children can be responsible for your happiness. Therefore, strive to find joy in what you have and within yourself. Maturity involves discovering happiness within rather than seeking it from others or through material possessions.'

Golden Nuggets

- Happiness is like a free application (app) inside our minds, readily available to download and use.

- The journey to happiness is not external but internal. It is entirely within your control to begin it.

- Happiness resides in our minds; you alone can discover it, and no one else can.

- Embracing happiness is a personal decision you make for yourself.

- Happiness is easily accessible if we take the initiative to find it. It all rests upon you.

- Happiness will never come to those who do not appreciate what they already have.

- Do not postpone your happiness. Cherish happiness now and open our hearts to all of life's wonderful experiences.

- Make the most of life's small moments by enjoying these little instances of happiness instead of only concentrating on significant victories.

- To enhance our happiness, we should take a moment to slow down and reflect on these experiences, ensuring they are firmly embedded in our memory.

Live in the Present and be Here Now

"Be happy for this moment. This moment is your life." the Persian Poet Omar Khayyam stated. Enjoying the present moment is a prerequisite for emotional and mental well-being. '**Being in the present is a precious gift,**' allowing us to enjoy each moment.

Our minds must be clear and focused on the present moment, not consumed by past regrets or future fears. One of the most common mistakes humans make is dwelling on the past or worrying about the future. The past often represents memories of sorrow and regret, while the future brings anxiety and uncertainty. The past should teach you a lesson; you can't change it, and it is over. I appreciate this meaningful proverb: "**You can't unscramble a scrambled egg**." You should not get stuck in it, like a prison. Don't be a prisoner of the past. The future is a mystery, and nobody can predict it. Most of our future thoughts consist of worries, fears, imaginations, and undue anxieties, which often won't happen at all. Most of our future predictions are wild guesses, and they are often wrong. So why do you still worry? The future is a clean sheet of paper with endless possibilities and mysteries.

Often, our minds become so cluttered with thoughts of the past or future that we completely lose sight of the present moment. A Harvard study found that 64% of our day is spent thinking about what has happened or is yet to come. Our main issue is **our lack of awareness of the present moment**, as we are lost in the haze of past reflections and future anxieties. We should rise from these dark clouds and shine brightly like the sun by appreciating every moment of our lives and enhancing our conscious awareness. **Enjoying the**

present moment is the 'real secret' to making daily meaningful. While we can't change the past or predict the future, we can savour the present. Instead of worrying about what has been or what might come, let's embrace the joy of now and make the most of our current days!

Have you noticed how great artists immerse themselves in their paintings? Watching them focus on each brushstroke, completely absorbed in their creation, is inspiring. We can take their cues and strive to engage fully in the present moment, giving our best in whatever we do. **The art of happy living is to 'be present in the here and now'.** This doesn't mean you have to forget your past or not think about the future at all. Wise individuals enjoy the present but remember the lessons learned from the past and pay attention to their significance. They also envision a bright future and use every opportunity that comes their way. They cultivate a sense of inner peace and happiness by focusing on the present.

Focusing on the present moment comes with so many wonderful benefits!

Living in the present moment allows one to listen '**more attentively and connect authentically'** with others. It also enhances one's ability to understand and empathise with people. Furthermore, being present improves one's focus on specific tasks, enabling better performance and increased productivity. Many people complain of 'being absent-minded or forgetful' in daily life. The main reason is a lack of conscious awareness of the present moment. With a cluttered mind, they are unable to retain the information gathered and feel as though they are experiencing mental fog or memory loss.

Living in the present moment brings us greater fulfilment and happiness each day. Influential figures like Buddha have embraced mindfulness, emphasising the importance of living in the now as a fundamental aspect of a fulfilling and contented life. Most people only partially enjoy their daily life experiences; we miss out on the present moment and lose opportunities for happiness daily. Imagine being on a beach holiday, sitting on the sand, feeling it beneath your hands and feet, watching the waves gently approach, accompanied by soothing sounds, the warmth of the sunlight, and the colours of the sky. When you are fully present, you start to notice the beauty in these small things in life, which can foster gratitude and increase your happiness and life satisfaction. However, even in such a serene setting, some people fail to truly enjoy the moment as their minds dwell on past events or worry about the future. They may believe that travelling or going on holidays will help, but it won't unless you learn the art of enjoying the present, which is necessary for such experiences to bring fulfilment. It is essential to learn to savour and live in the present moment.

Another point is that being in the present moment **helps you understand yourself more deeply**. People achieve true awakening by living in the present, appreciating the magic of life, and genuinely experiencing life as it unfolds. This is also referred to as enlightenment in technical terms. Achieving enlightenment involves mastering the art of being present in the here and now. You must be physically and mentally engaged in whatever tasks you undertake. Unfortunately, many people are physically present but mentally absent these days, which prevents them from enjoying the true essence of living. You must physically and mentally cherish the present moment by being fully present.

Some explore alternatives, such as individuals seeking revelation and enlightenment by visiting various shrines to discover temporary happiness through these practices. How can such practices benefit them long-term if they don't understand the importance of enjoying the present moment? The concept of enlightenment is beautifully illustrated in the book "Looking at Life Differently" by Indian monk Swami Sukhabodhanandha. A student asked his master about the difference between his experiences before and after enlightenment. The master replied, "Before enlightenment, I would wake up, bathe, eat, pray, and sleep at night. After enlightenment, I still do the same, but there is one difference: Previously, my mind was occupied with the past or future while performing these tasks. After enlightenment, my mind is focused on the here and now. When I eat, I eat; when I bathe,

I bathe." Thus, I truly live in the present. Being alive and conscious in the present allows one to enjoy each moment. He also states, 'If I can't be happy here and now, I will never be happy anywhere.' It is essential to recognise that enlightenment is always connected to the present and never to the past or future. Enlightenment involves understanding and perceiving happiness and peace while living in the present moment.

The phrase **"You can't add days to your life, but you can add life to your days"**—by Anonymous—conveys the idea that while we cannot control the length of our lives, we can enhance the quality of the days we experience. Finding happiness and fulfilment makes our days meaningful; enjoying the present moment is the real secret. In other words, it is not about how long we live but how well we live. This encourages us to focus on making the most of our time, appreciating the present, and engaging in activities that bring fulfilment, joy, and meaning to our lives. It emphasises the importance of living fully and valuing each day rather than merely counting the days we have.

Research indicates that a striking 95% of our worries are unnecessary! These concerns often arise from our tendency to dwell on the past or the future. Believe it or not, about 50% of these worries focus on future events that may never occur, while another 20% relate to things we can't change from the past. So, let's remind ourselves to appreciate the present moment more—it is much more rewarding!

Most people play their life's music in a "fast forward" (future) mode or "reverse" (past) mode. Try to play your life's music in normal play mode. Sometimes, you should press the pause button (stay in the present mode a bit longer), take a back seat, and enjoy the good things around you. Only then can you truly enjoy life. Relish the ice cream of life before it melts!

Let's explore mindfulness as a lovely next step towards enjoying the present moment in the upcoming chapter!

Golden Nuggets

- Stop dwelling on the past or fretting about the future.

- Develop the habit of focusing on the current moment and enjoying the simple pleasures of everyday life.

- The art of happy living is to 'be present in the here and now'. Embracing the gift of life means appreciating the present.

- Living in the present moment allows one to listen more attentively, connect authentically with others, and understand oneself more deeply.

- Living in the present moment brings our lives more 'fulfilment and happiness'.

- Achieving enlightenment involves 'mastering the art of presence in the here and now.'

Being Mindful and Not Mind-Full

"To have mindful connections, you must fight external distractions—disconnect to connect. In order to have mindful connections, you need to fight internal distractions—notice them and let go."—Clinical Psychologist, Chantal Hofstee (Mindfulness on the Run).

Mindfulness is a practice that cultivates awareness and focus. It involves being fully conscious of the present moment, fostering self-awareness through increased attentiveness and embracing each moment. Thus, mindfulness conveys the idea of daily developing a more profound sense of presence and attentiveness. We often live on autopilot, unaware of our surroundings. Mindfulness is about switching off this autopilot and shifting to conscious awareness. Mindfulness is awareness, which serves as the key to conscious living. It involves recognising your true conscious existence rather than merely existing on autopilot. To cultivate this awareness, you must deepen your understanding of your thoughts, emotions, beliefs, and preconceived notions. Awareness can help you manage people and situations, so strive to integrate mindfulness into your daily life.

Consider the mind like a monkey, jumping randomly from branch to branch of a tree—our thoughts often follow this chaotic pattern, leaping from one thing to another. Sometimes, we may find ourselves lost in thoughts about the past or uncertain about the future. However, we can influence the present moment. Mindfulness involves controlling this monkey mind and regaining command over our thoughts by focusing on the present moment. Essentially, we are training our minds to stay in the now. By doing so, we take control of the driver's seat and determine where our thoughts should go.

Mindfulness is **fundamentally about calming or slowing down the mind**. Integrate mindfulness into your daily activities by decelerating and enhancing your awareness of alignment in your actions. Ensure that these activities are performed slowly and with thoughtful consideration. Mindfulness can help you recognise distractions and effectively refocus your attention. Research in neuroscience shows that the insula (a small structure located deep within our brain's cerebral cortex) and its surrounding neural connections are thought to be responsible for several functions, including attention and awareness. The strengthening and activation of the insula are linked to increased awareness. Enhancing the insula can improve conscious awareness, allowing you to be more present in the moment instead of preoccupied with what has been or what might come. Evidence indicates that strengthening the insular network through mindful practice is essential for attention and awareness. Mindfulness practice tends to produce these positive effects within the brain.

When we consider our daily routines, such as eating or bathing, it is essential to take a moment to reflect on our experiences. Often, we consume our meals quickly without truly savouring them. Instead, we can embrace the concept of mindful eating! This involves tuning into our hunger levels and being aware of our portion sizes. It is all about appreciating our food's wonderful tastes, flavours, aromas, and colours, making the entire experience more enjoyable. Striving for balanced, healthy meals and eating in moderation nourishes our bodies and souls. Additionally, avoiding distractions like phone calls or television during meals can significantly enhance our mindful eating practice. This is why mindful eating is a valuable approach to our health and wellness!

Practising mindful bathing is about truly enjoying the experience and ensuring every part of your body receives the care it deserves. You can transform your bath into a profoundly relaxing retreat by being fully present, embracing the incredible bodily sensations and touching and appreciating different areas. Unfortunately, many people rush through their baths, missing out on the simple joy of the moment. While they may be physically in the bathroom, their minds often drift away, preventing them from fully soaking in the delightful bathing experience. Mindful listening involves immersing yourself in conversations and fully embracing the moment by listening without the immediate urge to respond. Like mindful eating, bathing, and listening, mindfulness can enhance various activities in life. By cultivating mindfulness, one can appreciate and enjoy each task they undertake. Without mindfulness, a person may feel scattered and miss out on the benefits of being fully present.

Being kind and non-judgemental is truly at the heart of mindfulness practice. When we find ourselves being judgemental, it often leads to impulsive reactions to situations. However, embracing a kinder and more mindful outlook empowers us to handle challenges with greater responsibility and effectiveness. As our minds grow quieter through mindfulness, we cultivate **the ability to respond thoughtfully to circumstances rather than simply reacting**. This encourages us to shift our mindset from judgement to mindfulness, allowing us to appreciate others' perspectives and foster understanding.

The mind often resembles heavy traffic, with thoughts flowing rapidly one after another. Mindfulness is not about acting like a traffic policeman trying to block your thoughts. Instead, it is akin to being a passive observer, standing aside and watching what happens without becoming emotionally involved. **Mindfulness is not about blocking unpleasant thoughts but acknowledging and observing them without attachment**. It encourages you to stay detached from this mental traffic and observe the events in your mind without judgement. With consistent practice, you may notice that the noise and chaos within your mind begin to quiet down, leading to a sense of calm. This experience can be truly special—a divine feeling that instils serenity. Research shows mindfulness effectively reduces stress levels, alleviates anxiety, improves mood, and decreases impulsivity. Additionally, mindfulness enhances physical health, emotional regulation, productivity, creativity, self-compassion, well-being, and happiness. **Learning to manage our inner states wisely is crucial.**

'**The mind acts like an enemy for those who do not control it.**' – the Hindu Scripture, Bhagavad Gita. It is vital to engage with your mind and work on gaining control over it; otherwise, the mind may dominate you. The purpose of life is to enjoy every moment and to experience different things truly, and mindfulness practice should become an integral part of our lives.

Mindfulness-based breathing exercises for stress reduction involve formal practice for five minutes. Begin by closing your eyes, breathing in through your nostrils, and exhaling through your mouth. Allow thoughts to come and go; observe them and your feelings without labelling them as good or bad, then return your focus to your breath. Use your breath as an anchor to centre your thoughts and calm your mind. The aim is to **detach from your thoughts and observe them** without getting caught up in them. It is like standing on the riverbank and watching the water flow by. The thoughts are allowed to flow. Mindfulness also helps you discover **"inner silence"** when you observe your thoughts without becoming absorbed. Instead, strive to witness these thoughts impartially. Gradually, look for "intervals of silence" between thoughts. Initially, the abundance of random thoughts may hinder your ability to detect these gaps. However, as your thoughts diminish in frequency, you will notice "more intervals," allowing you to immerse yourself in "**increasing moments of silence.**" Ultimately, mindfulness provides an expanded space of silence and enhances clarity in our thought processes.

Mindfulness can also be practised informally, with many one-minute practice suggestions in various books and resource materials. For example, while watching TV, you can mute the ads and focus solely on breathing until the commercials end. Additionally, you could set an hourly reminder to take a one- minute breathing exercise during your regular work schedule or breaks. These simple ways to practice mindfulness can easily fit into your busy lifestyle. They are practical and do not require you to sit still and meditate; they can be done on the go. Grounding techniques are excellent, simple practices that help you connect with the present moment. For example, feel your feet on the ground or pay attention to the sensations throughout your body. These little habits can make a difference! Encouraging someone to embrace mindfulness means reminding them that it is a journey, and every small step contributes to greater awareness and peace.

Ideally, mindfulness should be **'practised in all activities to gain maximum benefit'**, and it is possible to achieve it. People struggle to understand the difference between mindfulness and meditation. Being mindful can enhance awareness of the present moment and help slow down when we typically rush. But meditation helps to create singular thoughts. Mindfulness is a quality that can be practised all the time in your life, but meditation is a tool for which you involve dedicated practice. Practising meditation is more ritualistic, but mindfulness is not. Being mindful in all activities is crucial, and the utmost aim should be not **'MIND FULL'** of crowded thoughts.

Golden Nuggets

- Mindfulness conveys the idea of developing a 'heightened sense of presence and attention in daily life'.

- Mindfulness involves training our minds to develop the skills needed to be fully present and aware of our surroundings and actions.

- Mindfulness is about calming or slowing down the mind.

- Being kind and non-judgemental is at the core of mindfulness practice.

- Mindfulness is not about blocking unpleasant thoughts but acknowledging and observing them without attachment.

- Practice mindfulness during all your daily chores to enjoy every moment of your life.

"Know What You Want in Life"

Knowing what you truly want is essential to achieving happiness and fulfilment. However, many people need clarification on their goals and ambitions. When I provide career guidance to young adults, I often ask them what they genuinely wish to pursue. Most of them respond with vague answers or express uncertainty about their paths. I frequently hear the following statements:

"I don't know,"

"I'm still trying to figure it out,"

"I'm confused,"

"I am not sure," etc.

It is crucial to know what you want, why you want it, and how to achieve it.

It is essential to understand your desires, the reasons behind them, and the steps required to make them a reality. Needs are those expectations set by others and society, while wants are the things that truly resonate with our hearts. We must differentiate between what others require and what we want or desire. In addition to knowing what you want, **stay curious about why you seek them**. Question yourself thoroughly and explore the deeper reasons behind your wishes. Keep that curiosity alive, and consistently strive to understand what you truly want while seeking ways to achieve it. Once you understand your goals, focus your energy, put in the necessary effort, and begin investing in them.

Figuring out what you truly want in life involves two key steps –1) **reflecting on yourself** and 2) **understanding your interests and goals.**

I have been on small trekking trips with my friends, typically lasting a day or so. After a few hours of starting a trek, one of the most common questions we ask each other is, "Where are we right now?" To complete your trip, you must know your current location and determine the path to reach your desired destination. To achieve success, having a transparent mapping system for getting from point A to point B is even more critical. Without this guidance, wandering off track while trekking is too easy. This idea mirrors our lives, reminding us how to avoid feeling lost. First, you need to know where you are going and where you want to be in your life. Secondly, you should know where you are right now, and being aware of your current position is key. Lastly, you should consider how to navigate life's journey from 'where you are to where you want to be'. Through self-reflection, we can clarify what's working and what needs improvement. Take a little time to think about your interests, strengths, and what matters to you. Consider writing down your observations. You might want to jot down your thoughts; writing things out can bring a level of clarity that just thinking won't quite reach! Map out your objectives and find your calling.

Have you enjoyed watching a movie at a multiplex theatre? Before we head out, it is important to decide on the type of film that excites us—action, comedy, romance, thriller, or something artistic—before we grab our tickets. If we skip this step and choose a random movie without a clear preference, we might end up with a less enjoyable experience, which can diminish the film's fun and the entire theatre outing. Like selecting a movie, life offers us many choices, and it is important to **'take a moment to think about what we truly want'.**

The root of this issue lies in the need for greater clarity in thought processes. Remember, **"clarity is everything."** Clarity of thought regarding what you want in life is one of your greatest assets, yet many overlook its importance. You can choose anything, but you must be clear about your choices. This reflective work is essential for personal development. If there is a lack of clarity, confusion often increases, making it difficult to determine the correct outcomes. This confusion can lead to a state of indecision and inaction. Therefore, gaining clarity is essential for effectively determining what you want to accomplish in your life. Before planning to grow further, building a solid foundation is necessary. Clarity of thought is key, as it lays the groundwork for your journey. With a strong foundation, you can stand tall and confident.

Take the time to figure out what you truly want; that's perfectly okay! Many people even take a gap year to explore their desires or a sabbatical to reevaluate their priorities and take meaningful steps forward. If you are stuck, take time off to evaluate your life and establish clear goals for each phase of your journey. An unexamined life lacks meaning. As Socrates famously stated, **"The unexamined life is not worth living."** To develop a clear strategic plan, take a step back, reflect, and organise your life according to your goals and ambitions.

Once you have clarity, you can create a **strong rooting system** in your mind that will help you grow and thrive. Have you ever noticed a bamboo tree? For the first four years of planting the seed, you cannot see the plant above the ground because it is busy developing a strong root system. After that, it shoots up remarkably fast—sometimes growing several feet within 6-8 weeks! This teaches us that having a solid foundation is essential for future growth, and clarity is everything.

I was fortunate to have clarity in my thinking process from an early age. At the age of 10, I decided to pursue a science stream. By 15, I had committed to studying medicine because my strengths, qualities, feelings, and desires aligned with this choice. After completing my medical education at 25, I specialised in Psychiatry for my postgraduate studies. I aspired to practise it for the rest of my life, as it suited my abilities and personality better. At 35, I felt ready to start my hospital to offer services to the public, so I undertook the construction and opened a hospital. Now, in my 40s, I am running a successful 200-bed facility, introducing new mental health services, providing me with personal and professional satisfaction and financial success. The clarity of thought I developed at various stages of my life has helped me stay on the right path. I knew exactly what I wanted to do, and I feel fortunate to be doing it, which brings me success and happiness. Clarity of thought is vital in influencing decisions and achieving ambitions.

When choosing areas of interest, prioritise decisions that align with your preferences rather than being influenced by others. People often make this mistake and later regret it. Your career aspirations should stem entirely from your choices, free from the influence of others. The outcomes of what you desire in life must be an organic decision, not shaped by others. Many people regret their career choices at the end of their professional lives because they spent years pursuing what they did not want to do; those regrets cannot be undone.

'Your time is limited.
Don't waste it living someone else's life.'
– Steve Jobs

This quote reminds us to live authentically and avoid wasting our time by imitating or conforming to what others expect or desire. Instead, embracing your authentic journey opens the door to a more profound sense of purpose, fulfilment, and happiness. Sometimes, people **'compromise too much and end up living out the dreams'** **and ambitions of others.** Living someone else's life can lead to dissatisfaction and unhappiness—after all, it means you are not being true to yourself! This can hold you back from personal growth, self-discovery, and the chance to chase your passions and dreams. The golden rule is simple: never let anyone else steer the course of your life! Your choices will align beautifully with your values, interests, and ambitions, resulting in a much more meaningful and rewarding existence.

I have met so many young adults who find themselves pursuing degrees or going to university education because they feel obligated or because they want to fulfil their parents' dreams rather than their own. It is common for some to finish their bachelor's degrees but still feel uncertain about their direction. The pressures from parents and outside influences can lead to choices that don't resonate with their true selves, resulting in years spent on paths they never intended to take. If you are in this situation, take a moment to reassess your life, revisit your goals and dreams, and consider creating a personal development plan. **Only dead fish go with the flow. You should have a fighting spirit.** It would help you pursue your life ambitions based on your interests and not be influenced by others.

Ask yourself whose life you are living. Do you feel like you are truly living for yourself? Or are you just meeting the expectations set by others? If the answer is no, it is time to chase your aspirations and desires! Your goals and ambitions shouldn't be as fleeting as letters written in the sand; they should be carved in stone because they hold immense power. Make it a priority to engage in self-discovery, personal growth, and pursuing what truly matters to you. By staying true to yourself, you can craft a life that is uniquely yours and truly reflects who you are.

If you don't know where to start, then follow the three valuable questions suggested by Brian Tracy in his book (Master Your Time, and Master Your Life).

Question 1: "Ask yourself what you really want to do in your life."

Question 2: Ask yourself what you 'really, really' wanted to do in your life.

Question 3: "Ask yourself what you really, really, really wanted to do in your life."

When you move from questions 1 to 3, the questions become more serious, and you will get an answer. Try to move in that direction. Once you have established what you want in life, you can set clear goals, explore passions, visualise success, create an action plan and stay committed with persistence (which I have discussed in the next few chapters).

Golden Nuggets

- Life offers numerous choices; we must choose exactly what we want.

- It is essential to understand your desires, the reasons behind them, and the steps to turn them into reality.

- To determine what you want in life, take time for self-reflection and develop an understanding of your ambitions.

- If necessary, take more time to determine what you truly want. Make it a priority to engage in self-discovery, personal growth, and pursuing what truly matters to you.

- Your clarity of thought is one of your best assets. If you have clarity, it will empower you to take the next step towards success.

- Once you have a clearer vision of your goals, you can create a strong rooting system in your mind that will help you grow and thrive.

- Don't waste time chasing others' dreams. Value your goals and ambitions.

- To develop an excellent personal development plan, take a step back, reflect, and organise your life according to your goals in every phase.

Follow Your Passion and Bring the God within You

'Embrace your inner calling and the world will open'
– American writer Joseph Campbell

Passion is fuelled by enthusiasm. The word passion is derived from the Greek word *"Enthio,"* meaning "God within." So, bring the god (the passion that we all have) within you to the outside world. Find your calling. We all possess unique talents waiting to be embraced in meaningful pursuits. Discovering your calling doesn't mean abandoning what you are doing. Rather, it means integrating more of yourself into your work and **focusing on 'what you do best'.**

Passion is your calling. After all, the average person spends over 90,000 hours working throughout their lifetime, which accounts for one-third of their entire life. Therefore, it would be wonderful if that time were devoted to something you love. However, some people might not know what they truly feel passionate about. They lack clarity and feel stuck. Ask yourself what you want from life. Reflect on your long-term vision and the life you aspire to live. Pay attention to moments when you feel a natural pull toward a particular activity, area, or idea, as these feelings often indicate where your true passions lie. Ensure that you follow your curiosities; the attitude of curiosity is a strong indicator of potential passion. When you find yourself drawn to specific topics, activities, or discussions, take the time to explore them further. **Allow your curiosity to lead you to new experiences and insights.** If there is a lack of clarity, confusion often increases, making it difficult to determine the correct outcomes. This confusion can lead to a cycle of indecision and repetition. Therefore, gaining clarity is essential for effectively determining outcomes. Pay attention to your intuition. Allow your curiosity to lead you further.

'**The privilege of a lifetime is to become who you truly are**' - Carl Gustav Jung, the founder of the school of analytical psychology. True festivities of life involve 'pursuing our passions and living with purpose'. When we engage in activities that bring us joy and a sense of purpose, we enrich our lives and contribute positively to the world around us, living a more meaningful and fulfilling life. If you genuinely love what you do, you won't miss out on life's most incredible promises: happiness, peace of mind, and harmony. Anxiety about meeting others' expectations can push us to conform rather than follow our passions. It is crucial to navigate your journey and discover your passions independently instead of relying on parents, family, or friends for guidance.

Why is finding a passionate job essential? One of the best feelings is getting paid for what you love. Two key forces, the Law of Attraction and the Law of Repulsion, impact our bodies. These forces interact at the cellular level, which is a scientifically proven fact. Engaging in activities you love activates the Law of Attraction, reducing the effects of the Law of Repulsion. This leads to more energy, enthusiasm, and better sleep; you wake up feeling refreshed. Conversely, engaging in tasks out of obligation triggers the Law of Repulsion, resulting in low energy, mental fatigue, and tiredness. Thus, choose activities that align with your passions. While forced efforts may yield short-term success, they are not sustainable. Strive to find work you love for personal satisfaction and financial rewards. As Napoleon Hill wisely said, "Success in life depends upon happiness, and happiness is found in no other way than through service rendered in a spirit of love."

Passion is not about hobbies. People often confuse passion with hobbies or special interests, which are distinctly different. Passion is not merely about pursuing activities you enjoy—it **involves discovering your innate talents, at which you are good and probably even great, striving for self-mastery in those areas, and investing in your passion.**

'Follow your passion, and success will follow you'
– Quotation anthologist, Terri Guillemets

To assess your passion, read and follow these steps.

Step 1

Take a personal inventory. The first important step in self- reflection is to take a personal inventory to 'identify your interests and strengths.' Discover what excites you and what you are genuinely passionate about—essentially, find out what you love to do. It is crucial to uncover your talents and determine what you excel at; perhaps even identify areas where you could become exceptional. Start by listing activities that naturally draw you in. Evaluate how these interests align with your current skills. If you struggle to find your passion, think about what brings you happiness. Reflect on moments in your life when you felt delighted and fulfilled. What were you doing at that time? Who were you with? The answers to these questions can provide valuable insights into your passions. Choosing the right field can ease your progress while selecting the wrong one can lead to struggles. Choosing a focus area that aligns with your interests and skills for long-term success.

Step 2

After identifying your interests, **focus on embracing your strengths**. Everyone has unique talents that deserve recognition, and your strengths can reveal pursuits you might enjoy. Reflect on the qualities others value in you for insights into your passions. Recognising your core values and what matters is essential; this alignment guides your passions toward purpose. Understanding your personality is crucial, as is discovering what interests align with your skills. I discovered my passion for medicine as a child, finding joy in reading about science from age 10. Reflecting on my interests, I realised that subjects like biology and chemistry inspired me, and I enjoyed tutoring my peers in these areas. Visits to hospitals filled me with happiness, confirming my desire to belong in that environment. My empathy, strong work ethic, problem-solving skills, and ability to diagnose issues highlight my potential for medical success.

Step 3

Exploring different fields and experiences is key to discovering your passions. Reflect on fulfilling past engagements through school, work, or hobbies. Start this exploration early to identify interests; parents should enrol children in diverse classes like music, sports, and arts for early self-discovery. Consider skills you enjoyed during these activities, as this can highlight your passions. Assess your skill set by trying new activities—consider attending workshops, courses, or volunteering. Such exploration may unveil new interests and hidden skills. For instance, I have shadowed doctors, volunteered at hospitals, and participated in health fairs, revealing various aspects of medicine and healthcare.

Step 4

Another vital aspect is **experimentation—' embracing the process of trial and error.'** Understand that discovering your passion is a journey that often requires vigorous experimentation. Don't shy away from experiences that may seem outside your comfort zone. Each new endeavour, whether successful or not, can provide valuable insights into what you truly enjoy. Engage in activities that intrigue you, even if unfamiliar, as such experiences can lead to unexpected passions. For example, my friend used to play cricket and enjoyed it. However, a friend took him to a table tennis club one day. Although he entered reluctantly and played a few matches with hesitation, he soon realised that he was quite good at it; now he is a national player in table tennis.

Step 5

Seek inspiration from mentorship and feedback. Find experienced mentors in your areas of interest for guidance. Connecting with passionate individuals can reveal new paths and challenges. For example, conversations with physicians clarified the realities of the medical profession for me. Mentors like professors and older medical students motivated me with insights into their challenges and successes, encouraging my perseverance toward becoming a physician. Networking is essential; participate in workshops or community gatherings to connect with like-minded individuals. This can lead to new opportunities. Additionally, seek feedback from friends and colleagues about your strengths. Their insights can refine your understanding of what truly resonates with you

Step 6

Set Goals and Execute Your Plan - Once you have identified your passion through exploration and reflection, it is essential to define it clearly. A well-understood passion will empower you to take concrete steps toward it. **Create an action plan** that outlines how you will achieve your goals. This plan should include timelines, necessary resources, and specific actions. A structured plan will help keep you focused and motivated on your journey.

> **'If you don't execute your plans, then**
> **you don't reach anywhere'**
> – Indian Cricketer Sachin Tendulkar

Some individuals may take longer to discover their passion, which is fine. Once you identify what to pursue, take swift action; delaying this decision can be detrimental. If you have made past mistakes but have found your true passion, distance yourself from those earlier choices and pursue your passion with fresh insight and newfound wisdom. Ultimately, the only thing you might regret is not doing more of what you love.

"The only way to do great work is to love what you do. If you haven't found it, keep looking and don't settle." – Apple founder Steve Jobs. There is a Japanese legend that says, 'If you get on the wrong train, get off at the nearest station. The longer it takes you to get off, the more expensive the return trip will be.'

Start investing in your passion—time, money, energy, and effort—to grow. Identify your strengths and focus on enhancing your natural skills. Dedicate weekly hours to engage with your passion. For example, if you love playing an instrument, practice for 30 minutes daily to see significant improvement. Schedule specific times for this investment, as it is essential for mastery. **Consider it an important appointment with yourself.** Putting in effort is crucial to mastering your craft and achieving success. While not always necessary, financial investments may be required (e.g., classes, tools, equipment, resources, etc.. No matter your passion, there's always a way to monetise it. Today, starting now, there are more opportunities to profit from what you love.

> **"Investing in yourself - no one can take that away from you"**
> – American investor and philanthropist
> Mr Warren Buffett

Make a move and spring into action instead of waiting, as it won't produce results. **Explore opportunities to turn your passion into profit**. Sitting idly out of fear is not effective. Move forward, follow your passion, and monetise it. Enjoy the financial benefits of your investment in your passion. Give yourself a chance to earn a living doing what you love. Once you start monetising your passion, remain consistent and adaptable. Profits may not be immediate, but daily investment of time and energy is essential for progress. Commit to regular practice—passion demands dedication. Consistency builds skills and confidence over time.

Although I am a doctor, I also have a passion for teaching. After completing my postgraduate studies, I aimed to create a valuable course for doctors preparing for their exams. I started my teaching course in 2005 (see SPMM Course https://spmmcourse.com for details). Although initial profits were modest, this course allowed me to share my knowledge while earning an income. I dedicated time and energy each day to improving my situation. Despite early financial challenges, I found joy in teaching. Over time, my venture evolved into a successful business recognised as one of the top courses in the UK. If I had not taken that first step and committed to my passion, I wouldn't have achieved my current success.

I truly encourage you to explore ways to monetise your passions! It is indeed true that you won't discover your potential until you take that leap of faith. Getting wet is not bad—just dry off and try again!

Your next dive might lead you to a fabulous pool of opportunities. Take the time to identify your strengths and develop your skills; there are countless ways to earn money while doing what you love! **Pursue your passions, nurture your talents, and seek positive ways to share them with the world.** By aligning your habits with what genuinely makes you happy, you can shape your journey towards success!

Golden Nuggets

- Embark on a journey of self-reflection and personal inventory to uncover your passions.

- Pay attention to your intuition. Allow your curiosity to lead you further.

- Reflect on your interests and strengths. For long-term success, choosing a focus area that aligns with your interests and skills is crucial.

- Embrace your strengths. Everyone possesses unique talents that deserve recognition, and your strengths can indicate pursuits you may enjoy.

- Exploring different fields and experiences is key to discovering your passions.

- Embrace trial and error. Don't shy away from experiences beyond your comfort zone. Engage in activities that interest you, even if new to you.

- Seek inspiration from others and talk to people who have found their passion.

- Networking can lead to new opportunities.

- Start investing in your passion – time, money, energy, and effort – to grow.

- Take steps and spring into motion instead of waiting, as it won't yield results.

- Discover ways to convert your passion into profit.

Envisioning Your Aspirations and Picturing Your Ambitions

'Visualise the thing you want. See it, feel it and believe in it. Make your mental blueprint and begin to build'
– American author Robert Collier

Visualisation means imagining what you want to attain in the future as if it were happening today. It involves 'imagining yourself achieving your goals and successes, picturing yourself reaching your objectives and accomplishments'. Creating a mental image of your aspirations and dreams is a decisive step toward achieving them.

Consider what you would do if you had a magical wand. Write down all your dreams, goals, and desires in a notebook. **'Visualising your goals is crucial; envision achieving them and relishing the benefits of that success'.** Visualisation involves engaging all five senses: sight, hearing, smell, taste, and touch. To truly experience success, regularly immerse yourself in the feeling of triumph. For example, imagine you want to complete a 10 km marathon in your county. As you start your training, it is crucial to visualise the dream of finishing the marathon as if it were already a reality. You should envision yourself crossing the finish line and embracing the joy and elation of success. Create a mental movie with all the effects needed to make it a hit. Feel the satisfaction of achieving your goal and the happiness, pride, and emotions accompanying your victory. By immersing yourself in this vivid visualisation process, you can strengthen your determination and motivation, bringing you closer to realising your target.

From a scientific perspective, **visualisation is the most effective method for programming the subconscious mind.** Our subconscious cannot distinguish between reality and the visualisation process. Therefore, if you visualise your goals with strong emotions and vivid details, your subconscious will be convinced they are occurring. This belief provides motivation and ideas to help transform your life into the desired outcome. Training your brain and subconscious to envision success is crucial for future achievements. One intriguing fact about the brain is that it can be challenging to differentiate between imagination and reality. When you vividly visualise something, your brain activates the same neurons as you were experiencing it. The line between what is real and what is imagined becomes distorted and blurred. Whenever you envision positive emotions like success or happiness, your brain creates new neural pathways associated with those feelings. The more you focus on positive thoughts, the closer you move toward living them. Each time you visualise the life you desire, you are not merely daydreaming; instead, you are rewiring the neurons in your brain to align with that reality. When you imagine these scenarios long enough, they will no longer exist solely in your mind but will begin to manifest in your life. This approach offers a constructive way to envision your dreams and potentially transform them into reality.

Visualisation helps activate the subconscious mind, providing motivation and generating new ideas that can be implemented and turned into reality. Many psychiatrists and psychologists utilise visualisation methods to assist people in overcoming anxiety, PTSD (post-traumatic stress disorder), depression, and other psychological challenges. It is well-known that visualisation can lead to significant changes in one's thought processes, improving one's mental state.

Many high achievers and top performers worldwide are believed to use visualisation techniques to achieve their goals. We have all heard of Michael Phelps, who is regarded as one of the greatest swimmers of all time, with an astonishing twenty- three Olympic gold medals to his name. However, his success wasn't solely due to his intense training routines, which involved spending 5 to 6 hours a day in the pool, even on Sundays and holidays; it stemmed from something more profound: Phelps would visualise his races. He envisioned the perfect dive, the roar of the crowd, the rhythm of each stroke, and the sensation of the water. He also anticipated obstacles, such as a poor start or goggles filling with water. This visualisation process was crucial for him, allowing him to prepare for the specific situations he might encounter. As I previously stated, visualisation stimulates neural (nerve) pathways in the brain, leading to interpret everything as reality. This method encapsulated Michael Phelps's preparation for victory. In the final of the 200 m butterfly at the 2008 Beijing Olympics, his goggles filled with water halfway through the race. Most swimmers would have given up or struggled in that situation, but Phelps did not. He relied on his stroke count, executing it just as he had visualised, ultimately leading to his gold medal win and a world record.

I have had an incredible experience! As I approached my final year in medical school, I learned about the Pfizer Award given to top students for outstanding performance in their final year examinations. From early on, I envisioned the joy of receiving that award; I pictured the moment and the feeling of holding it in my hands, visualising this special occasion repeatedly. This served as a tremendous motivation for my studies. Eventually, my dream came true, and I was thrilled to be recognised as the top graduating final year student at my college, receiving both the award and a gold medal. This achievement is one of the most significant highlights of my life, rooted in my daily visualisations of success. Following this experience, I have started visualising success in other areas of my life, which has proven beneficial.

> **'If you don't have a dream, you can't really push yourself;**
> **you don't really know what the target is'**
> – Indian Cricketer MS Dhoni

Have you ever enjoyed watching football matches? Footballers truly need to know precisely where the goal is and picture it in their minds. They focus intently on the goal before taking a shot. Like them, we should all have clear dreams of the targets we want to reach and a wonderful plan to help us move forward. Having a clear vision is essential for achieving greater heights of success! What are you waiting for? '**Bend it like Beckham, Mend it like Messi, and run it like Ronaldo'.**

Have you noticed how major organisations proudly display their vision statements on their websites and lobbies? These statements beautifully outline their goals, ambitions, and objectives, all aimed at turning dreams into reality through dedicated efforts, often highlighted in the induction programme. We often refer to these vision statements to grasp the very essence of the organisation. However, this principle is not just for large organisations; it is equally important for individuals! **Everyone deserves a vision for their life and a vital mission** encompassing their dreams and desires. These visions should be **clearly defined, vividly imagined, and actively pursued.**

Speaking of inspiring journeys, let me tell you about Mr. Gukesh Dommaraju! He made history as the youngest person to win the World Chess Championship at just 18 years old! What's even more heartwarming is a video from when he was around 11 or 12, where he shares his dreams of becoming the youngest champion in the world. Isn't that incredible? Having a clear vision is truly essential! Gukesh not only dreamed big but also transformed that dream into a life mission, achieving everything he set out to do. We can say mission accomplished! Gukesh embraced his dream wholeheartedly and turned it into a real-life mission, reaching incredible goals. It is important for us to express our dreams clearly and take those first steps towards making them come to life! Achieving success is not just about dreaming or having a vision; **it is about cultivating a strong mindset that turns that vision into a successful mission.** Let's be honest: we shouldn't merely dream! Instead, let's work to transform that vision into a tangible mission that leads us on our path to success. And remember, it is wonderful to express our dreams clearly and take action to turn them into reality!

Having your vision statement for the future is crucial! Dreaming about achieving that vision is wonderful, and there's absolutely nothing wrong with wanting to fulfil your life goals. This is not just daydreaming; it is 'daydreaming with a purpose', and it is the first step toward realising your dreams. Visualising a specific outcome and reflecting on how it makes you feel inspires you to aim even higher. Remember, picturing your aspirations is vital to your journey, so don't underestimate it! It is equally important to imagine the positive outcomes you will experience once you accomplish your goals. Establish some friendly deadlines and target dates to keep yourself motivated, and then take those exciting steps forward!

> **"You have to dream before your dreams can come true.**
> **Dream, Dream, Dream.**
> **Dreams transform into thoughts,**
> **and thoughts result in action**
> – Former Indian President, Dr. Abdul Kalam

One of the wealthiest individuals in the world, Mr Elon Musk, is known for his ambitious vision for the future, which includes sustainable energy, space exploration, and transportation innovation. His work with Tesla aims to accelerate the world's transition to sustainable energy, while SpaceX focuses on making space travel more affordable and colonising Mars.

Visualising your goals and dreams for at least five minutes each day is advisable. You can do this when you wake up or before going to bed. Visualising is helpful for achieving bigger dreams and goals enhancing your day, and making it a good one for you. When you wake up, take a moment to close your eyes and visualise the essential activities you have planned for the day. Many people I know struggle with waking up late and feeling stressed throughout the day. To avoid this, try getting up 5 to 10 minutes earlier. You can sit quietly on your bed or lie down, close your eyes, take some deep breaths, and visualise what you want to achieve that day. Starting your day with this intention can set a positive tone; however, if your day begins in a rush, it can lead to chaos and stress, ultimately hindering your achievements. While pursuing long-term dreams is essential, addressing daily goals is equally important.

I have cultivated a habit of visualising my day each morning. It is immensely helpful to envision how I want my day to unfold, allowing my subconscious to guide me. This practice is both active and empowering, which is why it can be so beneficial.

Visualisation is a powerful tool for boosting energy and enhancing motivation. Pictures in your room that represent your dreams and goals can help remind you of them and assist you in visualising them regularly. If you examine the offices of many successful individuals, you will notice numerous images adorning the walls in various areas of the space. These visuals remind us to consistently work toward their goals, and this practice should be reflected in our environment to keep us motivated.

Many people have big dreams, but you must start taking steps towards those dreams to make progress. It is important to begin, even if it is with small actions. There is a famous quote '**Dream big, start small, but act now; take the first steps to turn those dreams into reality.**' Imagining your success is the first step in boosting your confidence and nurturing the belief that it can and will become a reality.. We need clearer visions of our targets to progress effectively. Visualisation is nothing short of a programmed time machine to the future. It serves as our time machine, allowing us to reach our desired future.

Golden Nuggets

- Visualisation is all about picturing yourself achieving your goals and celebrating your successes! Imagine realising your aspirations and regularly enjoying the rewards of that success.

- Visualisation is the most effective method for programming the subconscious mind and helps activate it. Each time you visualise your life, you are 'literally rewiring the neurons in your brain to align with that reality.'

- Everyone deserves a vision for their life. These visions should be clearly defined, vividly imagined, and actively pursued.

- Achieving success involves more than simply having a vision; it requires developing a robust mindset that turns that vision into a successful mission.

- Visualising helps you pursue larger dreams and goals, and it enhances your day, making it better for you.

- Visualising your goals and dreams for at least five minutes daily is recommended.

Be Smart to Set SMART Goals

The first important step towards achieving your goals is **to write them down and document them.** It is essential to verbalise your thought process and clearly articulate your goals. To accomplish this, you should write down your goals on paper. Research indicates a higher chance of success when you document your objectives. Specifically, individuals who write down their goals tend to experience greater success than those who do not. Studies show that only 2 to 3 percent of individuals write down their goals and actively pursue them. In contrast, the overwhelming 97 percent have their goals in mind but fail to document them or take actionable steps towards achieving them. Writing down your goals increases the likelihood of success by clarifying focus and motivating action.

The goals you write down should be simple and easy to understand. For instance, if you show your goals to a ten-year-old child, they should be able to comprehend them. This is what I mean by "simple and easy." By simplifying your goals, you make them more achievable and clarify them for others, streamlining the overall process. **Use the present tense and an action verb when writing down your goals.** This approach makes your statements more compelling, reinforcing your commitment to achieving those objectives.

Here are some sample statements written in the present tense with action words to enhance their impact:

1. I achieved X grades in my performance appraisal this year.
2. I earn £100,000 this year.

3. I drive a BMW car this year.

4. I secure a mortgage for £200,000 this year.

5. I completed three grades in my Music course this year.

6. I finished the first six modules in my training programme to become a Financial Consultant this year.

Having regular cues is helpful. I write my goals on paper and stick them in front of my computer screen, ensuring they are visible every time I sit down to work. These visual cues and reminders help me take incremental steps toward fulfilling my aspirations. Goals are equally important, whether small or big. Even small goals have high significance, so I take them seriously. Examples include drinking 6-8 cups of water daily, consuming fruits and vegetables as one-third of my regular diet, organising my room space weekly, and clearing my inbox of emails regularly.

Some people confuse their goals with their desires in life. For example, statements like "I want to be happy," "I want to have a good family life with my life partner and children," or "I want to be healthy" are not goals; they are merely wishes or desires. Understanding the difference between setting clear goals and having desires for your life is vital. Desires are broader feelings of wishing for something and reflect more of your personal inclinations. They can be general and less clearly defined, often driven by emotions and personal values. Conversely, goals are more specific and clearly defined, consisting of concrete and actionable steps. You can set goals that align with your deeper desires.

Setting goals and making plans to achieve our objectives are crucial for success. Your likelihood of success increases significantly with a clear action plan for your goals. A goal with a deadline and a consistent action plan will lead to success.

**'An idiot with a plan can beat a genius
without a plan'**
– American Investor Warren Buffett

Goals must be clearly defined, and it is recommended to follow the SMART acronym:

- S stands for specific

- M stands for measurable

- A stands for achievable

- R stands for realistic

- T stands for time-bound

Many people have heard of this acronym but don't know the true meaning of each letter, which I have explained. George T. Doran first introduced the term in the November 1981 issue of Management Review, where he advocated setting specific (or Simple), measurable, achievable, realistic, and time-bound objectives—hence the acronym S.M.A.R.T.

Take a sheet of paper and write down your goals, '**ensuring they are specific**'. For instance, clarify what you hope to achieve in six months. For example, 'I plan to complete my data entry and Microsoft Office courses within six months.'

If you don't know where your goals are or cannot see them, you are less likely to achieve them. We must be very clear about our targets and future plans. '**A lack of clearly defined goals**' is one of the most common reasons for failing to meet our objectives.

Don't focus on too many goals at once. Setting multiple goals simultaneously can be counterproductive. Once you know what you want, it is best to concentrate on one thing at a time and tackle it individually. It can be tempting to pursue many goals simultaneously, but this approach can complicate your journey. Focusing on a single goal enhances your chances of success. Complete one goal before moving on to the next.

The Chinese philosopher Confucius emphasised its significance by stating, "**If you chase two rabbits, you will catch none.**" Therefore, keep a clear focus on one specific goal at a time. When you have more than one goal in mind, it is helpful to prioritise them and tackle them one at a time. Creating a priority list can guide your focus, allowing you to put your energy into the most important tasks first. For instance, if you want to learn the keyboard and Zumba, but learning to play the keyboard is your top priority, make it a point to attend keyboard training classes regularly while keeping your other goals, like trying out Zumba, in mind for later!

Concentrating on a specific task, skill, or goal over time can help us achieve mastery. When we dedicate our attention to learning and improving towards one focused goal, we can become experts in our fields rather than juggling many interests without purpose.

Furthermore, goals should be measurable. **Measurable** means **'how will you or others know that you have achieved it'**. For instance, if you are engaged in a fitness programme, monitor your progress weekly using a smartwatch or fitness app. If you manage a business, regularly assess your income, expenses, balance sheet and net profit quarterly. A goal without a measurable outcome is like a sports competition without a scoreboard.

Ensure your goals are **achievable, meaning within your control.** Avoid setting objectives that are beyond your grasp. Setting excessively high expectations and pursuing unattainable goals can undermine your self-confidence. For example, starting a business in a distant location or entering an industry in which you have no experience may be impossible.

Additionally, goals must be **realistic and attainable within your current circumstances**. Be mindful not to set unattainable goals or pursue objectives out of reach. Aiming to achieve a milestone, such as running a 5-kilometre marathon in six months, losing 5 kg in five months' time, or learning to read and write a new language in 12 months, is realistic and can be achieved with the necessary effort, willpower, commitment, and dedication.

Lastly, goals must be **time-bound.** Ensure your goals have clear and realistic deadlines. **A goal without a deadline is merely a dream**. Goals should be time-sensitive and include a specific deadline. Most goals are attainable, but the deadlines must be realistic. Unrealistic timelines can hinder goal accomplishment, making it crucial to set goals with proper, achievable deadlines to ensure success. It is important to complete tasks by established deadlines that you believe are achievable on a subconscious level. To achieve your goals, you must establish clear timeframes, such as three to six months or one year. Establishing time-sensitive goals.

It is essential to review your goals periodically. Some individuals write them down but fail to revisit them. Avoid this mistake by revisiting your goals weekly, evaluating your progress, and determining the necessary actions. If you maintain a calendar, you can track your progress and assess the goals achieved and the direction in which you are heading. Reward yourself when you finish each step. Make a note in your diary or phone a friend or family member to monitor your progress.

If goals are bigger, break them into small, achievable objectives and tackle them in small steps. Take small, gradual steps towards achieving your goal. Make progress incrementally, starting from the bottom and working your way up rather than rushing through the process. Break It Down—Once you have your main goals, decompose them into smaller, actionable steps. This approach makes them less overwhelming and allows for steady progress. For example, if your goal is to start a blog, initial steps might include researching blogging platforms, creating a content plan, and writing your first post.

Goals can be categorised into **short-term, intermediate, and long-term categories for better structure.** You should aim to achieve short-term goals within the next few days, weeks, or by the end of the next month. Intermediate goals are intended for the next six months to a year, while long- term goals are those you hope to accomplish within five years. If you don't clearly identify your goals, you are less likely to achieve them effectively. Therefore, clearly define your short-term, intermediate, and long-term goals to succeed in your plans. Diligently working towards these goals is essential. For example, if you are passionate about photography, a short-term goal could be attending a photography workshop; an intermediate goal might involve creating a portfolio; and a long-term goal may be showcasing your work in a local exhibition.

Some people wanted to keep it even simpler, which is fine, too. They try to establish a "goal of the day." They also have goals for the week, month, or year, which serve as additional components of their action plan and help them work towards it.

While setting goals, **consider the various aspects of your life—** such as fitness, finances, personal growth, professional aspirations, material desires, relationships, social connections, and spiritual journeys—and establish clear, specific objectives for each as you plan your goals. For instance, you might aim to define your fitness goals to enhance your physical and mental wellness and identify personal goals that align with your passions and interests. You can identify professional aspirations to advance your career and achievements. Regarding finances, reflect on goals for saving, investing, and building a robust portfolio. You can also establish material goals for meaningful possessions you would like to acquire, relationship goals to nurture your connection skills, social goals to strengthen your friendships, and spiritual goals to enrich your inner self. Organising your goals this way can create a harmonious balance in your life as you pursue your dreams, ensuring you enjoy every step of the journey towards fulfilling your objectives in all these valuable areas.

You may need to make sacrifices and trade-offs while striving to achieve your goals. For instance, if you pursue an additional degree, you might have to forgo an hour of sleep each night to devote time to studying. This might mean spending less time on social media, reducing the frequency of going out with friends or cutting back on viewing on OTT platforms like Amazon Prime or Netflix. By making these sacrifices and compromises, you substantially increase your chances of achieving your goals.

You must have the right resources and strategies to reach your goals. This includes developing a clear plan and organising your resources effectively.

For example, when setting fitness goals, consider the following resources and strategies: A detailed diet chart and meal plan, a regular exercise routine, access to a gym or a basic home gym setup, fitness instruments (weights, bands, etc.), a coach for guidance and motivation, an accountability partner, and membership in fitness motivation groups or communities. As the saying goes, "Desire should be converted into action," and it is crucial that "goals are translated into action" for effective results.

Share your ambitions and goals for life with those close to you—your family, friends, and anyone you trust. When they know your goals, they can cheer you on and support you in making those dreams a reality. Talking about your goals with people who can offer help and encouragement is essential. By sharing what you want to achieve, you create an incredible support network that motivates and holds you accountable.

If you aim to wake up at 5 a.m., sharing this goal with your family can be incredibly helpful! They can help create a cosy and supportive atmosphere, like gently reminding you to head to bed early and waking you up when your alarm goes off at 5 a.m. This approach works wonders for all kinds of goals, whether small steps or big dreams. Connecting with the people who care about you can truly make a difference in turning those dreams into reality. Discussing your goals can be truly rewarding! Sharing your aspirations, especially with loved ones, presents a wonderful opportunity for support and encouragement. Not only can they assist you on your journey, but they can also make the process much more enjoyable. Keeping your ambitions to yourself can feel isolating and may make it harder to move forward. Therefore, being open about your goals can illuminate your path!

Recognising that problems and obstacles are a natural part of the journey toward achieving our goals is essential. When faced with challenges, we should not give up; instead, we should plan ways to overcome them using the strategies discussed in the other chapter, "How to Tackle Challenges Head-On." Setbacks may arise frequently, but overcoming these challenges and moving forward steadily in one direction is crucial. Don't lose your confidence; believe in your abilities throughout this process. Create an action plan: develop a detailed outline of how you will achieve your goals, including timelines, resources needed, and specific actions to take. **Having a structured plan keeps you focused and motivated.**

Be open to adjusting your goals and action plan as you learn more about your passion. **Flexibility allows you to pivot when necessary,** ensuring you remain aligned with your evolving interests and circumstances. It lets you shift gears when needed, helping you stay in tune with your ever- changing passions and situations.

Working together and teaming up with supportive individuals who share your goals can elevate your chances of reaching them! When you join forces with others who have similar goals and objectives, you create a wonderful understanding that enhances everyone's journey. For instance, having a workout buddy significantly increases the likelihood that you will hit the gym and explore new exercise styles together, inspiring one another. Collaboration fosters a beautiful blend of skills, experiences, and perspectives, transforming the path to success into a more rewarding and joyful adventure.

Remember that desire must be turned into action. Thus, goals should be pursued using the SMART strategy mentioned above.

Golden Nuggets

- Please write down your goals and document them.
- Focus on one goal at a time to improve your chances of achieving success.
- The goals should be simple and easy to understand.
- The goals must be SMART - Specific, measurable, achievable, realistic, and time-bound.
- Divide your goals into short-term, intermediate, and long-term categories.

- If goals are bigger, then break them into small, achievable objectives and tackle them step by step.

- Consider different areas of your life and establish clear, specific objectives when setting your goals.

- You may need to make sacrifices and trade-offs while striving to achieve your goals.

- To reach your goals, you must have the right resources and strategies.

- Share your goals with those close to you, as they can support you in achieving them.

- Collaborating with others who are supportive and aligned with your aspirations can significantly enhance your chances of success in achieving your goals.

- Goals should be implemented into action.

Thoughts are Incredibly Powerful

"The mind is everything.
What you think, you become."
– Gautama Buddha

Our thoughts are incredibly powerful, mainly determining how we feel and behave. **We must understand that thoughts, feelings, and behaviours are interconnected**. Changing our thoughts about a particular situation can alter how we feel and act. These three domains interact. Once you start generating more positive thoughts, you will cultivate more positive self-beliefs and nurturing self- affirmations. Positive thoughts can elicit uplifting emotions and inspire positive changes in your behaviour.

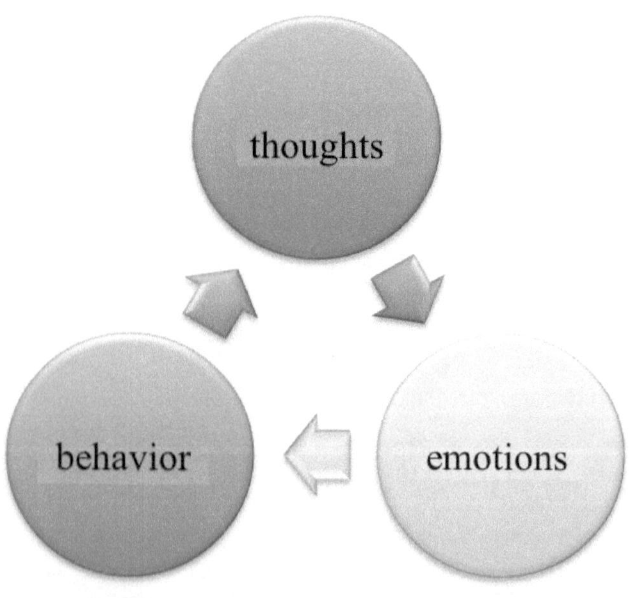

Let me share a situation to illustrate how our thoughts, feelings, and actions are interconnected and how individuals with positive or negative mindsets interpret them.

Imagine you are calling a close friend. During the conversation, you notice that your friend seems inattentive and is hurrying to hang up the phone. This situation can be interpreted either positively or negatively.

If you have a positive mindset and think positively, you might wonder why your friend is eager to end the call. You may think,

I wonder if he is feeling upset.

Is he having a tough time?

Does he need help?

Such thoughts can evoke worry, sadness, and anxiety about how you can assist your friend. These feelings can lead to positive behaviours, such as contacting them again to check in or visiting them in person to understand why they seemed upset.

Conversely, you might interpret your friend's behaviour differently if you have a negative mindset with negative cognition. You may think,

I wonder if he still likes me.

Why did he sound upset with me?

Why is he no longer interested in talking to me?

This line of thinking can generate anger, disappointment, and unhappiness. You might even feel disgusted by your friend's perceived attitude, which could lead to negative behaviours, such as refusing to contact them again, blocking their number, or sending angry messages expressing dissatisfaction with how they ended the call. The choice is ours to make. We can choose positive, inspiring, and creative thoughts, yet many people succumb to negative, fearful, or doubtful thinking.

Our brain is like a mini-computer. The various parts of our brain resemble the hardware of a computer. The chemicals released by the brain and the electrical changes function as the software of our bodily computer. The programming encompasses our thoughts, feelings, and desires. We are the programmers, wielding the power and control to shape it into a positive project. Focus your energy on what you can control, including your thoughts, emotions, behaviours, and responses to events.

Did you know that our minds have muscles just like our bodies do?

Our minds possess imaginary muscles that require regular training. We all have biceps; stretching them through regular workouts makes them more prominent and stronger. They remain thin and weaker if you don't work out and use them less. Similar things happen with our mental muscles. When you properly stretch these mental muscles, you will cultivate positive thoughts and become stronger. These mental muscles enable you to live well. However, if you overuse or underuse them, you risk straining them and producing negative thoughts. Therefore, concentrate on developing a positive thinking process in your mind.

Isn't it fascinating how our brains come up with thoughts?

Thoughts are the final products of electrical activities occurring in the brain and are shaped by neuronal interactions.

They are generated by brain cells and transmitted through synaptic clefts (the gaps between two neurons. The brain produces various types of thoughts—positive, negative, or neutral. It is crucial to prioritise and highlight positive and neutral thoughts while downplaying the significance of negative or fearful ones. Many individuals find themselves trapped in this cycle of negative thinking.

There is a famous saying: **"The quality of our thoughts determines the quality of our lives."**

Thoughts are compelling, and we should strive to cultivate positive rather than negative ones. People often ask me how to eliminate negative thoughts or express a desire for a mind entirely free of thoughts because they feel overwhelmed by negativity.

I always respond that our brains will keep generating thoughts as long as we are alive; they only stop when we die. The average person produces between 6,000 and 60,000 thoughts each day. We should learn to be good gatekeepers of our minds, prioritise the right thoughts, and give them more significance while allowing others to flow without importance.

Recognising that the fundamental cycle of thoughts, feelings, and behaviour is interconnected and universal to all individuals is crucial. Grasping the relationship among these elements offers greater insight into our perception of situations. This is the core principle therapists apply in Cognitive Behavioural Therapy (shortened to CBT, which the American Psychiatrist and pioneer of Cognitive Therapy, Mr Aaron Beck first described).

> **"The pessimist sees difficulty in**
> **every opportunity; the optimist sees**
> **opportunity in every difficulty."**
> – Sir Winston Churchill

The optimist with a positive thinking style sees a half- filled glass, while the pessimist with a negative thinking style perceives it as half empty. When wearing a cooler, the optimist looks through a coloured glass, whereas the pessimist interprets it as darkly tinted. No poison can kill a positive thinker; positive thinking is a protective shield. No medicine can cure a negative thinker, and with negative thinking styles, you remain a slave to your mind.

Many wonder whether negative life experiences or situations cause more pain and how to avoid these adverse events. No one is immune to such occurrences. We often label certain life experiences as negative or destructive, leading to significant pain and hurt. However, it is not these so-called negative experiences that cause pain; rather, **our perceptions and thoughts about these experiences determine the extent of our suffering.** It is not the situation that makes us sad but our reactions and perceptions. These perceptions, shaped by our thoughts, ultimately influence our feelings and behaviours.

> **"Your mind is a magnet. If you think of blessings,
> you attract blessings. If you think of problems,
> you attract problems. Always cultivate good thoughts
> and always remain optimistic"**
> – Chinese businessman and philanthropist
> Mr Jack Ma

You can think of a **strong mindset like iron**, which is not easily destroyed. The only thing that can weaken or destroy it is its rust. Similarly, no one can negatively influence you if you maintain a positive mindset. However, if you have a negative mindset, it can greatly impact your success and well-being. Individuals who consistently harbour negative thoughts often stagnate and struggle to progress.

Albert Einstein famously stated that **"everything is energy,"** emphasising that energy is the fundamental essence of all things in the universe. This energy cannot be destroyed; it can only be transformed from one form to another. This concept underscores the idea that our experiences, emotions, and thoughts exist within this energetic framework. By adopting a more positive outlook, **we change our internal energy and influence the energy we project into the world around us.**

Therefore, the key to overcoming negative energies lies in one's mindset. By consciously shifting our perspective, we can transform negative thoughts and emotions into positive ones. This transformation involves recognising negative thoughts and feelings and actively choosing to reinterpret them to foster growth and positivity. For instance, overwhelming challenges can initially be reframed as learning and personal development opportunities.

Golden Nuggets

- Thoughts, feelings, and behaviours are interconnected and universal for everyone.

- Changing our thoughts about a situation can alter our feelings and behaviour.

- Thoughts are the end products of electrical activities in the brain, generated by neuronal processes. They are always present.

- Focusing on positive or neutral thoughts is essential while diminishing the impact of negative or fearful thoughts.

- Our brains generate thoughts while we are alive; they cease when we die. We should learn to prioritise positive thoughts and attach greater significance to them.

- Individuals experience significant mental anguish in various situations. It is not the challenging life experiences that lead to pain and suffering; instead, our perception of these experiences, influenced by our thoughts, determines the level of our distress.

- The key to overcoming negative energies lies in one's mindset by consciously shifting one's perspective.

Identifying Thinking Errors

Thinking errors are irrational thought patterns often observed in individuals facing stress, anxiety, and depression. Many people encounter these errors in their thinking, which can result in unnecessary distress. Thinking errors, technically called cognitive distortions, can impact one's progress in life, success, and happiness.

I would like to share thoughts on overthinking before delving into thinking errors.

'The most common reason for our unhappiness is overthinking. Stop overthinking and don't create problems that don't exist.'

During my seminars, people often ask me why life is so complicated. I typically provide a straightforward answer: life is quite simple, but we tend to complicate it by overthinking, overanalysing and overjudging situations. As Roman philosopher Seneca wisely said, **"We suffer more in imagination than in reality."** The secret is to recognise that you are someone who overthinks, a tendency that most people don't share; therein lies the problem. Once you gain this insight, you can understand why you are doing it and gradually reduce your overthinking altogether.

Imagine a minor cut on your skin. If you keep scratching the wound, you will ultimately cause more damage, leading to bleeding and infection. If you leave it alone and try not to worry too much about it, it will heal quickly. Similarly, we should avoid overthinking and give ourselves time and space when we have worries. Constantly revisiting the same issue can lead to more mental anguish, further complicating your situation. The key lesson is to avoid overthinking matters, as it can lead to cognitive (thinking) errors.

The more stressed and upset you feel, the more your thinking errors affect you, and the more your thinking errors affect you, the more stressed and upset you feel. To break this vicious cycle, **you must first identify your thinking errors.** Many people are unaware of their thinking process errors and how deeply they are entangled in this cycle. Consequently, they dwell on negative thought patterns and associated emotions repeatedly; this is akin to conducting a postmortem examination on a deceased body. You internalise your mind, meticulously revisiting all the negative thoughts, emotions, and experiences. This repetitive mental process complicates matters further, exhausting your mind and cognitive functions.

First, it is important to understand the various types of thinking errors that can arise in our minds. I have had the pleasure of conducting cognitive behavioural therapy (CBT with many of my clients, and one key focus of this therapy is identifying these thinking errors, as they often lie at the core of our challenges. I have shared my observations to help others reading this book recognise the presence of these errors, and in the upcoming chapter, I will provide examples of how to effectively challenge them.

Some common thinking errors with simple examples are given below.

'All-or-nothing thinking, also known as black-or-white thinking'', is a cognitive error in which people assume that if a 'situation falls short of perfection, it is viewed as a complete failure'. Individuals with this mindset struggle to recognise the grey areas in between and only focus on extremes.

For example, one might think, "Unless I achieve my goal without mistakes, I have failed my test." Similarly, someone might conclude, "If he doesn't visit me today, then he doesn't love me at all." Somepeople are particularly hard on themselves and engage in "should" statements. They tell themselves that things should be the way they hoped or expected them to be. These individuals often make 'extreme statements and set impossible standards'. They frequently use words like "should," "always," "never," and "typical." Their "should" statements are directed at themselves and others and the world, which complicates things.

For instance, they might think, "I should be a perfect parent," or "I should always make the right decisions for my children." They might assert, "I must always do my job perfectly and never make any mistakes," or "I want to be the perfect boyfriend and should not make any errors in my relationships." They may even strive to embody all the positive traits of a "typical human being." This self-imposed pressure can lead to increased misery, as they find it difficult to escape the vicious cycle of setting impossible standards and making extreme statements. **These unrealistic expectations and high standards are often not dictated by others or external circumstances,** yet individuals feel burdened by them, nonetheless. They tend to have a rigid mindset or are dogmatic in their beliefs about how things ought to be and may be described as engaging in absolutist thinking. This thinking can lead to a lack of flexibility and openness to alternative perspectives.

'**Catastrophizing**' is another cognitive distortion that involves '**predicting the worst-case scenario and jumping to dire conclusions**'. In this thinking error, people often exaggerate the consequences of an event or situation and blow it out of proportion. They can't think of different possibilities other than the worst outcomes. For instance, if someone experiences chest pain, they might think there is something severely wrong with their heart and fear they are having a heart attack. Likewise, if someone has a headache, they may worry that they are on the verge of a stroke. If a person close to them does not answer their phone while travelling, others might irrationally assume they have been in an accident and possibly died. Similarly, if a child does not return home on time, it may be assumed immediately that they have been abducted. In all these situations, individuals jump to the worst possible conclusions and begin to believe that the most catastrophic outcomes are imminent.

Another significant cognitive error is **overgeneralisation,** which involves **drawing conclusions based on minimal evidence.** This thinking error leads individuals to assume that if something occurs once, it will always occur. For instance, after experiencing a setback, such as failing an exam, someone might conclude, "I failed once, so I will always fail." Similarly, after a relationship failure, they might believe they are doomed to an endless cycle of defeat. Consequently, they may miss opportunities in life without giving it a fair try. People who engage in overgeneralisation often use "always" or "never." For example, if someone feels anxious in a crowded supermarket, they might think, "I'm going to feel anxious every time I go out."

Another common cognitive error is **jumping to conclusions** without evidence, technically called **arbitrary inference.** This involves interpreting situations negatively without real facts to support such beliefs. For example, if a daughter does not visit, her mother might assume that the world hates her. There may be valid reasons for this absence, such as being occupied with work. However, those who engage in this thinking error tend to overlook alternative perspectives, believing nobody likes them, and that the entire world is against them.

Have you heard of the term **"mental filter,"** technically called **'selective abstraction'**? In this thinking error, individuals focus on their failures and mistakes while ignoring positive aspects and achievements. They dwell on specific adverse events and struggle to see the brighter side. Those with this thinking pattern view situations through a dark-tinted lens, perceiving a glass of water as half empty rather than half full. For instance, after delivering a presentation to a group, a person might receive numerous positive comments; however, if one person offers mild criticism, they may fixate on that critique instead of appreciating the positive feedback. Individuals might ruminate on this negative comment for days, filtering out any positive reinforcement. Similarly, students could achieve several A's and A stars in their exams but focus solely on a single C they received, overlooking all their accomplishments. Their mental filter prevents them from recognising their strengths and leads them to concentrate on their failures.

They often dismiss positive experiences by insisting they "don't count." They become their own harshest critics, overlooking their strengths while fixating on their weaknesses and downplaying the importance of their positive traits. They may also amplify the significance of their problems and shortcomings. For instance, even after performing well, they might tell themselves, "It could have been done better," or "Anyone could have done it better, not just me."

Another thinking pattern is '**personalisation**, often coupled with labelling.' Individuals who engage in this pattern take on excessive blame and unfairly assume responsibility for events beyond their control. They internalise negative occurrences and feel personally accountable even when they are not directly involved. Consequently, this labelling fosters feelings of shame, guilt, and inadequacy. For example, a woman whose friend died in a car accident might irrationally label herself as responsible, believing her driving was to blame rather than considering factors like her friend's failure to wear a seatbelt or the involvement of another driver who drove recklessly in the accident—issues that were completely beyond her control.

Due to altered thinking patterns, some individuals become intriguing **mind readers**. They often attempt to read others' minds and feel those around them react negatively without verifying their assumptions. They develop a negative perception of others view them and second-guess what others might think. For instance, they may think, "I can tell from their expression that they believe I am a fool," or "I know from their gestures that they dislike me."

Some of them become **fortune tellers in their minds.** These "fortune tellers" adopt a negative and gloomy view of the future, making pessimistic predictions. They assume that things will turn out badly, even when they cannot accurately foresee the outcome. For example, they might think that the housing market will likely worsen, the stock market will decline, their relationship will not improve, or their job interviews won't go well.

At the end of this chapter, you might question whether you exhibit some of the thinking errors discussed above. **Humans are all**

prone to making these mistakes in our thinking, ranging from mild to more severe forms. The important thing is to acknowledge that these errors exist and are frequently experienced by many people.

The first step is to **identify and understand thinking errors**. Once we recognise these errors and gain insight into them, we can challenge and address them through a technique known as **"thought challenging,"** which I will describe in the next chapter.

Individuals who experience mild thinking errors can often learn to ignore, adapt to, and manage their thought patterns effectively. Some educate themselves about these issues, while others utilise self-help measures or seek counselling or therapy. However, most people lack awareness and continue to struggle, which hampers their success and happiness. The more severe these thinking errors become, the more problematic they can be, impacting a person's happiness and success in various aspects of life.

Upon realising these patterns later, many individuals say, "I never understood the existence of these errors. I didn't know anything about them," etc. They express regret, stating that if they had been aware of these errors earlier, they believe they could have achieved greater success and happiness.

After reading this book, readers must understand that cognitive distortions do exist and can be addressed and that many strategies exist to overcome such cognitive errors. The technique of "thought challenging" is one useful strategy for overcoming these extreme forms of thinking, which I discuss in the next chapter.

If cognitive distortions or thinking errors are not identified and addressed, they can have several negative consequences. When individuals rely on distorted thinking, it may impair their problem-solving abilities and result in impulsive decisions that are not always optimal. These thinking patterns can evoke feelings of fear, guilt, and anxiety, which in turn can lower one's mood and self-esteem. Those who grapple with these thoughts for an extended period may withdraw from various life situations, limiting their growth and opportunities. Additionally, these patterns can cause misunderstandings and conflicts that strain relationships, leading some individuals to feel increasingly isolated. Cognitive distortions can hinder the ability to see alternative possibilities, narrowing one's perspective. Unfortunately, this can contribute to mental exhaustion and may lead to issues such as long-term stress, anxiety, and depressive disorders. In some cases, these struggles could even result in physical health problems like chronic headaches, stomach aches, obesity, and an increased risk of heart issues.

> **'The happiness of your life depends upon the quality of your thoughts'**
> – Former Roman Emperor Marcus Aurelius

Golden Nuggets

The first step is to identify and understand what thinking errors truly are.

- 'All-or-nothing thinking, also known as black-or-white thinking', is a cognitive error in which people assume that if a 'situation falls short of perfection, it is viewed as a complete failure'. They frequently use words like "should," "always," "never," and "typical."

- 'Catastrophising' involves 'predicting the worst-case scenario and jumping to dire conclusions. They can't think of different possibilities other than the worst outcomes.

- Overgeneralisation involves drawing conclusions based on limited evidence. This cognitive error leads individuals to assume that if something happens once, it will always happen. People often tend to use the terms like "always" or "never"

- Jumping to conclusions without evidence involves interpreting situations negatively without facts to support such beliefs and those who tend to overlook alternative perspectives.

- Mental filtering is a cognitive error where individuals focus on their failures and mistakes while overlooking positive aspects and achievements. This mental filter hinders them from recognising their strengths and causes them to dwell on their shortcomings.

- Personalisation is a standard cognitive error. Individuals who engage in this thinking pattern take on excessive blame and unfairly assume responsibility for events beyond their control. They internalise negative experiences and feel personally accountable even when they are not directly involved.

- Mind readers attempt to interpret others' thoughts and may feel that others are reacting negatively towards them without confirming their assumptions and second- guessing what others might think.

- Some envision themselves as fortune tellers. These "fortune tellers" adopt a negative and gloomy view of the future and make pessimistic predictions.

- We all tend to make these mistakes in our thinking, which can vary from mild to more severe.

How to Halt and Challenge Your Thoughts

There's a famous saying: **"Choose your thoughts like you choose your food."**

We must choose the right foods to nourish our bodies and maintain good physical health. Similarly, to achieve mental peace and happiness, we must select constructive thoughts that enhance our mental well-being and foster positive relationships with others. The great news is that we have the power to choose helpful thoughts. We possess the 'power of choice' to select our thoughts, which is a profound empowerment, granting us control over our mental health.

Have you ever enjoyed a buffet lunch? There is such a delightful variety of food choices waiting for us! People who practice mindful eating love to select nutritious options and savour their meals in moderation. Likewise, we can nurture our minds by focusing on enriching thoughts for a healthier mindset.

Negative thoughts are like **black holes in outer space.** When we allow ourselves to dwell on recurring negative thoughts, it is akin to approaching a black hole that pulls us in with its immense gravitational force, causing us to feel completely lost. Similarly, negative thoughts consume our mental space, making it difficult to escape their grip.

When I see young adults, I often encourage them to view negative thoughts as akin to Voldemort and positive thoughts as like Harry in the Harry Potter movies. Negative thoughts, like Voldemort, may always linger in the background. Still, we should strive to overcome them, learn to conquer them and grow into individuals with positive thoughts like Harry, brimming with courage and confidence in the films.

Heaven and hell are not in space; they are inside your mind. Many people search for heaven and hell, often overlooking the significant role of their thoughts. If you cultivate positive thoughts, you are essentially living in heaven; conversely, if you dwell on negative thoughts, you find yourself in hell. Ultimately, it is all in our minds, determining whether we experience heaven or hell.

> **"Your worst enemy cannot harm you as much as**
> **your unguarded thoughts"**
> – Gautama Buddha. If your thoughts are unguarded,
> they can become your worst enemy

We have the power to choose the thoughts we entertain. We can act as **gatekeepers, allowing positive and neutral thought**s to pass while blocking negative ones. Imagine being a watchman for a gated community, permitting entry only to those with passes. Similarly, within your mind, you can establish a system that allows only positive thoughts for further processing while negative thoughts are stopped at the gate. Learning to be a filter and a 'proactive mind watchman' is crucial for blocking negative thoughts. This filtering process requires practice, but mastering it will lead to greater happiness and fulfilment. Become a proactive watchman guarding for peace and joy by allowing positive thoughts to enter your mind.

Thought-stopping is a useful technique for managing recurrent, unhelpful negative thoughts that linger and can be bothersome. Consequently, people may experience persistent ruminations of these negative thoughts. To practice the thought- stopping method, you must learn to catch yourself in the act of rumination. The first step is to label these thoughts as negative when they arise. When you realise you are ruminating on negative thoughts, immediately shout "Stop," either aloud or in your mind. Some find it helpful to wear an elastic band around their wrist and snap it as they shout. A negative thought needs attention, much like a child throwing a tantrum.

Therefore, please do not give it your attention. If you provide more attention, you will encounter more mental tantrums. After this, **try to divert your mind by 'directing your attention to a fantasy'** you have prepared, focusing on it for 30 to 60 seconds. Creating a list of pleasant fantasies to help rescue yourself in such situations can be beneficial. These pleasant fantasies may include a beautiful place you visited recently, memories of an enjoyable holiday, joyful moments spent with close friends or family, funny jokes, instances of past glory, thoughts of someone who inspired you, or hobbies you genuinely enjoy. Having this list as a "rescue list" can assist you in shifting your mindset while practising thought-stopping.

Aim to focus on the pleasant fantasy for 30 seconds to one minute. There may be a tendency for unhelpful thoughts to return during that time. If this happens, pause again and repeat the fantasy. For this exercise to be effective, it must be practised consistently until the troubling negative thoughts go away.

Initially, you should do these 10 to 20 times per day; however, with repeated practice, t hese unhelpful thoughts will likely become less frequent and eventually disappear. (Ref-Change your thinking-Dr Sarah Edelman

Thought diversion through engaging in activities leading to distraction- Instead of indulging in a fantasy, focus on an alternative activity that can divert your mind, such as calling a close friend to discuss a neutral topic, going for a walk outside, enjoying something you love—like listening to music, watching comedies, or following sports—or tackling household chores or work. This will help keep you busy and engaged.

What is the technique of thought challenging, and how do we achieve it?

Challenging our thoughts is an essential skill to develop and carry with us throughout our lives! When we notice thinking errors that weigh us down, the next step is to gently identify and question those thoughts. This journey involves closely examining the less helpful aspects of our thinking and discovering more realistic and positive ways to view our situations. It is all about exploring our core beliefs and identifying any false assumptions we may hold while clarifying their meanings. We can dig a little deeper and lovingly challenge those assumptions! This approach is often referred to as the Socratic Questioning technique. Once we embrace these strategies, we gain the power to transform unhelpful or negative thoughts into something much more uplifting.

Step 1

During the thought challenging process, you must confront your worries or negative cognitions. The foremost step is to '**write down your worries or anxious thoughts**'—this will help you identify the negative thoughts.

For example, you might think, "I will never be successful in my job interviews and career after a failed job interview." (The faulty thinking is overgeneralisation. If something happens once, you think it will always happen.)

Step 2

The next step is to '**examine the evidence for and against this negative thought**'. It is beneficial to write down the evidence supporting and contradicting your thoughts. For instance, the evidence for this negative thought could include the fact

1. that you did not get the last several jobs for which you interviewed

2. leading to feelings of discouragement and anxiety about attending future interviews.

On the other hand, the evidence against this negative thought might include:

1. the skills and qualifications you possess.

2. positive feedback from previous employers and colleagues.

3. the numerous opportunities still available for future applications.

4. the knowledge that many successful people faced numerous rejections before achieving success.

Step 3

The following step is to **'challenge the thought and question the validity of the negative belief'.** Rather than searching for proof, you should assess the accuracy of your thoughts and seek other explanations. In this case,

1. It is essential to ask whether it is true that you will never be successful and define what success means to you from your perspective.

2. Reflect on your personal life and think of many small successes you have had, even if they are unrelated to job interviews. This setback doesn't negate your potential or achievements.

3. It would help if you also considered examples of people who overcame failures to achieve success.

Challenge your negative or doubtful thoughts, as well as your fearful or dark thoughts, by questioning them with prompts like 'What if?'

Step 4

The fourth step is to **'generate alternative thoughts.'** This will help the individual develop more balanced and realistic perceptions. Inquire what you would advise a friend facing a similar situation and how that friend might respond.

For instance, friends might say that

1. Setbacks do not define our future, and we can learn from our experiences.

2. Success is an ongoing journey that involves numerous failures along the way.

3. With further practice, you can improve your skills and increase your chances of success.

4. This is just one step along the journey; success takes time and persistence.

Additionally, it helps the individual **'reframe their thoughts'** so that they are no longer harmful or pervasive. For example, this interview was a chance to gain experience and insight into what employers and organisations are looking for and use this knowledge to prepare better for the next one.

Step 5

The final step is **'developing an action plan'** that encourages the person to take constructive steps.

1. To build confidence, They should practise interviewing by scheduling mock interviews with a friend or mentor.

2. Seeking constructive feedback after these interviews and asking for areas of improvement can be immensely beneficial.

3. Additionally, establishing specific small goals—such as applying to a set number of jobs each week—can help you stay focused on the process rather than the outcomes of individual interviews.

4. It can be advantageous to consider courses or workshops to enhance skills relevant to the desired job field. It is crucial to ensure that applicants possess the essential and desirable qualifications listed in job descriptions.

Step 6

Finally, regular **'reflection on progress' is crucial**. Encouraging the person to maintain a journal where they note their thoughts and feelings after interviews can be helpful. It is also wise to celebrate small victories, like securing an interview or receiving feedback on performance.

By utilising these thought challenging techniques, people can shift their mindset from defeat to growth and success. The same principles and steps can also challenge other thinking errors.

However, for some individuals, their challenges may be so overwhelming that they cannot manage them independently. In such cases, seeking help from a therapist and engaging in cognitive therapy with a trained professional can be beneficial.

Golden Nuggets

- Choosing your thoughts is as important as choosing your food.

- We have the 'power of choice' to select our thoughts, a profound empowerment that gives us control over our mental health.

- If your thoughts lack protection, they can become your worst enemy.

- Learn to be a proactive guardian of your mind, welcoming positive thoughts that foster peace and happiness within you.

- Combining thought-stopping with a shift to a pleasant fantasy is an effective technique for overcoming disturbing negative thoughts.

- 'Thought-challenging' involves closely examining the unhelpful and harmful aspects of one's thinking and questioning one's thoughts, beliefs, and assumptions.

- Thought challenging will help the individual develop more balanced and realistic perceptions.

Affirmation is a Powerful and Empowering Tool

Affirmations are positive statements that help overcome negative thoughts and challenge them. Self-affirmations are powerful declarations that allow us to recognise our worth and value as individuals. They can promote self-confidence, resilience, and a positive mindset.

Affirmative statements are like seeds: when planted in our minds, they develop into positive thoughts and beliefs, ultimately growing into larger trees that transform us into more positive individuals. This positivity enhances our lives and attracts people and situations that resonate with us, aligning with the Law of Attraction. Reviewing and incorporating these affirmations into our daily routines is vital, just as one would water a plant daily to ensure healthy growth.

Positive self-talk and affirmations are powerful tools. Your inner voice can become your best friend or worst enemy, depending on the affirmations you hold. Therefore, it is essential to nurture yourself through positive self-talk. Replace negative thoughts with positive affirmations that emphasise your strengths and capabilities. This practice can enhance your confidence and self-esteem. Regularly affirming positive statements can boost your self-worth. Many of us tend to worry about small and trivial matters constantly. For instance, if a food particle gets stuck between our teeth, our tongue may focus on removing it rather than enjoying the meal. Similarly, our minds often default to obsessing over negative experiences instead of focusing on the positive. The internal dialogues in our minds resemble the movements of our tongues that draw us toward negativity, causing us to overlook life's brighter aspects. **Positive affirmations act like toothpicks**, helping to remove the distractions that prevent us from appreciating the moment.

Let's explore some great strategies to incorporate them!

Speak them aloud! Repeating your daily affirmations can truly reinforce positive self-talk. It is even more powerful when you say them in front of a mirror, gazing at your reflection as you share those uplifting words. Just imagine standing there: if you envision yourself as a fierce tiger, that's what you become! Or if you picture yourself as a cat, that's what you become too! It is all about recognising your strengths and expressing them through encouraging dialogue.

Visual reminders can powerfully reinforce affirmations. They help keep your affirmations front and centre in your mind and present in your daily life. Write your affirmations on sticky notes, flashcards, vision boards, artwork, posters, and photo frames, and place them in visible locations. The positive affirmations expressed through sticky notes and journaling are vital for enhancing mental well-being and overall effectiveness.

Affirmation apps and digital reminders - Many affirmation apps for positive affirmations exist. You can use your positive affirmations as wallpapers and screensavers on your computers. You can have calendar alerts and send you daily notifications to allow you to create reminders of your affirmations.

Personalisation: Create a personalised list of affirmations that resonate with you and reflect your aspirations and values. Based on your needs and goals, you can make them more impactful and effective. Use positive language and make it in the present tense. Make your affirmations specific and believable. Use 'I statements' and keep it short and simple.

For them to be effective, affirmations must be positive, powerful, and meaningful. You can create your affirmations and focus on areas where you want to build confidence and foster positivity. Here are some key themes to consider when creating these affirmations:

1)Self-Care, 2) Feeling Safe, 3) Unconditional Positive Regard, treating yourself with love and respect, 4) Strength and Self-Belief, reminding yourself of your potential, 5)Trust Your Intuition and believe in your inner guidance, 6) Improving Self-Respect and recognising your worth, 7)Bravery and Resilience, with the ability to bounce back, 8) Moving Towards Success and achieving your dreams.

Some examples of affirmative statements

I can do it

I prioritise my well-being and take time for myself

I have a lot of support I can ask for help

I love who I am

I am a strong person

I am the best

I will be able to get this done

I am getting better day by day

I was born to do great things

I see my goals clearly

I have a bright future

Making affirmations a routine part of our lives can transform how we view ourselves and interact with the world. Consistently using affirmations can help rewire our brains, fostering a mindset filled with positive thoughts. Our subconscious mind requires regular reprogramming, and one effective method to achieve this is through positive affirmations.

Affirmations cultivate a positive mindset. Individuals with a positive mindset tend to see challenges as opportunities for growth and learning. They are more likely to embrace change and innovation, viewing setbacks as stepping stones to success. A positive mindset often fosters resilience, enabling these individuals to bounce back from failures while maintaining motivation and enthusiasm. They are generally more receptive to collaboration and teamwork, creating a supportive environment that encourages shared ideas and solutions.

In contrast, individuals with a negative mindset often focus on identifying problems rather than solutions. This can lead to a pervasive sense of dissatisfaction and hinder personal and professional growth. A negative outlook may result in a reluctance to take risks, as individuals might be excessively preoccupied with the fear of failure. This mindset can strain relationships, as ongoing criticism can engender a lack of openness and cooperation from others. Therefore, cultivating a positive mindset can greatly enhance an individual's ability to navigate life's challenges and foster a more productive and fulfilling environment. Encouraging others to adopt this perspective can create a ripple effect, leading to collective growth and innovation.

I am sharing my practice of using affirmations, which has greatly benefited my mindset and overall well-being. I find it incredibly helpful to write positive statements and post them as sticky notes on my computer, fridge, and office desk. This practice allows me to visualise these affirmations regularly, generating positive energy.

Here are a few examples of the affirmations I use:

- "I am a wonderful human being."
- 'I am a good doctor, believe in my abilities and trust my
- judgement.'
- "I add immense value to people's lives through my great work for humanity."
- "I love using my skills and talents to help make the world a better place for everyone."

These affirmations have greatly enhanced my self-esteem and nurtured a positive mindset that embraces resilience. They constantly remind me of my abilities and purpose, helping to counter any negative self-talk that may arise. By fostering positive dialogue in my mind, I am better prepared to face challenges and maintain a constructive outlook. Incorporating such practices can be transformative for ourselves and the teams and communities we belong to. Consistency is essential, so integrating them into a daily routine can enhance their impact. I encourage everyone to adopt these practices and witness the positive effects this empowering approach can have on your growth.

Golden Nuggets

- Affirmations are positive statements that help to overcome negative thoughts and challenge them.
- Positive self-talk and affirmations can promote self-confidence, resilience, and a positive mindset.
- Affirmations need to be positive, powerful, and meaningful to be effective.
- For affirmations to be effective, it is important they are specific, believable and stated in the present tense.
- Incorporating affirmations into daily life can be transformative for both one and the teams and communities to which one belongs.

Experience, Embrace, and Express Your Emotions

We all experience different emotions, including joy, sadness, fear, pain, disgust, and anger. If these feelings are suppressed, they can eventually become more destructive. When people experience pain or hurt caused by their loved ones, we often assume they have the right to feel this way. As a result, we allow hurtful feelings to fester within us. We may avoid discussing these emotions, choosing to keep them bottled up. While this might provide temporary comfort, it can lead to significant internal damage over time as we lock these feelings deep within our minds. Bottling up sadness and hurt is detrimental. **'Acknowledging and processing our emotions is healthier for us'** physically and mentally. It is crucial to understand that expressing our feelings is acceptable; therefore, embrace and accept them openly.

It is essential to learn how to express these emotions constructively. **'Emotions are meant to be experienced and expressed,'** says Shama Patel (in her book twenty-one Ways of being happy). Unfortunately, many people overanalyse their feelings and struggle more.

We must learn to manage our emotions; one way is to express them.

We can all express our emotions through writing, talking, or therapy.

There are various ways to articulate emotions. A meaningful approach is to **write them down.** Expressing feelings in writing can be therapeutic for many. Documenting the events that have caused mental conflict and noting the associated feelings is essential. Writing can often enhance your emotional state. You can review your writing, but don't be self-critical of the style. Journaling can be very therapeutic. It reduces symptoms of stress, anxiety, and depression. Through journaling, you put thoughts and emotions on paper, which helps you process and release them with clarity and calmness. The journaling process also allows you to identify patterns, gain insights, and develop a deeper understanding of yourself.

The next meaningful way to express your emotions is by **talking things out**. Look for a close friend or family member with whom you can share your feelings and thoughts. There is a famous quote from the Royal College of Psychiatrists in the UK: '**Worrying changes nothing, and talking changes everything**.' Therefore, stop overanalysing and worrying; instead, have a discussion. You should feel confident they won't judge or criticise you for what you are experiencing. **Discussing our feelings** is one of the most effective forms of emotional healing. Suppose you can't find someone on a casual level. In that case, you can also seek help from a professional to talk to a neutral party who won't judge or criticise you regarding your emotional experiences and associated feelings. Simply talking to someone about how you feel can be beneficial. This conversation can help distract you from stressful thoughts or release tension through discussion. We should avoid suppressing our emotions, as this may offer short-term relief but ultimately lead to accumulation. Eventually, this buildup can reach a breaking point, resulting in an explosive outburst that can negatively affect yourself and those around you. However, bottling up negative feelings will keep them trapped in your mind, ready to erupt like a dangerous volcano, leading to dire consequences. It is better to get it off your chest.

'**Unexpressed emotions will never die.**
They are buried alive and will come forth later in uglier ways'
– Psychoanalyst Sigmund Freud

There is a mature way of expressing one's feelings. Some people habitually express their negative emotions and frustrations by doing something positive. In psychological terms, humans adopt this defence mechanism to prevent conflicts inside their minds. The defence mechanism is **sublimation, where people channel all negative feelings positively**. For example, when they experience negative emotions, they try to cope by engaging in sports or music activities, playing games, doing artwork, etc. In my counselling and therapy sessions, I often advise people that one of the best ways to cope with negative emotions like anger or frustration is to engage in some form of physical activity. Going out and participating in a workout can be incredibly beneficial. When you engage in physical activity, you gradually become aware of the reactions occurring in your body and can feel those negative emotions exiting. This is something you can undoubtedly notice and acknowledge. Personally, I enjoy dancing, which is highly therapeutic, especially when I feel overwhelmed by negative emotions. After a tough day, I often come home and dance in my room. Recently, I have developed an interest in boxing, and every time I attend a practice session, I experience a sense of relaxation. By the end of the session, I can feel my negative energy dissipating, leading to a profound sense of relief. This positive way of expressing emotions is often called sublimation in psychological terms.

In contrast, some individuals cope with negative feelings through unhealthy habits, such as consuming alcohol, smoking cigarettes, using recreational drugs, overeating, sleeping excessively, spending too much time on the internet, or engaging in social media. These behaviours rarely provide relief and can harm both physical and mental health. Instead, I encourage you to channel your negative emotions positively by participating in meaningful activities like sports, music, or art.

Consistently expressing your feelings allows you to share your emotional state with others, deepening your self- understanding and relationships. Regularly expressing these emotions can also help prevent long-term issues. It is equally important to help others release their emotions and to empathise with them. When someone approaches you to share their feelings, resist the urge to turn a deaf ear or to be judgemental. Avoid offering advice immediately, even if you are tempted to do so. Instead, allow them the space to express their emotions and reassure them that what they're feeling is valid and completely natural.

The next time you encounter a strong emotion—whether your own or someone else's—try to acknowledge, accept, and embrace it. Most importantly, find a healthy way to express it; everyone deserves that opportunity.

You may have encountered the recent terminology **"emotional intelligence."** This concept encompasses several key elements, including:

A. Being self-aware of one's emotions and understanding and expressing your own emotions.

B. Recognising those emotions and noticing how you and others feel helps you respond appropriately.

C. Pausing before reacting to situations allows you to respond healthily and not impulsively.

D. Empathy towards the feelings of others builds trust and deepens relationships. Maintaining these aspects of interpersonal interaction cultivates and strengthens relationships.

If you can gain insight into these components, you have achieved 'emotional intelligence,' a term coined by Peter Salovey and John Mayer in the 1990s and later popularised by Daniel Goleman.

"Experience your emotions, Embrace your emotions, Express your emotions, and empathise for others' emotions too"

Let me add a few points to clarify some myths about emotions.

People prefer only positive emotions and avoid experiencing negative ones. However, **'negative emotions are essential for our survival'.** For example, fear is a crucial emotion. When people find themselves on a mountaintop near a cliff, they may feel fear; nonetheless, this fear can heighten their awareness, prompting them to exercise extreme caution while navigating the area near the edge. Such negative responses are vital for survival. Similarly, consider the role of experiencing anxiety during a job interview. When you feel anxious, your focus and performance can improve. This heightened alertness lets you absorb interview questions and understand the information better, ultimately enhancing your overall performance. Negative emotional responses, in this context, serve a necessary purpose. It is important to recognise that while negative emotions are essential, they should '**not dominate your daily life or become paralysing.**'

Many individuals mistakenly believe that happiness is the only positive emotion, overlooking the value of others, such as satisfaction, contentment, confidence, optimism, gratitude, inspiration, love, kindness, and compassion. Due to this misunderstanding, people often perceive positive emotions as occurring less frequently than negative ones. We must embrace a broader spectrum of life experiences and behaviours to shift from negative to positive emotions. "**To change negative into positive emotions, add experiences and behaviours in your life that can foster happiness**" - Christine Carter mentioned in her podcast, Finding Work-life Balance. For instance, daily nurturing feelings of satisfaction, contentment, optimism, hope, and faith can shift emotional balance. Concentrating on these experiences can help individuals understand how to feel various positive emotions beyond just happiness and focusing solely on happiness as a positive emotion in the first place. Moreover, developing curiosity and exploring new interests is another avenue for generating positive emotions. Engaging with the world around you and seeking new experiences can significantly improve your emotional health and life satisfaction.

Gratitude is an effective way to foster positive emotions. A **gratitude log involves recognising positive emotions, remembering and reciprocating them, and can be a transformative practice.** This tool is powerful for cultivating appreciation and mindfulness, allowing individuals to reflect on positive experiences and their emotions. Start by identifying and understanding what positive emotions are. Common examples include joy, gratitude, love, contentment, and pride. These emotions often arise from specific experiences or interactions. Set aside time each day to reflect on moments that made you feel positive. This could be as simple as appreciating a compliment or enjoying a delicious meal. Write these moments in your gratitude log. Pay attention to what triggers these positive emotions in your life. Is it spending time with loved ones, achieving a goal, or engaging in a favourite hobby? Recognising these triggers can help you seek out and create more uplifting experiences. Another point is to express gratitude for the people and experiences contributing to your positive emotions. This can be done through notes, messages, or face-to-face conversations. Letting others know their impact can strengthen your bonds and elevate their spirits. **Please make it a habit to regularly reflect on what you are grateful for.**

Additionally, **mindfulness practices, such as meditation,** have been shown to enhance positive emotions. Regular meditation practice is essential for nurturing emotional well- being.

Why do people make mistakes, like saying inappropriate things and making wrong decisions during emotional states? The answer lies in **"amygdala hijacking",** a term psychologist Daniel Goleman coined in his book Emotional Intelligence. The amygdala is a small, almond-shaped structure in the brain that plays an important role in processing emotions. The front part of our brain, the prefrontal cortex, usually evaluates situations and helps us make rational decisions. However, during states of high emotion, 'the amygdala hijacks the role of the prefrontal cortex,' triggering the fight-or-flight response to threats—real or imagined— before the prefrontal cortex can evaluate the situation. This can lead to impulsive reactions that contradict rational thought. In intense moments, the amygdala can overwhelm cognition or thought processes, leading to emotional responses such as anger and anxiety, often neglecting context. Stressful situations or specific triggers may provoke **aggressive behaviour or withdrawal** in response to perceived threats. Such outbursts can damage relationships, as individuals may unjustly lash out at loved ones with negative emotions. Understanding this clarifies our emotional reactions that contradict our intentions. By enhancing emotional awareness, we can better manage our responses.

Recognising amygdala hijacking allows individuals to adopt coping strategies such as mindfulness and deep breathing, which restore the balance between emotional and rational responses. Understanding amygdala hijacking offers insight into why we sometimes react emotionally in ways that may not align with our intentions or values. **"Be intellectual rather than becoming emotional, as our intellect can be clouded by our emotions due to amygdala hijacking"**. By developing emotional awareness and strategies for regulation, we can enhance our responses in such situations.

Viktor Frankl stated, **"Between stimulus and response, there is a space. In that space is our power to choose our response."** During high emotional states, 'pausing with some silence' before reacting to situations allows you to respond healthily and not impulsively. Between a stimulus and a response, there exists a space. When provoked emotionally by any stimulus, we have a moment to decide how to respond. During that time, we possess the power, freedom of choice and capability to choose our response, which can be positive, negative, or neutral. Our response can have a significant impact, so wisely using that space and time is crucial to provide the most appropriate reaction.

Research indicates that the ability to express one's emotions is associated with various positive outcomes, such as improved stress management and heightened psychological resilience. Therefore, we must begin communicating our emotional states effectively.

Golden Nuggets

- Recognise and accept your emotions.

- Discover ways to express your feelings and do not suppress them, as this can lead to many complications in the long-term.

- Expressing your emotions means healthily communicating your feelings through words, actions, or creative activities.

- Everyone deserves the opportunity to express their emotions in various forms.

- Empathise with others' emotions and give them the space to express themselves.

- It's not just positive emotions, but negative emotions are also essential for our survival.

- To shift from negative to positive emotions, we should embrace a broader range of life experiences and behaviours daily.

- Keeping a gratitude log, participating in mindfulness practices, and practising meditation are effective methods for cultivating positive emotions.

- Understanding amygdala hijacking provides insight into why we sometimes react emotionally in ways that may not correspond with our intentions or values.

- In high emotional states, taking a moment of silence before reacting allows you to respond thoughtfully rather than impulsively.

- Stay rational rather than becoming emotional, since our feelings can cloud our intellect.

Release Negativity and Eliminate Toxic Emotions

'Learn to let go, that is the key to happiness'
– Gautama Buddha

'Letting go of negativity' is one way to process our emotions. What does this mean? When you try it, it doesn't imply that what 'happened in the past was okay' or that you will 'let it happen again'. Instead, you are releasing the emotions, which helps you **'move on without being stuck'**. You need to learn to let go to be free, peaceful, and happy.

The emotional toll of holding onto negativity is immense. Retaining negative feelings is like clutching rotten meat; at first, it may seem manageable, but over time, it spoils and emits an unbearable stench that can permeate your entire life. Just as spoiled meat can ruin a meal, unresolved emotions can taint our thoughts, relationships, and overall well-being.

Carrying negativity and emotional baggage is like having a phone overloaded with unnecessary data, such as unwanted applications, large files, videos, and messages. Have you ever considered the impact this has on your phone? You are correct; it slows down the device's performance and efficiency, eventually leading to storage issues where it can no longer handle additional information. Just as it is important to delete those large files and applications to free up space and improve your phone's efficiency, we must also learn to let go of emotional baggage and negativity in our daily lives. Holding onto past regrets and burdens can weigh us down mentally and emotionally. Remembering this phone analogy is essential: just as we should regularly delete unwanted data from our devices, we must also work to release memories and emotions that bring us misery. This practice can help lighten our emotional load, allowing us to function more effectively. **By reducing this emotional baggage, we can maintain our vitality, which is crucial for our well-being.** If we don't address these issues, we may find ourselves unable to embrace new experiences or challenges, hindering our ability to function in daily life.

Consider the film 'Titanic.' If you have not seen it, I highly recommend it, as it is often regarded as one of the greatest movies ever made. The story portrays the tragic sinking of the Titanic, where Jack and Rose are thrown into the freezing water as the ship succumbs to the depths of the ocean. In a heartbreaking moment, Jack sacrifices himself, ultimately freezing to death. While Rose initially clings to him, she comes to realise that holding onto Jack, who has died, only adds weight to her precarious situation. 'Letting him go' frees her, as she would not have survived if she had clung to his dead body. This choice allows her to float to safety and eventually signal for help. This pivotal decision symbolises the 'power of letting go.' Similarly, we must learn to release the past regrets and burdens that weigh us down for survival.

Let's explore helpful strategies to release toxic emotions and refresh your mind from negativity! We often find ourselves in minor conflicts with others on the road, especially when stuck in traffic. However, these moments of frustration are typically best forgotten within 10 minutes. We free ourselves from negativity by not holding onto anger and resentment and allowing such instances to pass. This principle can also be applied to overcome negativity in other areas of our lives. Avoid letting fleeting negativity become a part of your long-term memory by repeatedly revisiting and dwelling on past negative experiences. Instead, practice letting go of any grudges associated with those moments. If we can forgive strangers, why can't we extend that same concept of forgiveness to our family and friends? Clinging to past hurts or unresolved emotions can weigh us down, preventing us from enjoying life's joys and opportunities. Letting go of these burdens lightens our emotional load and opens the door to new possibilities, healthier relationships, and a more positive outlook.

Likewise, to reach greater heights, **you must shed 'all emotional baggage and maintain a light spirit'**. Birds flying high in the sky must be light; they struggle to ascend if they are too heavy. When they fly high, they get a better view of the world and enjoy their flight. It would help if you also learned to let go of the past; only then can you rise higher, gain a better perspective on life, and fully appreciate the world around you. Imagine this uplifting metaphor: Fly high like a graceful crane soaring above 10,000 feet! Let go of everything that holds you back—your past mistakes, regrets, and resentments, along with overthinking, negativity, the fear of failure, and the opinions of others. The more you release, the higher you will rise!

An illustrative example is a teacher who held up a small glass filled with water and asked her students to estimate its weight. Various students offered different responses. One insightful student suggested that the weight of the glass depended on multiple factors. For instance, just holding the glass for a minute might feel slightly challenging, and if you were to hold it for an hour, it could put more strain on your arms. Carrying it around all day could become overwhelming and may really start to hurt, potentially making it extremely hard even to lift your hand and hold the glass at all. This analogy mirrors our lives— if we cling to insults, negative comments, and hurtful actions, our emotional weight will increase based on how long we hold onto them. Just as it is advisable to put down the glass after a moment of carrying it, it is crucial to let go of hurtful events and insults periodically. Continuously revisiting and reliving such incidents is akin to repeatedly picking up the glass and holding it for too long, serving no beneficial purpose. You can effectively manage your inner state by mastering the ability to release these emotional burdens, minimising the toll on your mind and soul, and becoming a light spirit soaring high in the sky of life.

Have you ever encountered the Law of Detachment? The Law of Detachment involves letting go of emotions to manifest our desires.

Embrace the comforting mantra, "**Release and let go.**" This beautiful spiritual practice invites us to shed worries and negativity, allowing life to unfold in its wonderful way. It is essential to recognise that clinging to painful emotions and being overly sensitive can obstruct our path to peace and happiness. By welcoming the philosophy of detachment, we can truly transform our lives. When we remain detached and avoid taking things too personally, we navigate life's challenges with greater ease and compassion for ourselves and others. This approach significantly supports our journey toward emotional well-being.

I appreciated the technique for effectively letting go described by Chantal Hofstee, a clinical psychologist, in her book Mindfulness on the Run. The final step in processing our emotions is to let them go so we can move forward. One effective method is to place one hand on your chest and the other on your stomach. Take a deep breath. Relax and drop your shoulders as you breathe out. Then, say or think, **"I let it go." Repeat this a few times.** Your body and emotions are deeply interconnected; if your feelings are not processed, they can lead to tension in your neck and shoulders, causing your breathing to become shallow. By taking conscious deep breaths and dropping your shoulders, you adjust to your body, which helps your mind process the emotions and ultimately let them go.

Another effective way to rise above negativity is to address unfinished business with others and seek closure. Often, individuals pursue closure, which can be crucial for moving forward. Letting go of past hurts will create a mental space for peace and happiness.

For instance, consider a woman named Sarah who experienced a difficult breakup after four years in a relationship. Unfortunately, it ended abruptly, leaving her with many unanswered questions and unresolved feelings. For weeks, she felt trapped in negativity, constantly replaying the events in her mind and grappling with feelings of hurt and confusion. Closure can be viewed as the emotional and psychological resolution we seek after significant life events. Realising this, Sarah reached out to her ex-partner for a final conversation a few weeks after their breakup. During their meeting, she expressed her feelings and sought clarity about why the relationship ended. Her partner shared their perspective, acknowledging the good times they had together and the reasons for the breakup. By having this conversation, Sarah gained a better understanding of the situation. She felt a sense of relief and closure, recognising it was time to let go of the past and move forward. With this newfound clarity, she focused on personal growth, reconnecting with friends, and exploring new interests. As a result, she began to break free from the negativity that had held her back, allowing her to embrace a more positive outlook on life. Sarah's example illustrates how seeking closure can help individuals process their emotions and transition from a negative phase to a more positive and forward-looking mindset.

Regarding the reduction of negativity, **limiting exposure to negative news cycles on television and social media is vital**, as they have recently generated much negativity. The media landscape is saturated with adverse events, leading to increased anxiety and worry about our current circumstances and the future. Many people become anxious about their health or financial stability when exposed to constant streams of distressing news. This barrage of negative events can significantly impact mental well-being, fuelling feelings of despair and influencing overall mood. Instead, consider spending just 10 minutes scanning newspaper headlines for updates on current events rather than immersing yourself in extensive coverage from television, radio, and other media outlets. Additionally, we should learn that we don't have to react to every negative and bothersome occurrence. Sometimes, we need to know how to breathe, let it go, and maintain our peace.

> **'The past is like a rear-view mirror.**
> **Glance at it, but don't keep staring or**
> **you will miss what's ahead'**
> – Indian Spiritual Leader Gauranga Das

When past thoughts and feelings burden us, our 'emotional baggage becomes heavy' and hard to carry. Life is a journey on a long river; on this journey, our "boat" should travel with minimal baggage and navigate the waters smoothly. It will be pulled down if we tie large stones to our boat. These large stones are like past emotional baggage. Dwelling on past events & thoughts and trying to carry their burden can weigh us down and hinder our ability to navigate the river of life comfortably. If our emotional baggage is causing us more strain, we must learn to cut the ropes and release these burdens in such situations. Excessive baggage is not a loss; it is essential to untie these weights for survival. Therefore, we should quickly sever the ties to misery, regrets, and other negative thoughts. '**Releasing these burdens is far better than holding onto them**'.

They say holding on to grudges and mulling over them is like drinking a glass of poison and expecting the other person with whom we have grudges to die. It will destroy you more than the other. Why would you want to harm yourself more? Instead, let go of grudges and toxic emotions. There's a lovely Indian proverb that says, '**The tree does not bother about flowers that fall**,' which beautifully captures the idea of letting go. So, let's embrace this wisdom and try to be like that tree together!

Golden Nuggets

- Releasing negativity is one of the best ways to process our emotions. To thrive, we must learn to let go of the regrets and burdens of the past that weigh us down.

- Holding onto grudges only brings negativity and hurts your emotional well-being. Practice releasing any grudges and negativity.

- Shed all emotional baggage and keep a light spirit. Constantly revisiting and reliving painful events and insults from the past offers no beneficial purpose.

- Prevent letting fleeting negativity become part of your long-term memory by continually revisiting and dwelling on past negative experiences.

- Embrace the mantra, "Release and let go." By remaining detached and not taking things personally, we can navigate life's challenges more effectively.

- To emerge from negativity, we must 'address unfinished business with others', find closure for our emotional resolution, and reduce psychological pain.

- Minimising exposure to negativity in every possible way is crucial for our emotional well-being.

Fostering Good Habits

There's a common saying that it takes 21 days to form a habit and 90 days to create a lasting lifestyle change. **If you commit to your goal for 21 days, it will become a habit**. If you commit to your goal for 90 days, it will become part of your lifestyle. Most neurolinguistic studies indicate that developing new habits takes between 21 to 30 days, though there may be some variations. With some flexibility, I strongly recommend dedicating 30 days (one month to creating new habits. Establishing new neural circuits in the brain for habit formation typically takes 3 to 4 weeks, and once habits are formed, they can last a lifetime. Consistent effort during this period is crucial for instilling these habits. Once established, regular practice becomes essential for achieving success.

It is important to develop a daily routine that includes focused work time. Such routines can help train your brain to better concentrate and reduce distractions. I had always wanted to practice meditation but had delayed it due to concerns about establishing the habit. However, I eventually mustered the courage and commitment needed. It took me three to four weeks to learn this new habit, and I have consistently practised meditation since 2022. Similarly, I faced challenges in going to the gym for body workouts in the year 2002. I made it a lasting habit by committing to a month of regular gym visits without breaks. I have maintained this habit for over twenty years, and it has become integral to my routine.

Isn't it fascinating how our brains change when we learn a new habit? Let's dive into the proven science that explains this amazing process!

Neuronal connections in the brain form pathways through repeated engagement in specific behaviours or activities, eventually leading to habits. These new connections function similarly to the coded software used by programming professionals. In the same vein, these codes become embedded in the brain and establish new neural circuits and pathways. As connectivity strengthens, tasks become easier. Therefore, we must acknowledge that task repetition, consistent practice, and reliability are advantageous. The more you practice, the more quickly you can develop new habits. **Repetition eventually leads to mastery.**

What's even more interesting is that behaviour becomes more automatic. Habit formation is a process through which **behaviour becomes more automatic through repetition**. The frequency of repetition in adopting a new behaviour makes a significant difference. It doesn't matter how long it takes for a habit to become automatic; the practice itself is what matters. With repeated activities, the brain undergoes structural changes, strengthening connections between neurons to become more efficient at that task. This neurological phenomenon is known as long-term potentiation, which refers to the strengthening of connections between neurons based on repeated patterns of activity. With each repetition, neural signalling between nerve cells and connectivity increase. Donald Hebb first described this concept in 1949, famously articulated as **"neurons that fire together wire together."** Therefore, repeatedly practising a habit can lead to physical changes in the brain. Structural changes within the brain and the formation of new neural pathways facilitate the performance of tasks without much conscious effort, potentially resulting in remarkable improvements. Eventually, the brain develops a process known as automaticity, the ability to perform a particular behaviour without deeply contemplating each step. As a result, the unconscious mind takes over, making the task significantly easier to execute.

Have you ever walked through a forest? If so, you might have noticed a "trail path" formed by many people taking the same route over time. It begins as a simple line, but with repeated use, it develops into a well-defined path. This happens not just because a few individuals choose the same way, but because many people walk on it consistently. Interestingly, our brains operate similarly. When we aim to build new habits, we must engage in the behaviour or task regularly and with ample practice. This repetition enables our brains to forge new connections, creating strong neural pathways as we learn and grow!

We all have a wonderful opportunity to cultivate either good or bad habits. Imagine people living in the jungle; they often choose safe pathways leading to a stunning valley filled with sparkling rivers, fruitful trees, and beautiful gardens. They embrace the forest trails that guide them toward strong, sturdy roads. However, they could also take an unsafe path filled with lurking dangers and darkness. It is their choice which path to follow. Similarly, your journey is shaped by your habit choices and how you construct those pathways in your mind. Therefore, let's focus on building neural circuits that promote positive behaviours and encourage good habits!

Starting a new habit can be exciting! Let's explore the steps together.

When initiating a new habit, **it is essential to allocate a specific time and location for it.** This structured approach ensures that you consistently adhere to the habit, regardless of life's circumstances. Be clear and specific about the location, timing, and other details. Ensure you clearly understand when and where you will perform your actions. Without these specifics, you may find it challenging to develop a new habit. For instance, I initially planned to meditate at night. However, after a few nights, I found it difficult to adhere to this routine. Therefore, I decided to be more precise by selecting a specific location and time.

Try to fill out this sentence

I will ------ (new habit) at ---- (time) in (location)

For example, I will practise meditation for 10 minutes every night at 9 pm in my study room immediately after shutting down my computer.

By being precise about the habit, timing, and location, you are more likely to adhere to it. This specific routine helps me stick to the habit consistently. Therefore, setting the right timing and location is vital—it becomes part of your personal space. Developing new habits with defined time frames and locations is a crucial aspect of the process. Treating this commitment with the same importance as a specialist doctor's appointment serves as a helpful analogy. Just as you wouldn't want to miss such appointments, strive to honour your commitments to your new habit. Approaching habit formation with a mindset of utmost importance is essential. Treat it with the same significance as a consultation with a specialist. By prioritising your new habit as you would necessary appointments, set designated times and locations for practice without fail. This practice signals to your brain that you are dedicated to this habit and must consciously devote effort towards its success. Consistent practice with repetitions is key to mastery.

Next, let's explore Mr Fogg's fantastic idea of '**anchoring new habits**' and discover how it can help us create new routines. **Instead of linking your new habit with a specific time and place, you can associate or connect it with an existing habit you are already practising.** This method is known as "anchoring," a concept developed by BJ Fogg as part of his Tiny Habits programme. During habit anchoring, the key is to pair your desired new behaviour with something you already do daily. You can integrate these new habits into your existing routines. **Connecting an existing habit with a new one creates a beneficial chain reaction** where one action naturally leads to the next. When developing a new habit, consider how different behaviours are interconnected, and leverage these connections to your advantage.

For instance, after eating lunch, I will drink two glasses of water.

The anchoring formula is: "After (the current habit) ----------------, I will (the new habit) ----------------."

Fogg calls this the anchor moment, which is the 'existing routine', but this moment also reminds you to do the 'new behaviour' or habit that you wanted to form. Therefore, you do the new behaviour immediately after the anchor moment.

Here are some additional examples:

After brushing my teeth in the morning, I put on my workout clothes.

After changing into my night pyjamas, I will meditate for five minutes.

After arriving at the office and sitting at my desk, I will create a to-do list for the day.

After dinner, I will place my plates directly into the kitchen sink dishwasher.

The secret to creating a new habit through anchoring is selecting the right cue to initiate it. **When starting a new habit, ensure it is based on 'specific environmental cues'.** Redesign your environment to make these cues more noticeable and accessible. These cues can motivate you by acting as a game plan for your future actions. The key is to select the right cues, as they will assist you in developing and maintaining good habits. You must decide when and where to incorporate this new habit into your daily routine, as this can make a significant difference. Start by brainstorming your daily habits and creating a list. Once you have established this list, you can identify specific times and locations to slot these new habits into your routine. Remember that no habit exists in isolation; rather, habits are interconnected actions that lead from one to another. Leverage the interconnected nature of your behaviours to your advantage when cultivating a new habit. After completing the current habit, seamlessly transition into the new habit. For instance.

- If you want to practise playing the piano, consider placing it in your living room.

- If you want to drink more water, keep your water bottle on your workspace as a reminder to stay hydrated.

- If you aim to start your day with morning exercise, keep your workout clothes beside your bed as a reminder.

- If you plan to end your day by reading a book, keep it next to your pillow.

- If you want to eat at least one fresh fruit daily, keep it on your dining table.

- If you want to talk to a close friend or family member once a week, write it down on your noticeboard.

This visual reminder can motivate you. An essential new dietary habit I have incorporated into my life is prioritising fruit consumption before meals. I keep fruits on my dinner table and make it a point to add them to my plate before the main course. This practice ensures that I consistently consume enough fruit by having them visibly present. Placing them at the forefront allows for easy access and immediate consumption. Visual cues like this have been instrumental in supporting and maintaining my healthy eating habits.

Let me explain a psychological phenomenon called shaping, which is used to develop good habits. Shaping is a psychological technique that involves reinforcing successive approximations of a desired behaviour until the target behaviour is achieved. It is based on operant conditioning concepts described by the American Psychologist and behaviourist Mr. Skinner. Instead of expecting the individual to perform the desired behaviour perfectly from the start, shaping allows for gradual improvement by rewarding closer and closer attempts toward the desired behaviour. To explain it in a simpler way, rather than expecting someone to get it right from the very beginning, **shaping encourages gradual progress by celebrating each step they take toward the desired behaviour.**

Here is how you can apply the concept of shaping to develop a delightful habit of doing body workouts at the gym every day:

For example: Developing an exercise routine a nd going to the gym

Identify the Desired Behaviour - Let's create a fun and enjoyable routine of working out at the gym daily! Start small and choose a step that feels totally manageable.

Process of Shaping - Change into workout clothes as soon as you arrive, then step outside. After achieving success, walk to the nearby park three days a week. Following this, walk to your gym and back three days a week. Next, walk to the gym, exercise for 15 minutes of cardio, and return three days a week. After each gym visit, take a moment to celebrate your success! This could be as simple as treating yourself to your favourite snack, enjoying a lovely and relaxing bath, or pausing to appreciate your own efforts. Positive reinforcement by rewarding yourself and celebrating small successes at every step is key to making that habit stick!

Then, drive to the gym and exercise for 30 minutes of cardio before returning three days a week. Occasionally, reflect on your progress and acknowledge how far you have come. Feel free to adjust your goals as needed, too! And if 30 minutes seems like a lot, don't worry! You can always scale back to 20 minutes and gradually work your way back up.

Gradually Increase the Challenge: Start by driving to the gym, exercising for 15 minutes of cardio and 15 minutes of weight training, and going three days a week. As you become more comfortable with the process, you can increase the frequency of your visits and gently enhance your routine by setting specific goals. Don't forget to reward yourself after each workout session! **Celebrate each time you commit more to the process.**

After these significant steps, drive to the gym and engage in cardio, weights, and high-intensity training four days a week. Following this, drive to the gym and participate in cardio, weights, and high-intensity training five days a week. Build up your workout duration—once you regularly visit the gym several times a week, focus on gradually extending your workouts, eventually aiming for a full hour! Select specific days and times for your workouts and allow this routine to become a delightful part of your daily life. **Consistency is key.** Remember that celebrating and treating yourself to small rewards is crucial in shaping your journey!

If you are still deciding when to begin, why not start on the first day of the week or month? Starting when you feel motivated, energised, and optimistic makes it easier to create a new habit and can help you get the momentum going!

'Embrace every little opportunity' to foster positive changes! **Seize each chance to make small adjustments and cultivate beneficial habits.** For example, you could opt for the stairs rather than using the elevator at work. Small actions, such as stretching every 30 minutes during your breaks or enjoying a refreshing short walk every four hours for about

15 to 20 minutes, can significantly impact you! Instead of focusing on excuses, let's aim to find every opportunity to establish those fantastic new habits. The key is identifying the right cues that encourage positive habits and capitalising on every opportunity.

The incredible influence of small daily habits on our long- term goals is truly inspiring! Just saving twenty-five dollars a day can add up to an impressive 10,000 per year. Did you know that if you read just ten pages each day, you will quickly finish ten books in no time? It is amazing how these small habits can lead to significant results, so let's keep that in mind and embrace their power. Tailoring your habits to your personality is crucial.

Identifying the right areas of interest that align with your personality and skills is essential. **Based on your personality, develop habits that suit you best.** It is worth remembering that '**Habit-changing can become life-changing.**' What are you waiting for? Most people read this and understand a lot, but more action is required. Buckle up and enjoy learning new, positive habits.

Golden Nuggets

- Establishing new neural circuits in the brain for habit formation generally takes three to four weeks. Once solid habits are formed, they can last a lifetime.

- Consistently practising a habit can lead to physical changes in the brain, resulting in a process called 'automaticity' that allows individuals to perform specific behaviours without deeply considering each step.

- When developing new habits, set a specific time and place.

- Habit anchoring involves connecting a new habit to an existing one that you are already practising.

- Revamp your surroundings to enhance the visibility and accessibility of these cues, fostering new habits.

- Shaping involves gradually learning a new habit or behaviour by reinforcing successive approximations toward the desired behaviour. It's all about celebrating each small step you take toward building a new habit over time until it becomes fully integrated

- Seize every opportunity to make small changes and develop positive habits.

- The duration of learning alone is not important; what truly matters is how often tasks are repeated and the consistency of your practice.

Breaking Free from Bad Habits

Overcoming bad habits can be tough, but with effective strategies, it is completely achievable. While forming new habits is relatively easier, breaking old and negative habits can be demanding and requires more discipline. Understanding our habits can help us determine whether they are beneficial, harmful, or neutral. Ultimately, our perspective shapes how a habit is categorised. By consciously evaluating habits and classifying them as good, neutral, or bad, we can focus more on enhancing positive habits and reducing the frequency of negative ones. Common triggers that maintain bad habits I have observed in my practice include boredom, isolation, lack of activities, lack of proper structure, and stimulation during the day, as well as spells of untreated anxiety.

One of the simplest ways suggested in many books and websites to break a habit is to **"follow the three-day rule"**. Stop engaging entirely for three consecutive days to eliminate a habit. Allowing a habit to lapse for more than three days can make it challenging to start again. Therefore, aim to refrain from the behaviour for three straight days. One day is merely a pause, two days are a break, and three days mark the beginning of a new pattern. If you don't want to establish the behaviour as a pattern, avoid doing it for those three days. However, this may apply only to some and "requires a more structured approach".

Identifying the bad habit and understanding the triggers is the first significant step. Identify the bad habit: for example, you might check social media sites on your phone at night in bed. Recognising that this is a bad habit you want to change is vital. Understand the triggers: identifying these triggers is also crucial for change. The triggers could be the notifications you receive on your phone, and you tend to check for new messages when you are not sleepy. One of the most highly effective methods to break a bad habit is to **'reduce exposure to the cues that trigger it'**. A critical psychological phenomenon known as 'cue-induced wanting' indicates that an external factor can trigger a compulsive craving to repeat a bad habit. Once you notice or encounter something associated with the habit, you will likely develop a desire for it. Therefore, it is essential to minimise exposure to these cues to address bad habits at their source. I can give you a few instances to minimise the exposures.

If you habitually check your phone at night, consider leaving it in another room to ensure you get a good night's sleep.

If you struggle with drinking alcohol, you might want to avoid routes that take you past places where alcohol is sold.

If you are playing video games too much, unplugging the console and storing it away can be effective.

Making these changes can make the cues less noticeable or even invisible. As the saying goes, **"Out of sight, out of mind."** By removing these critical cues, your habits can gradually fade away. Consequently, modifying your environment to diminish visibility or access to triggers can facilitate positive change.

Stop trying to change bad habits in just 24 hours. Attempting to make such a significant change in that short time frame often results in failure and can lead to disappointment. Instead, focus on starting small and taking one step at a time. Adopting an "all-or-nothing" mentality is ineffective for making behavioural changes, especially when it comes to breaking bad habits. People often have multiple bad habits, but **trying to change several at once can be overwhelming and challenging.** Changing too many habits simultaneously can also lead to discouragement, so it is best to concentrate on one bad habit at a time. I have seen people who wanted to quit alcohol and smoking at the same time, which led to discouragement and failure. In such situations, dedicate your full attention to breaking one bad habit, and once you feel confident in your success, you can move on to the next one.

If you want to break down destructive habits, the next important step is to 'set clear goals with rules, make a plan to break the existing habit, and replace it with alternative healthy habits. Set realistic goals and aim to "approach rather than avoid," as the objective is to substitute a bad habit with a healthier one. For example, if someone tends to bite their nails when stressed, they might replace that habit with a stress ball. If someone frequently overspends while shopping, they can limit their purchases by using a small basket instead of a large cart. When attempting to replace a bad habit, ensure that your plans are specific and realistic.

While doing so, **you should work hard, put in extra effort, and endure challenges.** For instance, I used to have the bad habit of snacking frequently at night when I felt hungry. This habit led to weight gain due to unhealthy late-night snacking. So, what did I do to overcome this habit? I decided to stop buying snacks and instead purchase more fruits and nuts. I completely stopped purchasing unhealthy snacks. It was tempting and challenging to give up something I enjoyed. I removed them from my online shopping cart, so I no longer ordered them despite the strong temptation. By doing this, I eliminated the opportunity for unhealthy snacking at night. Instead, I developed a new habit of adding more fruits and nuts to my shopping cart, which I kept in my fridge. Whenever I felt hungry and craved something, I ate fresh fruit at night. This helped me overcome my unhealthy snacking episodes, and I started losing weight without significant dietary restrictions. The good news is that I eventually liked them more than unhealthy snacks. Initially, it may be difficult for some people to adjust to healthy snacking, but eventually, they will start to enjoy it, just as I did. However, I am not too hard on myself and still allow for indulgences during holidays. I still buy popcorn, nachos, and drinks at the cinema. I view this as a special reward for achieving something I wanted, which brings me joy.

For instance, I can identify two negative habits of my own, which I recognised and replaced: 1) Checking my phone for messages frequently and aimlessly scrolling through social media, now replaced by reading books at bedtime, and 2) watching television instead of engaging with my children during family time, now replaced by playtime and chatting with my children about their day. Replacing a bad habit can take two to three months or longer, but adhering to your plan will gradually become easier. Here are some examples I have given to my clients who have replaced old habits with new ones. When you sit down for a meal, why not start by enjoying some delicious vegetables before diving into the main course? Embracing this can become a wonderful new habit. Instead of slipping into too much TV time, try swapping it for some invigorating exercise. Your body will thank you!

The key principles from the book Atomic Habits by James Clear suggest that when breaking a habit, you should make it less obvious **using three strategies which are 'avoiding cues, making it less attractive, and making it more challenging to engage in'.**

We have discussed avoiding cues or triggers.

To break a habit, another thing you can do is **"make it more unattractive".** To do this, you must list the disadvantages of continuing a particular habit and make it less attractive. Reframe your mindset by considering the disadvantages of continuing bad habits. For example, if you were to continue drinking alcohol, then list down the disadvantages of continuing this habit. It impacts your health by damaging your stomach, liver and nerves; it affects your mind, leading to anxiety and depression. It costs you a lot of money. It disrupts your sleep pattern at night. It affects your relationship with family members and friends with frequent fights. It diminishes work performance leading to lateness and frequent absences . Lets look into another example, if you continue to eat fast food and takeout frequently, list the disadvantages of maintaining this habit. Craving fast food and frequent takeaways can impact physical health and well-being. Key drawbacks include: Fast food is high in unhealthy fats, sugars, and sodium, leading to nutritional deficiencies. Many options lack essential vitamins and minerals. High caloric content can cause weight gain and obesity, while large portions encourage overeating.

Unhealthy fats may increase cholesterol and blood pressure, raising heart disease risk. High-sugar and high-carb diets can lead to insulin resistance and type 2 diabetes. Processed foods can cause digestive issues like bloating and constipation. Diets rich in sugar and unhealthy fats can result in mood swings, anxiety, depression, and fast food addiction. Regularly buying fast food can cost more than home-cooked meals, and reliance on takeaways can reduce family meal opportunities, impacting social and emotional health. Making a list of disadvantages and thinking it through can help make those habits feel less appealing, which can motivate you to adopt healthier habits instead.

How do you make habits more challenging to engage in?

You can break bad habits when barriers or obstacles make it difficult to engage in unwanted behaviours. Below are a few simple strategies that can help make these habits even harder to maintain. By applying these strategies, you can effectively create a supportive environment for breaking unwanted habits and promoting positive behaviour changes.

Consider Adding Physical Barriers: For example, if you frequently snack late at night, consider placing snacks in a hard- to-reach location or removing them from your home entirely.

Limit Accessibility: If you find yourself distracted by certain websites or want to reduce screen time on your devices, you can use specific applications to block and minimize temptation and decrease excessive social media usage. By removing social media apps from your phone, you can reduce the time spent scrolling through social media, which will help lessen the urge to check your accounts.

Implement a Waiting Period: Introducing a waiting or "cool down" period before indulging in your habit can be effective. For instance, if you feel the urge to smoke, try waiting 30 minutes before deciding whether to act on that impulse. This delay can help reduce impulsive behaviour, distract you, and aid in overcoming the urge. If you find yourself shopping online more frequently, be mindful of these triggers. To lessen temptation, consider turning off your Wi-Fi for a couple of hours and enabling it later. If you are still tempted to buy, consider waiting 24 hours before clicking the order button. Use this time to research and reflect on whether it is something you truly need. Believe me, you are less likely to go back and make the purchase

Establish Reward Systems: Create a reward system for yourself. Reward yourself for resisting bad habits by offering positive incentives to avoid them.

Establish Penalty Systems: Think about introducing a penalty system whereby indulging in the bad habit results in financial costs, such as donating money to a cause you dislike every time you engage in the habit.

Adjust Your Environment: Change your surroundings to remove triggers associated with your bad habits. For example, if you often drink fizzy beverages, take out all such drinks from your home and workplace. If watching too much TV is a problem, think about taking the television out of your bedroom.

Include Accountability Mechanisms: Sharing your goals with friends or family fosters a sense of accountability. Knowing that someone is watching can discourage you from indulging in the habit.

Psychologists utilise a powerful tool known as the '**commitment device**' during their sessions. This device involves seeking support and sharing goals with friends or family.

A commitment device is a tool or strategy used to help individuals stick to their better habits or behaviour in the future, especially when they face temptations that might lead them off course. Psychologists and psychiatrists often use the term "commitment device," particularly concerning individuals with addictive behaviours. For example, people struggling with alcohol dependence or recreational drug dependence can ask their friends and colleagues not to invite them to parties, which helps reduce the temptation to drink or take drugs. Another common example involves children: when they play video games or use gadgets, parents can programme the devices to shut off automatically after an hour of agreed-upon playtime. Such devices are useful; you can use them to avoid succumbing to temptations. Employ these commitment devices and seek support from others to limit your future choices to those that benefit you.

Having an '**accountability buddy**'—whether a friend, partner, family member, or coworker—can be beneficial in overcoming bad habits and serving as a distraction. Involving others can enhance the effectiveness of commitment devices. Action plans may vary from person to person, so it is helpful to establish barriers against your bad habits with the support of accountability buddies. For instance, if you struggle with overeating, avoid keeping junk food at home and refrain from ordering takeout through delivery apps. Your accountability buddy can provide a distraction. If you find yourself checking your phone too often, consider placing your phone in a locker and going for a walk with your accountability buddy instead of scrolling through social media.

Commitment devices can include external mechanisms that establish consequences for failing to honour commitments. For instance, a person might agree to pay a penalty if they do not achieve a specific goal. Let's consider an example of a commitment device designed to quit a harmful habit, such as smoking, by looking at a man named Paul who has struggled to stop smoking for years. Paul often finds it difficult to resist temptation, especially during stressful times. To support his efforts to quit, Paul decides to implement a commitment device that imposes external constraints. He sets a goal to quit smoking completely within three months and establishes a financial penalty: if he smokes even one cigarette during that period, he will donate $500 to a cause he strongly opposes (for instance, a political party or organisation). To enhance his accountability, Paul shares his goal and the details of his commitment with his close friend, Peter, who agrees to be his accountability partner. Peter will verify whether Paul has smoked during the three-month period. If Paul smokes, he will be required to make the $500 donation to the agreed-upon cause. Paul maintains a journal to track his cravings, triggers, and successes along the way. Peter checks in with him regularly to provide support and encouragement. The substantial financial penalty associated with smoking motivates Paul to resist cigarettes and seek healthier coping mechanisms for stress. By the end of the three months, Paul successfully quits smoking without making any donations, feeling proud of his achievement and relieved to avoid the financial penalty. This experience helps Paul develop healthier habits and reinforces his commitment to staying smoke-free, ultimately contributing positively to his overall health and well-being. In this example, the potential loss of $500 to a cause he opposes is a powerful external constraint supporting Paul's commitment to quitting. Moreover, involving others in the process, like Peter, can enhance the effectiveness of commitment devices; sharing goals with friends or family can create a sense of accountability. By utilising commitment devices, individuals can better align their actions with long- term goals and values, effectively enhancing self-control and decision-making.

Celebrate small victories and successes while working to eliminate bad habits. For example, treat yourself to a spa session for every incremental goal you achieve, such as maintaining a regular exercise routine for four weeks. After following a healthy diet for a month, reward yourself with a manicure and pedicure. Remember that setbacks can happen and facing them is part of the journey. Reflect frequently on why you are engaging in this habit. Tracking your progress with a calendar and marking milestones can keep you motivated. After breaking a bad habit, continue to follow your new routines consistently. Regularly practising these new habits will embed them more permanently in your mind. Consistent practice strengthens the neural pathways in your brain.

Golden Nuggets

- Stop attempting to change bad habits in just 24 hours.

- Adjusting multiple habits simultaneously may lead to discouragement, so it is advisable to concentrate on overcoming one negative habit at a time.

- Identifying the negative habit and recognising its triggers is an essential first step.

- Set clear goals with rules as you plan to break the existing habit and replace it with healthier alternatives.

- One essential piece of advice is to avoid those cues. By reducing exposure to and eliminating cues associated with bad habits, you can break free from them more effectively

- To break a habit, make it more less attractive and list the disadvantages of continuing this habit.

- One more effective strategy for breaking a habit is to make it more challenging to engage in.

- Celebrate small victories and successes as you work to eliminate your bad habits.

Keep Distractions at Bay to Maintain Your Momentum

An interesting quote says, **"A focused fool can achieve more than a distracted genius."** Staying focused is essential; not getting diverted or distracted helps us achieve more.

Overcoming distractions in daily life is crucial for maintaining focus, productivity, and goal achievement. Distractions often lead to mistakes, which require additional time to correct. They can scatter our energy and dilute our efforts, making it tougher to reach our objectives. Staying focused allows for deeper engagement with tasks. When distractions are minimised, individuals can complete tasks faster and with more creativity, enhancing overall efficiency.

The first step is to identify the everyday distractions that disrupt your focus.

There are two types of distractions: internal and external. Internal distractions primarily arise from our body or mind and significantly affect our ability to maintain focus. They can manifest as a torrent of thoughts racing through our minds, shifting rapidly from one topic to another and hindering us from concentrating. These thoughts may include negativity, fear, randomness, and personal worries. Any disruptions to our physical health, such as pain, hunger, thirst, dehydration, or fluctuations in body temperature, also function as internal distractions.

External distractions stem from one's environment, whether at home – such as family members – or in an office setting, like colleagues. Technology is also a significant distraction, including television, social media, emails, phone calls, and loud surroundings. It is essential to avoid becoming overly dependent on social media and phones. Simple environmental factors can be quite distracting. For instance, an uncomfortable room temperature can cause distractions, whether too hot or too cold. Additionally, disruptive noises from transportation also contribute to distractions.

What is the scientific explanation for becoming so hooked on electronic distractions? We are frequently interrupted by various electronic elements, including emails, WhatsApp messages, phone notifications, and social media alerts. Each time we receive a new message, a small amount of dopamine is released as part of our body's novelty response to new stimuli. This process creates a sense of pleasure and stimulation. However, the unfortunate reality is that this feeling lasts only a brief time. Eventually, the mind craves the next message, leading to a compulsive checking of notifications that becomes addictive. This constant cycle can hinder productivity throughout the day as our bodies seek short bursts of dopamine. The release of dopamine produces a sensation of euphoria for a brief period, comparable to consuming small quantities of stimulant recreational substances like amphetamines or cocaine. These distractions can trigger dopamine release in the brain, referred to as **"bad dopamine."** They create a habit loop, making it difficult for individuals to quit. Ultimately, people become addicted to electronic gadgets, representing another form of addiction equivalent to smoking, alcohol, and drugs. Therefore, it is crucial to take control of these modern electronic distractions.

Electronic distractors, such as mobile phones, televisions, mobile applications, the Internet, and social media, have wholly invaded our spaces—at home, in the office, and into the broader community. It is an invisible form of pollution, yet it is real and occurs everywhere. Due to technological advancements, we have become overly reliant on these devices, which negatively impact our living and working environments and our health and well- being. I consider this a new and perhaps the most detrimental form of pollution, **which I call technological pollution.**

What happens to our brains when you are spending too much time on screens and gadgets?

Spending excessive time on electronic devices and gadgets—checking emails, WhatsApp messages, and surfing the internet—can cause your brain to overwork, resulting in increased fatigue and mental exhaustion as the day progresses. Neuropsychological studies indicate that this constant disruption can lead to a drop of **up to 10 IQ points** as the day continues. By day's end, you may feel so drained that your brain struggles with even simple decisions—like catching a bus or train home, deciding what to cook for dinner, whether to go to the gym, or how to spend your evening. Personally, I usually check my emails only twice a day: at 11:30 a.m., just before noon, after completing three to four hours of productive work in the morning, and then again at 4:00 p.m., after three more hours of work in the afternoon. By 4:00 p.m., my brain feels fatigued, so I dedicate this time to less demanding tasks, such as checking and replying to less urgent emails. This strategy helps me use my time more productively.

One of the most significant distractions of modern times is **social media.** We are constantly bombarded with updates and information from social media platforms. Research in social psychology indicates that the average adult spends about three and a half to four hours each day **(210 to 240 minutes)** checking emails, texting, browsing social media platforms, and using various applications. Most of this time, approximately two and a half hours daily (Ref-Datareportal), is devoted to social media platforms. While these applications provide some enjoyment and entertainment, they also result in significant time wastage and are harmful distractions for people worldwide. Mindlessly scrolling through social media without any real purpose can consume several hours of your time if you are not mindful of it. When engaging with social media, the first important step is to control how you use it to maximise its benefits and minimise any adverse effects. Establish clear boundaries and limit your daily time spent on them. For instance, I typically allocate 30 minutes daily to check for updates and post on social media. You may opt to dedicate additional time, perhaps up to an hour, but it is crucial not to exceed this limit.

Consider turning off notifications and sound alerts for incoming messages and limiting your exposure to electronic distractions.

"Disable non-essential notifications." This step can help you avoid the temptation of constantly checking your phone and social media platforms, as you won't receive alerts for new messages or updates. When you are ready to engage with social media during your designated time, turn notifications back on and enjoy using the various platforms.

First, create a strong barrier, a virtual wall to guard against distractions. The most essential step is to create a work environment that fosters focus and enhances productivity. It is crucial to recognise that interruptions can reduce work quality and increase errors.

Research indicates that when you face interruptions, "it can take 23 minutes to regain focus" (University of Columbia Irvine Study). Regaining focus is more complex, so it aims to avoid interruptions and distractions.

To protect myself from distractions, I have established several strategies that serve as **"virtual security guards."** I have minimised clutter, noise, and visual distractions in my office. It is also essential to reduce interruptions; I hang a "Do Not Disturb" sign on my door to inform colleagues that I am busy. I set my phone to "Do Not Disturb" mode and keep it out of sight in a drawer, checking it only during my scheduled breaks. To further reduce distractions, I disable notifications and alerts on my laptop. When working alongside others, I wear noise-cancelling headphones. I take restroom breaks every three hours. I keep a bottle of water on my desk to stay hydrated. Having my computer calendar open helps me manage my schedule and ensures I don't miss any necessary tasks. These simple strategies have significantly improved my focus at work. However, others may wish to develop their methods for minimising distractions. Additionally, I inform my family to contact the main reception in case of an emergency so they can relay urgent information to me during work hours. Only in emergencies should administrative staff knock on my door to inform me.

Establish boundaries with coworkers. Setting clear boundaries helps others recognise your need for concentration. When sharing office space with distracting colleagues, politely inform noisy or talkative individuals that their behaviour disrupts your work and suggest using AirPods or headphones as a subtle signal. Conversations with disruptive coworkers, especially if they are your supervisors, require a tactful approach. It may be necessary to have a one-on-one discussion to express that frequent interruptions hinder your progress politely. Consider sending a carefully crafted message to address the issue if face- to-face communication is awkward and difficult.

Techniques such as the **'Pomodoro Technique'**, which is derived from the Italian word for tomato, are highly effective. This method entails working in focused bursts followed by short breaks—specifically, a 25-minute focused work session followed by a 5-minute break—which helps to maintain concentration, improve task completion, and increase productivity. Set specific times for work sessions and breaks. **I recommend starting with 25-minute focused work sessions and 5-minute breaks.** I refer to this focused session as my 'Concentration Sprint,' followed by regular breaks. When you complete one concentration sprint of 25 minutes and then take a 5-minute break, I consider it one 'Pomodoro Set.' To enhance productivity, aim for 5-6 Pomodoro Sets in the first session, followed by a long lunch break of 45-60 minutes, and then another 5-6 Pomodoro Sets in the second session. If you are working full-time, try to target 10-12 Pomodoro Sets a day, with a minimum of ten Pomodoro Sets daily to maximise productivity.

Working from home can be challenging due to distractions and the need to create a productive workspace. It is essential to communicate with your family members about your work schedule and let them know when you need uninterrupted time to work.

Establish a dedicated workspace free from distractions. This area should be linked to work to help maintain your focus. Manage your technology use by disabling notifications on your devices and scheduling specific times to check emails, preventing constant interruptions. Implementing these straightforward strategies can create a conducive work environment at home, reduce distractions, and enhance productivity while working remotely.

Staying focused is essential; it helps us achieve more by maintaining our attention on our tasks. Focus without distractions truly drives productivity, and concentrating on our work leads to better outcomes. With fewer distractions, we can work more quickly and creatively, significantly boosting our efficiency. In summary, while managing time is important, developing the ability to focus deeply and without distractions is key to achieving outstanding results. Nurturing our focus enhances our productivity and brings a sense of fulfilment and accomplishment in our work.

Golden Nuggets

- Maintain a clear and focused mind and avoid distractions, as they can derail progress.

- Focusing intensely without distraction plays a crucial role in achieving better results.

- When we are distracted, mistakes occur, which can take even more time to correct.

- The first step is to identify the everyday distractions that disrupt your focus.

- Build a strong barrier, a virtual wall to protect against distractions.

- Having dedicated work periods and regular break times during work hours is essential.

- Establish boundaries with coworkers, colleagues, and family to minimise interruptions during focused work time.

- Additionally, your productivity will naturally increase by consistently minimising the time spent on negative distractions.

Make Prioritisation Your Priority to Enhance Productivity

"Prioritisation of your priorities" refers to identifying and organising tasks or responsibilities based on their significance and urgency. **This means determining which tasks are most crucial and must be addressed first**. It involves assessing the value (how important it is), urgency (how soon it should be attended to), and potential impact of each task. Being able to distinguish 'what is urgent' from 'what is important' is essential for prioritising effectively and planning our days purposefully. By prioritising, you commit to a structured approach to managing your workload. This practice ensures you address the most critical tasks to achieve your goals efficiently and effectively. Prioritising tasks is vital to your time management and decision-making strategy.

Have you heard of the Pareto principle, also known as the 80/20 rule? It states that 80% of outcomes come from 20% of causes. To put it simply, 20% of what you do yields 80% of your desired results. The value of a task or activity is more significant than the number of activities. "Just 20% of your critical tasks can achieve 80% of your work, so focus on those priorities". Therefore, prioritise the most vital tasks and keep the 80/20 rule in mind.

Regularly assess the value you bring to each task, job, meeting, or assignment to ensure you make a meaningful contribution and effectively fulfil your responsibilities. If you feel you are not adding significant value or if others don't appreciate your contributions, it is best to avoid wasting time in such situations. For example, I used to attend all the meetings, but I realised I was not contributing anything significant. As a result, I have become skilled at sending apologies for meetings where my involvement is minimal, choosing instead to review the minutes afterward and contribute if necessary. Attending only the most relevant meetings or sessions where I can add value has proven to be a more effective use of my time.

Try to start your day with a clear visual plan in your mind. The brain requires a proper structure and planning to execute tasks. If you spend the day without a plan, it is like starting your journey without a proper roadmap. You will waste a lot of time without direction or purpose. Without a visual plan for the day, you can easily get sidetracked and waste even more time.

Focus on high-priority tasks, followed by medium-priority and then low-priority ones. Have you heard the story of the rocks, pebbles, and sand? It emphasises the importance of prioritising how we spend our time. In this story, a professor stands in front of his class with a large, empty jar. He fills it with rocks, each about 2 to 3 inches in diameter. Next, he asks the class if the jar is full, and they all agree. Then, he adds a box of small pebbles, measuring 2 to 3 centimetres in diameter, giving the jar a gentle shake to allow the pebbles to fill the gaps around the rocks. Once again, he asks if the jar is complete, and the class agrees.

Finally, the professor takes a box of sand and pours it into the jar, filling the tiny spaces between the rocks and pebbles. Once more, he asks if the jar is full, and this time the class laughs and agrees that it is. The professor then explains that the 'jar represents our lives'. The big rocks symbolise the most important things that should be prioritised and completed first. The pebbles represent moderately essential tasks that we need to accomplish daily. Finally, the sand signifies the least important tasks with minimal priority. Now, imagine if you were to fill the jar in reverse order, starting with the sand. There wouldn't be enough space left for the rocks and pebbles. This analogy applies to real-life as well. If we spend too much time on less important tasks (the sand), they occupy so much of our time and energy that we won't have enough left to focus on higher-priority tasks (the big rocks). Therefore, it is crucial to prioritise the big rocks first, followed by the medium-priority pebbles, and leave the sand for last. The sand will always find space in our day and can be accomplished after the more significant tasks are addressed. (Ref- Prioritising your life: Mindful Practices)

Grasping the difference between urgent and important tasks can truly transform how you manage your workload, find job satisfaction, and stay focused. Learning to prioritise tasks is a valuable skill that, with a little practice, can become second nature and really boost your productivity. It is all about balancing the urgent tasks with those that matter most in your life. Being able to tell 'what is urgent' from 'what is important' is essential for prioritising effectively and planning our days purposefully. The wise words of the **Eisenhower Matrix** remind us that '**what is important is seldom urgent, and what is urgent is seldom important**,' guiding us in making thoughtful choices every day!

One simple and effective technique to use when you are uncertain about what to do is to create a '**Must Do - Should Do - Could Do' list**. This is a technique that I created for myself. This is my daily strategy that I wanted to share with you because I believe it could help! Here is how it works: first, determine whether a task belongs to the 'Must Do', 'Should Do', or 'Could Do' category, and then prioritise your activities to ensure you easily meet your deadlines.

'**Must do**' tasks are essential activities that require immediate attention or must be completed within a specific timeframe. They are non-negotiable, urgent, and critical to complete. These tasks are crucial for achieving your goals with tight deadlines and fulfilling your responsibilities. Must do tasks are both more urgent and more important, and they have consequences if not addressed. For example, if you have distressed customers needing immediate assistance, those tasks should be prioritised and handled promptly at the start of your workday.

Next, we have '**Should Do' tasks**. These are important but not urgent — they contribute to your overall progress and should be handled after the Must Do tasks. Think of Should Do tasks as 'more important but may be less urgent' activities that are part of your daily routine. This could include regular responsibilities such as interacting with customers if you are a bank manager, providing consistent care and bedside rounds to patients as a doctor, or managing routine accounting duties as an accountant. Although these are essential and should be done daily, they can wait until you have addressed the most urgent matters. Completing these can improve productivity and contribute positively to your goals.

Finally, there are **'Could Do' tasks.** These are optional and would be nice to complete if time allows. It can be taken on if you find that you have extra time and resources. While they may enhance your work or offer additional benefits, they are not critical—consider them as 'less urgent and less important' tasks that can patiently wait. This includes responding to non-urgent emails or messages, making casual phone calls, attending social gatherings, or planning for the future. You can enjoy these tasks during your free time. They may help with long-term goals and personal development.

Remember to create **'buffer times'** to handle unexpected and emergency tasks and to include time for your break, relaxation, and well-being.

Using "must do," "should do," and "could-do" tasks is a clear and effective way to prioritise your tasks. It can reduce overwhelm and increase effectiveness. This terminology provides a more actionable framework. Overall, it is a practical way to categorise tasks based on their significance and urgency. This approach resonates well because it emphasises the importance of each task's urgency and necessity, helping you focus on what truly matters while keeping track of lower priority items. You should decide on them by the start of the day and plan them. Just make sure to review and adjust your lists as priorities change regularly.

You can succeed in every area of your life by making the most of your time. So, take charge of your time today and see the fantastic things you can accomplish. You can apply this technique to all aspects of your life, including work, personal time, family time, health and fitness, physical activities, and financial decisions. Remember, time management is a crucial principle that should be followed in every walk of life to achieve success and maintain a healthy work-life balance.

To improve your productivity, follow these steps.

STEP 1: Start by creating a list of tasks to complete.

STEP 2: Prioritise the tasks in order of importance. (The Must Do – Should Do – Could Do) and divide your tasks into three categories

STEP 3: Concentrate and focus on the most critical tasks and complete them first. Do not start on the Should do tasks until you have completed all the Must do tasks on your list.

STEP 4: Don't spend too much time on one task. Set time limits and divide the time between all tasks for the day.

STEP 5: Reflect on your progress. Track it periodically and adjust your plans as needed.

Following these steps can increase the quality and quantity of your work, leading to phenomenal positive results and outcomes. Results and outcomes matter, and your productivity will automatically increase.

In cases where individuals may work for organisations, companies, or industries whose priorities may not align with their own, it becomes critical for everyone employed by the organisation to understand the organisation's vision and goals clearly. Employees need to be aware of the priority tasks within the organisation, allowing them to adjust their work approach accordingly. In such organisational contexts, leaders play a pivotal role in effectively communicating the organisation's objectives to the staff, aiding them in task prioritisation, and boosting their motivation. Leaders must communicate regularly with their subordinates, providing guidance and fostering alignment with the organisation's goals and objectives. Employees can learn how to prioritise tasks effectively, maximising their organisational contributions through this approach.

The Must Do, Should Do, and Could-Do method is a great way to prioritise tasks effectively. Here is how an HR manager in an IT company uses it on a typical day: The same principles can be applied to other fields.

Example Task List

Must Do (Critical Tasks)

1. Finalise job offers for selected candidates; timely communication is essential to secure talent.

2. Address employee grievances, which are crucial for maintaining morale and workplace harmony.

3. Prepare for the performance review meeting with senior management, as it affects employee engagement and retention strategies.

Should Do (Important but Not Urgent Tasks)

1. Conduct orientation for new hires, which is essential for onboarding.

2. Plan the upcoming training session, which is vital for employee development while allowing for some flexibility.

3. Review and update HR policies, which are essential for compliance and efficiency but not immediately critical.

Could Do (Low-Priority Tasks)

1. Organise HR files and documentation – necessary, but this can be done later.

2. Research and explore new HR tools – useful for future improvements but not urgent.

3. Schedule team-building activities for the next quarter and email relevant staff – Good for team morale, but can wait until more pressing tasks are completed.

Golden Nuggets

- Prioritising tasks is crucial for your time management and decision-making strategy.

- It is crucial to differentiate tasks based on their urgency and importance clearly. Understanding the distinction between urgent and important tasks can significantly change how you manage your workload.

- It is essential to evaluate whether tasks or commitments add value and prioritise accordingly.

- Using "must do," "should do," and "could do" tasks is a clear and effective method for prioritising your tasks. Overall, it is a practical approach to categorising tasks based on their significance and urgency.

- First, prioritise high-priority tasks, then tackle medium-priority tasks, followed by low-priority ones.

- Focusing on high-priority tasks enhances your goal achievement, boosts your time management, and elevates your productivity.

- Once you learn to focus on your most essential and high-priority tasks and begin completing them, it will become a habit, enabling you to achieve more over time.

Elevating Productivity and Upgrading Performance

Productivity involves two key components: **improving your focus and concentration on the task at hand and reducing distractions that can adversely affect your performance.** Some people believe that time is what matters, but that is not the case. It is primarily the focus, free from distractions, that allows you to achieve more. A focused individual can channel their energy into high-quality work, leading to better outcomes. Many people claim to be busy, but being busy is different from being productive. You can feel busy without accomplishing much. Remember, being busy is not the same as being productive.

Improving Focus on a Deeper Level is necessary to improve productivity. Our brain is a vital organ for enhancing our focus and concentration. To improve your focus, it is essential to ensure that your brain receives adequate glucose, oxygen, and hydration. Consistently drink water regularly and incorporate healthy snacks like fruits, nuts, and seeds. You don't need to consume large meals to keep your brain active; in fact, eating smaller meals can be more beneficial. Eating larger meals can improve blood circulation in your gastrointestinal tract (splanchnic circulation) but may reduce blood flow to the brain (cerebral circulation). Mental fatigue occurs when there is reduced cerebral blood flow to the brain. Healthy snacks help maintain blood glucose levels, which are vital for enhancing focus and concentration. Additionally, taking deep breaths regularly for a minute or two can significantly improve mental clarity. It can promote better blood circulation and oxygen levels in the body. Practising deep breathing can relax your brain, enabling it to operate more efficiently. Moreover, enjoying a cup of coffee or tea can help keep you alert and boost your productivity.

Regular breaks are important for boosting productivity. It is essential to take breaks every 30 minutes. During these breaks, try to avoid thinking about work or commitments; the brain slows down like computers that run continuously without breaks, and therefore, they are essential. Short breaks throughout your work period will significantly enhance your productivity and focus. If you work for hours without proper breaks, you may complete tasks, but the quality and efficiency of your work can decline. Therefore, it is vital to take regular breaks throughout your workday. Take a moment to close your eyes, breathe deeply, sit in silence, enjoy a cup of coffee, stretch your muscles, have a snack, or go for a short walk during your short break time. This topic is discussed further in the chapter on 'Allow Yourself Breaks.'

Focus on Single-Tasking, which is a Key to Improve Cognitive Efficiency. Monotasking benefits the brain, which is inherently not adapted to multitasking. The human brain is designed to handle one task at a time. Focusing on a single task increases your concentration on a deeper level, leading to 'focused attention' and improving the quality of your work. For instance, when you are on a phone call, strive to give the conversation your undivided attention and avoid checking your emails at the same time. Similarly, when writing emails, maintain a friendly tone and clear communication without the distraction of phone calls or other conversations. This approach can significantly enhance the quality of your work. During the writing process of this book, for example, I devoted my energy exclusively to gathering and articulating my thoughts positively and cohesively. Many people view themselves as skilled multitaskers. At first glance, they may appear to be highly efficient. However, multitasking often reduces the overall quality of work due to divided attention. Moreover, it takes time for our brains to switch from one task to another, which can further affect the quality of the work produced.

This division of attention can sometimes result in longer completion times for tasks as well! Moreover, multitasking can make individuals more impulsive and fatigued. The constant switching of focus required in multitasking drains the brain's energy, leaving individuals feeling tired and overwhelmed. Unlike a smartphone or computer, which can run multiple applications simultaneously, the human brain can only concentrate on one task before shifting to another. While a few individuals may claim to achieve success through multitasking, it frequently leads to increased exhaustion and gives a false impression of high productivity. The efficiency of the output often decreases.

Although a small number of people may have genuine multitasking abilities, this is more of an exception than the rule. Committing your full attention to a single task increases your chances of achieving better results. Without proper breaks, added multitasking leads to cognitive overload with decrease d ability to think clearly and decreases productivity. Therefore, it is beneficial for everyone to focus on completing one task at a time.

Some folks multitask by juggling two things at once as they claim to have no other option. However, it is important to remember that while handling two tasks simultaneously is possible, one should be something you can do on autopilot. For instance, you might chat on the phone while cooking a new recipe or write a routine email while assisting a child with math homework. In the situations above, cooking a new recipe and assisting a child with math homework are more demanding tasks than the other two. Our brains typically handle only one complex task at a time, **so when multitasking, it is wise to prioritise the more demanding task** while allowing the easier one to take a backseat. Switching between tasks can be time-consuming and requires deep thought or critical analysis. In such cases, tackling them one at a time is frequently the most effective strategy.

Batching tasks—When you switch from one task to another that is very different, your brain needs time to adjust to the new focus. This transition can occasionally lead to lost time. If individuals constantly bounce between tasks, even more time may slip away. A great strategy is to group and address similar tasks during a dedicated time block. For example, when I see patients in my clinic, I typically see ten people before moving on to the next task. When I write a discharge summary, I complete several summaries before proceeding to the next task. This approach allows you to work more efficiently and maximise your time!

Identify your golden time, also known as prime time during the day, and aim to be the most productive during these periods. Recognise your optimal timing and work accordingly. Golden time is when your thoughts and cognition peak, allowing you to perform at your best. Utilise this time for your most challenging tasks and minimise distractions, especially during golden hours, to boost your productivity. You should be highly focused during your productive hours. Identify your peak productivity times, which could be any period, like early morning or late at night; it truly doesn't matter. Everyone is unique, and biological clocks differ. Your prime time may shift as you age and take on new responsibilities; for example, as a teenager, my prime time was early mornings, whereas in my mid-forties, it has shifted to the evenings. Therefore, it is crucial to remain adaptable. Remember, your biological clock is one-of-a-kind, and there's no need to compare yourself to others.

Have you heard of the 2-minute rule?

This is a concept from David Allen's workflow management method called GTD (Getting Things Done. This rule simply states that if you encounter a task that can be completed in two minutes or less, you should do it immediately instead of postponing it or adding it to your to-do list. The two-minute rule is a productivity concept introduced by David Allen in his book "Getting Things Done." The idea behind this rule is that if a task can be completed in two minutes or less, it should be done immediately rather than being put off or added to your to-do list. This approach helps prevent small, manageable tasks from accumulating and becoming overwhelming. By promptly addressing quick tasks, individuals can maintain a sense of organisation and efficiency in their daily activities.

Minimising Distractions and Interruptions - True productivity means minimising interruptions and distractions. To improve your focus and productivity, eliminate physical and digital distractions to maintain sharp focus during your productive times.

(This has been discussed in the other chapter.)

Managing your email inbox and responding to WhatsApp messages are integral aspects of saving time and improving productivity. I would like to share a few thoughts on managing emails and WhatsApp messages.

Begin by quickly scanning your emails. To organise your emails effectively, **follow Barbara Hemphill's 'File, Act and Toss' methodology.**

'F' stands for filing, ' A' f or a cting, an d 'T ' for trashing or tossing.

When reviewing emails, delete unnecessary ones immediately, and then proceed with filing and acting on the rest. The first priority is to eliminate or delete irrelevant emails by moving them to the trash. The next focus is to categorise emails that require filing. Create specific folders based on organisations or individuals for easier retrieval later. This ensures that essential emails are stored chronologically and are readily accessible. Thirdly, for emails that require action, prioritise those needing immediate responses; if an email can be answered in a minute or two, do not hesitate to reply promptly. Flag important but less urgent emails to address them during your workday. Non-urgent emails can be filed in your office management tools for later attention. For tasks that require more time, schedule them in your calendar or add them to your task management system. By following this systematic approach, you can effectively manage your inbox, ensure timely responses, and easily track important emails for future reference. This method allows you to manage your work while efficiently attending to email correspondence and promptly addressing inquiries.

Individuals needing minimal email engagement can check their emails twice daily—once in the morning and once in the evening—

spending only 10-15 minutes. This approach keeps important messages visible and ensures communication effectiveness.

For those in email-intensive roles, such as an eight-hour workday, it is best to establish a routine. To address urgent emails, check emails periodically during set times, such as hourly or every two hours. Turn off notifications between checks to prevent distractions and maintain focus on work tasks.

In urgent situations, people may call your phone multiple times for immediate contact. Prioritise answering these calls for critical matters. However, keeping your email inbox open can be distracting due to the influx of unwanted emails from companies and marketers. If emails are overwhelming, consider unsubscribing or blocking senders to reduce inbox clutter. Apply these principles to WhatsApp. With its rise as a key communication tool, manage notifications to reduce distractions. Set a schedule for checking messages every two to three hours, dedicating 5 to 10 minutes each time. Timely responses to direct messages address urgent issues, while focusing on important group chats promotes structured engagement. Identify groups that significantly impact your work or personal life for more efficient interaction; periodic updates can replace immediate replies. Leave groups that no longer add value to avoid message overload. For low-engagement groups, check in every few days.

A lack of trust can often hamper productivity. Since we spend a significant portion of our lives together, it is important to understand the work culture and your colleagues. By collaborating, sharing a laugh, and creating a supportive atmosphere, we give everyone the chance to feel comfortable and play their part.

Golden Nuggets

- Enhancing your focus and concentration at a deeper level boosts productivity, while avoiding distractions remains essential.
- Fostering focus can profoundly transform our work, resulting in greater achievements and enhanced personal fulfillment.

- Remember, being busy does not mean being productive.

- Regular breaks are essential for enhancing productivity.

- Single-tasking, or monotasking, enhances focus, reduces stress levels, improves work efficiency, and aids in successfully completing tasks.

- Many claim to be proficient multitaskers; however, productivity and work quality generally suffer as a result.

- Identify your golden time, also known as prime time, and strive to be most productive during these periods. This term refers to a time of day when an individual or organisation operates at peak performance or productivity.

- Maintain Focus in particular during Productive Time.

- To organise your emails effectively, apply Barbara Hemphill's 'File, Act and Toss' methodology.

- Respond promptly to urgent emails and schedule less urgent matters for later in your calendar or task list.

Time Management is Life Management

Time management is life management,' stated Brian Tracy in his book. (Master Your Time, Master Your Life).

Time management is about effectively **'managing yourself and your life'**. It simply refers to planning and organising how you allocate your time to various tasks and activities effectively. Time is a very valuable resource because it cannot be earned back. Once you lose time, it is lost permanently, making time management even more essential for maximising your potential. By managing your time well, you can achieve a better work-life balance, reduce stress, and increase overall satisfaction. Time management is essential to help you achieve your goals and lead a successful life. In today's complex and fast-paced world, effectively planning and organising one's work and organising your time will improve productivity.

'The most precious thing we have with us is TIME'
– Apple founder Steve Jobs

We all have 24 hours a day, and we should strive to make the most of this time frame.

Managing time effectively is synonymous with managing life and prioritising tasks within these 24 hours. Good time management fosters confidence, satisfaction, and productivity. Therefore, we must use our time for what truly matters to us.

Many people have asked me how I manage to juggle so many responsibilities and activities in my life, as I am a full-time doctor in India, an entrepreneur, an active social media figure, a teacher running courses in the UK, and a father of two children. They say they don't have the time to accomplish this. My first thought is that they also have time but struggle to manage it effectively. You cannot save time, but you can utilise it wisely. Effective time management helps you prioritise tasks in life and focus on the most crucial ones. Spend your time on things you truly value, such as being with family and friends, enjoying leisure activities, or working on important tasks. Before taking on any task, ask yourself: Is it worth your time? If it holds good value, go for it; if it doesn't, avoid it.

As we progress through different stages of life, "**our priorities change.**" Therefore, it is important to allocate our time according to our age, priorities, and life circumstances.

If you have just joined the workforce, your priorities may include managing finances, focusing on personal growth, and advancing your career. If you are newly married, your priorities likely shift towards nurturing your relationship with your life partner, spending quality time together, and enhancing relationships. If you are a parent, your focus may be on child- rearing, saving for the future, and ensuring family time while balancing work commitments. If you have retired, your priorities typically revolve around health, safety, and managing retirement funds. Identifying and focusing on your priorities should be the foremost consideration in your 24-hour routine. Then, you can manage time and achieve your goals. Focus on what is important to you, mainly the high-priority tasks first, followed by the medium-priority and low-priority ones.

Some common time management strategies include a) Creating schedules, b) Setting priorities, c) Breaking tasks into smaller manageable parts, d) Using productivity tools, e) Avoiding distractions, and f) Practising good time estimation with realistic expectations. It involves setting goals, prioritising tasks, and managing time to maximise productivity and efficiency.

A. Task Journaling and Task Scheduling

> **Task journaling** involves creating a to-do list, which can be done using a notepad. You can do this daily, either in the morning or the night before—whichever suits your

preference. Some people prefer to journal first thing in the morning, while others like to do it as their last task at night. You can also jot down tasks for the next day in a notebook before going to sleep. This practice can help prevent you from dwelling on unfinished tasks, since knowing you have written them down assures you that you will address them tomorrow. This method can promote a more peaceful and restful night's sleep. Physically journaling is generally more effective than relying solely on digital devices, as you might overlook tasks displayed on a screen. However, if you prefer digital tools, feel free to use Excel sheets or task calendars. I also find it helpful to include a "not-to-do" list.

Task Scheduling - Having a daily plan is crucial. Before you begin work, ensure you clearly understand the tasks you intend to complete and when. Organise your to-do list by priority This practice, known as task scheduling, is a more structured way to help minimise distractions and allow for focused work. Check off tasks as you complete them to foster a sense of achievement and well-being. Creating a schedule involves planning your day or week to allocate specific times for tasks, meetings, and activities. Try to schedule your activities by dedicating 10-15 minutes at the beginning of the day to plan out your tasks. By setting aside 'dedicated blocks of time for focused work, breaks, and personal time,' in your calendar or diary, you can stay organised and maintain a balanced workflow. Regularly reviewing and adjusting your schedule allows you to adapt to unexpected changes and remain productive.

I constantly review my workload, which includes the number of patients I must attend to in the hospital, both in the outpatient and inpatient settings. I also allocate time for administrative and managerial tasks, although my focus remains on clinical work. Planning and preparing in advance have proven to be very beneficial. Additionally, I ensure that I set aside buffer time each day to handle any unforeseen emergencies. Sometimes, our 'to-do' list can overwhelm us, a common cause of stress. Accept that you cannot do everything simultaneously, and start prioritising and diarising your tasks.

B. **Setting priorities** identifies which tasks or goals are most important and should be tackled first. Please make a list of all the things you need to do and list them in order of genuine priority. Make sure your activities align with your highest priorities, such as career advancement, health improvement, and nurturing relationships.

Designing a consistent daily schedule will help you achieve your top priorities in areas like health, finances, and relationships.

Organising tasks according to this three-tiered cabinet system (High Priority - Medium Priority - Low Priority) automatically establishes priorities based on their importance.

Setting reminders and allocating dedicated time on specific days of the week can ensure the completion of these tasks on time. This approach can also be applied at home to manage household chores and other tasks that require completion. Prioritisation is discussed in one of the previous chapters.

C. **Breaking down tasks**: When you divide a large task into smaller, manageable parts, it becomes much less overwhelming, allowing you to stay focused and progress steadily towards your goal in small increments. This technique transforms extensive projects into bite-sized, actionable steps, making them feel significantly more achievable. Focusing on one small piece at a time helps you maintain your momentum and motivation, track your progress quickly, and avoid procrastination. Start with baby steps and build up gradually. Every significant achievement starts with a small action by taking baby steps. Tackling them in smaller chunks makes the process easier and more rewarding. Moreover, this approach is beneficial for time management, providing you with a clearer idea of how long each part will take so you can effectively plan your time accordingly.

D. **Always have a calendar, such as a Google Calendar or a task management tool**. In the calendar, mark important dates and appointments. Use calendars that help you schedule tasks and set reminders. By leveraging these resources, you can streamline your workflow, collaborate effectively with others, track progress, and organise tasks to align with your priorities and deadlines, ultimately improving your overall productivity. These could include parent-teacher meetings, doctor appointments, or crucial business meetings, etc. By adding these appointments to the calendar, you can plan and prioritise the tasks you need to complete during the week. However, be careful not to overload the calendar with small or trivial tasks, as this can lead to feeling overwhelmed and demotivated when tasks are left incomplete. A well-designed calendar that highlights your important tasks can be a great way to visually organise your commitments. It not only clarifies your schedule but also helps you manage your time more effectively and feel more in control!

Consider using task management tools to manage smaller tasks efficiently. Plenty of task management tools and software are available on the Internet, which can be downloaded and used on computers and phones. Use tools to prioritise tasks based on their importance and urgency. These tools can help you track daily appointments and chores and assist in completing many tasks within specified timeframes. Understanding and maintaining the calendar and effectively utilising task management tools is crucial. Rather than giving up after a short trial, commit to using these tools for at least a month to experience their benefits. Developing a routine with your calendar and task list can improve productivity and consistently complete tasks on time. These tools can range from task management apps like Trello or Asana to calendar applications like Google.

E. **Avoiding distractions** is crucial for maintaining focus and completing tasks efficiently. In our increasingly connected world, distractions can take many forms, such as notifications, emails, phone calls, social media, internet surfing, and environmental factors. (Detailed discussions on distractions are covered in the previous chapter)

F. **Practising time estimation with realistic expectations** is vital. Effective planning and precise time estimation for tasks enable you to develop a practical schedule. You can better allocate your time and resources when you clearly understand how long each task will take. When you underestimate how long tasks will take, you risk taking on more work than you can handle. This can lead to missed deadlines, increased stress, and burnout. Realistic time estimation helps you understand your limits. Knowing how much time each task will require can help you maintain focus and motivation. It encourages you to stay on track and work efficiently, knowing that you have a set timeframe for completion.

Let's look at an example of writing a report. The task allotted is to write a 10-page report. Instead of estimating that it will take one day, assess the steps involved: research (2 days), outlining (1 day), writing the first draft (2 days), revising (1 day), and finalising (1 day). Make a realistic expectation of 7 days, allowing additional time for unexpected issues such as needing more research or revisions. Extend it to 10 days. Always have buffer time for unforeseen delays.

Golden Nuggets

- Time management is about effectively 'managing yourself and your life'.

- Effective time management helps you prioritise tasks in life and focus on the most crucial ones. Spend your time on things you truly value.

- We must allocate our time based on our age, priorities, and life circumstances.

- Journaling practice can help prevent you from dwelling on unfinished tasks. Knowing you have written them down assures you that you will complete them.

- Creating a schedule involves planning your day or week to allocate specific times effectively.

- A thoughtfully designed calendar that highlights your important tasks can be an excellent way to visually organise your scheduled commitments.

- Common time management strategies include task journaling, task scheduling, setting priorities, breaking tasks into smaller manageable parts, using productivity tools, avoiding distractions, and practising good time estimation with realistic deadlines.

Overcoming Procrastination and Defeating Delays

Procrastination involves postponing tasks, even though one knows this delay often leads to negative consequences. **Winners make progress, losers make excuses.'** People put things off with excuses, even when they recognise their importance. Some prioritise comfort over progress, while others prefer to remain disorganised and chaotic. Procrastination impacts productivity and performance. Therefore, it is essential to promote proactive behaviour and overcome procrastination.

People use different kinds of statements to give excuses for procrastinating:

"Too busy, too tired, too overwhelmed."

"Too many things to do, too much in my way," etc.

Understanding the root cause of procrastination is helpful and often gives more insight into overcoming it. Let's investigate the reasons for engaging in this behaviour and the reasons that reinforce this habit.

There are several reasons why people procrastinate. The first is **developing an aversion (something you dislike) to specific tasks.** Often, individuals may not enjoy a particular task or may lack motivation to engage in it. In such cases, they tend to postpone these tasks. To overcome this, we must change our perspective and focus on the outcomes we want to achieve. Sometimes, despite our reluctance, certain tasks remain necessary. By shifting our focus to the bigger picture and emphasising outcomes, we gain new insights that help us overcome procrastination rooted in aversion. (Ref- Mindfulness and mindset podcast- Alok Taunk)

The next reason for procrastination arises from the **complex nature of tasks.** When faced with complicated tasks, our brains can struggle to cope, as they naturally prefer simpler tasks that require less mental energy. Complex tasks demand greater cognitive effort and often lead to avoidance. It is helpful to break tasks down into manageable components and follow a graded approach to manage this complexity. Dividing larger tasks into smaller, easier-to-handle parts is beneficial. By addressing tasks step by step, we can simplify the overall process, making it easier for our brains to engage. **"A journey of a thousand miles begins with a single step"** is a well-known proverb attributed to the Chinese philosopher Laozi. It stresses the importance of taking the first step, no matter how daunting a task or goal may seem. Every significant achievement or journey starts with a small action. Even the largest and most complex endeavours can be tackled by breaking them down into manageable parts.

For example, when trying to eat a large portion of chicken, it is impractical to consume it all at once; instead, we can take small portions, making it easier to digest and ultimately finish the meal. Starting with small tasks can significantly help in overcoming procrastination.

The third reason is that **feeling overwhelmed or fatigued by routine tasks,** along with a lack of energy to pursue set goals, can lead to procrastination. Fatigue can manifest in both physical and mental forms, creating a sense of exhaustion that makes even simple tasks seem daunting. Routine tasks can become dull and monotonous, diminishing enthusiasm and motivation, thereby fostering a sense of being stuck in a cycle of unending responsibilities. When faced with a long list of routine tasks, it is natural to feel overwhelmed, making it particularly challenging to start. Eventually, individuals lose energy and focus, which leads to procrastination. Procrastination arises from the sense of being overwhelmed by these tasks and not knowing how to begin. In such situations, starting by prioritising the most essential tasks and gradually building up activities can help alleviate feelings of overwhelm. If you struggle with procrastination and have difficulty completing tasks on time, it is advisable to increase your activities gradually. It is important to begin with smaller tasks and increase them gradually to avoid feeling overwhelmed.

Establishing a routine and making it a habit can help you stay on track and achieve your goals. For instance, if you want to go to the gym, adjust your routine accordingly and keep your gym clothes and shoes within reach of your bed. Once you wake up and change into your workout attire, you are more likely to stick to your daily physical health ritual. If going to the gym is not feasible, consider alternatives such as purchasing a treadmill or engaging in different forms of exercise at home. As you cultivate a routine, you will start to feel a sense of achievement and boost your energy levels. This principle applies to all aspects of life, not just exercise. A lack of discipline, absence of routine, and insufficient structure can lead to procrastination.

Similarly, when mastering a skill, starting slowly rather than avoiding it is a good idea. Gradually increasing the time and effort spent can build momentum and help prevent feelings of overwhelm and discouragement. Follow the mantra of '**Start Low and Go Slow.**' For difficult tasks, begin with the one-minute rule or extend to five or ten minutes based on the task's complexity and your level of resistance to starting. For instance, you might commit to a new task for just one minute every day. This could include one-minute meditation, one- minute sit-ups, or one-minute skipping each day. Make sure to schedule this activity for the same time every day. This routine will help develop a habit within a month, after which you can gradually increase the duration. Start with one minute, then extend to two minutes, three minutes, four minutes, and eventually five minutes, and so on.

Make sure your goals and outcomes are clear. A lack of understanding of the desired outcomes of goals is a reason for procrastination. Initially, it is crucial to understand the potential outcomes of the goals that have been planned to have a clear idea of what one aims to achieve. Otherwise, individuals often feel stuck, unable to make progress and easily distracted. When your goals and outcomes are clear, you are more likely to make progress.

Anxiety about facing situations can lead to procrastination by delaying or avoiding these situations. This only exacerbates the problem and increases anxiety. There is no benefit in postponing tasks, as doing so will only worsen the situation, heighten your anxiety, and trap you in a vicious cycle. Instead, let's break this cycle, emerge from the shell of anxiety, and confront it. The feeling of anxiety won't linger for long; it will subside after a few minutes of taking bold steps to break free from your avoidance.

Fear of failure makes it difficult to take significant steps, resulting in negative thoughts that induce fear and erode self- confidence, ultimately leading to procrastination. Instead, take the initiative. Only when you step into a river will you gauge its depth, not by merely standing at the edge. Ultimately, concerns about potential failure in specific tasks lead to a general lack of progress.

"Most procrastination is caused by either fear or conflict," says Christine Li, a clinical psychologist specialising in procrastination.

Some people waste a lot of time trying to do it the best possible way, leading to procrastination. From the very beginning, they want to achieve perfection. Striving for perfection can lead to wasting too much time and not achieving the agenda. So don't worry about being the best or perfect; start doing things and getting into action.

Don't waste time searching for the best. For instance, the best diet to follow, the best exercise to lose weight, etc., will only lead to wasting time and not achieving productive actions. They won't produce positive outcomes. Too much preparation can sometimes become some form of procrastination. So, get into the practice habit as quickly as possible. If you want to master a habit, the key is repetition and not thinking about perfection. You need to start practising it, which is repetition rather than focusing too much on achieving perfection. Planning and execution are more important than achieving perfection. Perfection is impossible.

There are two types of procrastination.

The first type is **mindless procrastination,** which involves 'habitual patterns and persistent habits formed over time' that lead individuals to postpone tasks in various aspects of their lives, often with detrimental effects. This behaviour lacks an apparent reason or purpose, as it is typically driven by distractions rather than intentional choices. For example, mindless scrolling on social media and binge-watching TV shows illustrate this tendency. It hinders progress and can foster guilt and frustration as essential responsibilities remain unaddressed. Our minds can sometimes wander like restless monkeys, shifting from one situation to another. In today's world, people often spend substantial amounts of time online and browsing social media platforms. This can consume a significant amount of time, resulting in individuals losing focus and track of their priorities, ultimately reinforcing the habit of procrastination. Overcoming mindless procrastination requires self-awareness, taking control of actions, resisting distractions that dilute efforts, and cultivating positive intentions alongside healthier habits that emphasise meaningful engagement with tasks.

The second type is **mindful procrastination, also known as conscious or wilful procrastination in psychological terms.** In this type, individuals consciously decide to postpone tasks. Regarding mindful or wilful procrastination, tasks are often delayed because they are perceived as lower priority. When individuals recognise that certain tasks are less urgent, they assign them less importance. These tasks may be significant but not pressing, resulting in delays in decision-making. Another reason is that individuals may choose to take extra time when making major decisions. Essentially, they are purchasing thinking time to consider these important choices and may delay them for a while, which can be beneficial in certain situations, especially for significant ones.

To overcome procrastination, consider trying the five-minute hack suggested by Mr. Kevin Systrom, the founder of Instagram. He advises, **"If you don't want to do something, make a deal with yourself to do at least five minutes of it. After five minutes, you'll**

likely end up doing the whole thing." When you find it challenging to dive into a task, tell yourself you will work on it for just five minutes. Often, once you get started, you may discover that it is easier to continue working straight through until the task is completed. The true purpose of this five-minute rule is to help you enter a "flow mode" that goes beyond the initial five minutes. Once you begin a task, the mind can maintain what is known as a flow state after a few minutes. During this flow state, we can become so absorbed in the activity that we engage with it on a deeper level. After five minutes of intense engagement and work, you can overcome the initial hurdle of getting started, even if the project is massive or something you are hesitant to begin.

Procrastination can serve as an advantage in a few situations and is not always a bane.

In some rare situations, mindful procrastination can benefit significant decisions, allowing time for further contemplation and resulting in wiser choices. Procrastination has proven to aid in thoughtful decision-making and foster creativity; it is particularly advantageous in creative endeavours. For instance, while writing this book, I have experienced intermittent bouts of procrastination, which I view as essential thinking time rather than a hindrance. This period of reflection allows me to conduct thorough research on the topic before beginning the actual writing process. Similarly, a friend who writes songs for artists has shared that stepping away from immediate composition enables him to access his creative energies more effectively, leading to better results. It is crucial in creative work to balance demonstrating progress to others while also dedicating time to the creative process. Therefore, procrastination or delaying decisions is not always harmful.

During many great wars before the Industrial Revolution, there were instances when an army would besiege a fort. If the soldiers inside the fort had lost the battle, they might not venture outside but instead remain inside and continue engaging the enemy. The more powerful opposing army often refrained from immediately entering the fort, as doing so could result in significant casualties due to the defenders' ability to attack from multiple vantage points. In such situations, kings and commanders frequently postponed the decision to breach the fortress walls, waiting outside for days, weeks, or even months. It is a mindful procrastination, and this strategy could be advantageous; the besieging army allowed the defenders to exhaust their resources by delaying their attack. The people inside the fort would gradually deplete their food supplies, ultimately forcing them to emerge. Once this happened, the besieging army could launch their assault and enter the fort. This example illustrates how delaying a decision and withholding immediate action can sometimes be beneficial. Similarly, in modern life, many situations exist where deferring decisions can lead to greater success.

Golden Nuggets

- By shifting our focus to the bigger picture and emphasising outcomes, we gain new insights that help us overcome procrastination rooted in aversion (something you dislike).

- To overcome procrastination caused by complex tasks, it is helpful to break them down into manageable components and adopt a step by step approach.

- If procrastination stems from an overwhelming number of tasks and uncertainty about where to start, prioritising the most essential activities and gradually adding more can help alleviate feelings of being overwhelmed.

- The key to overcoming procrastination is starting with small tasks and gradually building up to more significant levels of activity.

- Anxietyaboutfacing situations can lead to procrastination, as doing so only worsens the problem, heightens your anxiety, and traps you in a vicious cycle. Instead, let's break this cycle, emerge from the shell of anxiety, and confront it.

- Mindless procrastination, which involves habitual patterns developed over time that cause individuals to delay tasks in various aspects of their lives.

- Overcoming mindless procrastination requires self-awareness, positive intentions, and healthier habits that emphasise meaningful engagement with tasks.

- To overcome procrastination, consider trying the five- minute hack. If you don't want to do something, make a deal with yourself to do at least five minutes of it. After five minutes, you are likely to end up completing the entire task.

Self-Discipline is Crucial for Success

There is a famous quote:
**'All successful people have one thing in common'
– discipline**

Self-discipline is one of the most important principles that we should all follow. **Discipline means doing what needs to be done and when it needs to be done, even if you don't like it.** Self-discipline is not about doing things you enjoy; it involves tackling tasks that, at times, you may not want to do, even when you feel uncomfortable or unmotivated. Nonetheless, you still need to engage with them to achieve positive outcomes. This requires hard work and commitment, and the results will be rewarding.

Self-discipline is essential for success. Without it, achieving important life goals and milestones becomes impossible. Most individuals who have achieved significant success attribute their accomplishments to discipline, which enables them to accomplish more in a shorter timeframe, thereby making them even more successful than others.

It is essential to understand the difference between motivation and discipline. Motivation is an intrinsic part of us, regardless of the circumstances. It remains constant, while discipline is a strategy we choose to implement continuously. Motivation is fuelled by emotion and desire; the initial spark ignites excitement or inspiration to take steps. However, motivation can be fleeting and often depends on our feelings. It may come and go, and when the enthusiasm fades, it is easy to lose momentum. Discipline, in contrast, is about taking consistent action, irrespective of your emotional state. It represents the ability to adhere to your goals and routines even when motivation wanes. Discipline fosters long-term success grounded in commitment and habit rather than transient emotions. In summary, motivation initiates your journey, while discipline sustains your progress. When you are motivated, you feel the desire to act; when you are disciplined, you may not feel that desire, but you know you should proceed anyway, so you do it regardless.

Michael Phelps, the Olympic swimmer, discusses what separates elite athletes from their competition: **'I think if you look at the greats in anything, in any walk of life, the greats do things when they don't always want to, and that's the separation.'**

This statement does refer to self-discipline. It highlights the idea that highly successful individuals—often called "the greats"—tend to push through challenges and continue to perform tasks even when they may not feel motivated or inclined to do so. This ability to act consistently and focus on their goals, regardless of their immediate feelings or circumstances, is a key aspect of self-discipline. Self-discipline involves making choices that align with long-term objectives rather than succumbing to short-term desires or discomfort. People who succeed have long-term goals and perspectives on what they aim to accomplish.

Self-discipline demands significant sacrifices, often requiring giving up immediate pleasures and joys to maintain self-control. For instance, I have committed 10 to 12 years of study as a doctor, forgoing other activities. This dedication has enabled me to become a proficient doctor, fulfilling my life's purpose and primary goal of serving society. Achieving success through discipline requires commitment and sacrifice. Staying self-disciplined is essential for achieving personal and professional goals, and it involves cultivating specific qualities and habits. Here are four essential pillars that contribute to building and upholding self-discipline:

1. **Goal-Oriented with Clear and Specific Goals:** Establishing clearly defined, specific, and achievable goals helps maintain

focus and direction. This clarity ensures you know what you are working towards, minimising distractions and aiding in informed decision-making. Steve Jobs was known for his intense focus on product quality and design excellence. His disciplined approach guided Apple's groundbreaking innovations and exemplified how a commitment to a vision can transform industries and leave a legacy.

2. **Commitment:** A strong commitment to your personal values necessitates a willingness to see tasks through to completion, even when challenges arise. This will strengthen your self-discipline over time.

3. **Motivation:** Cultivating intrinsic motivation, the internal drive to achieve personal satisfaction, is crucial in reinforcing self-discipline. This type of motivation often leads to more sustained efforts and a deeper commitment to tasks.

4. **Consistency and Developing Routines:** Establishing daily routines fosters a sense of normalcy and discipline in your actions. Consistent practice reinforces habits, making them easier to maintain over time. Serena Williams, renowned for her rigorous training schedule and strong focus on her goals, has demonstrated extraordinary self-discipline throughout her tennis career. Her daily routines and mental fortitude have led her to achieve a record number of Grand Slam titles, underscoring how perseverance and commitment contribute to professional achievement.

> **"The distance between dreams and**
> **reality is called discipline"**
> – Paulo Coelho, Brazilian lyricist and novelist.

The statement suggests that achieving one's dreams or goals requires effort, commitment, and consistent action—qualities embodied by discipline. It implies that simply having dreams or aspirations is not enough; one must also be willing to work hard and make sacrifices to turn those dreams into reality. In essence, discipline is the bridge that connects the idealised vision of what one wants to achieve (the dream with the practical steps and actions needed to achieve it (the reality). Without discipline, dreams may remain just as mere fantasies while discipline transforms them into tangible outcomes through perseverance, focus, and dedication.

One common challenge we face in our discipline **is the tendency to choose the path of least resistance.** It is essential to recognise that when confronted with two choices—one requiring more effort and the other offering an easier route—most naturally gravitate towards the easier option. We often seek shortcuts or simple solutions instead of embracing the tougher journey. While taking a shortcut can seem appealing, we must remember that truly worthwhile achievements rarely come without effort. Many of us find ourselves tempted to select the easy route instead of embracing the challenges that lead to success. Persistence and discipline are crucial for sustainable success. People who take shortcuts or cut corners to find a quicker route may achieve temporary success. Still, long-term success is better attained by those who work diligently and maintain self-discipline. Lack of discipline kills more dreams than a lack of resources ever will.

Self-discipline is the key to success. To succeed in tasks, one must follow four steps: write down your goals, create a plan, set priorities, and start with the most crucial task. All these steps were discussed in the earlier chapters. Participating in these steps requires a significant degree of self-discipline.

Every goal requires two things: discipline and consistency.

'The rarest of all human qualities is consistency'
– English philosopher Jeremy Bentham

One of the most potent forces that operates in parallel is consistency. Consistency serves as a fundamental key. Among the most formidable forces in life is the principle of consistency. The ability to perform a particular task repeatedly is how one initiates significant moments and achieves substantial results. It is through these incremental successes each day that progress is made. Everything appears challenging before it becomes manageable; initially, every task presents difficulties. However, with the passage of time, activities tend to become more manageable and ultimately intuitive. Motivating oneself to develop discipline is essential, and, in time, tasks will become more straightforward, resulting in enhanced satisfaction.

Brian Tracy shares a fascinating insight in his book: many individuals who find themselves in the top 20% started from the bottom 80% and gradually climbed the ladder of success. A select few astute individuals have even reached the top 4%. While it is true that some of the wealthiest—like millionaires and billionaires—have inherited their fortunes, countless others have transitioned from the bottom to the top through hard work, self-discipline, and perseverance. This journey is not only possible but realistic. Anyone with self-discipline, a passion for their work, and a willingness to embrace innovative ideas can achieve it. On a personal note, I have experienced this journey myself, moving from the bottom 80% to the top 20%. My long- term goal is to reach the top 4%. If I, as an ordinary person, can accomplish this, I genuinely believe that others reading this book or listening to this message can, too.

'**Cultivating commitment, willpower, and self-discipline is essential for a fulfilling life.**' When you're dedicated to something, it enables you to take that crucial first step and set things in motion. You can maintain those actions and achieve your success goals through dedication and discipline! Remember to cherish your commitments—if you lose sight of them, you may also lose some of that incredible energy and motivation to keep moving forward. Commitment is a significant choice, so focus on goals that resonate with your strengths and capabilities. Avoid overcommitting tasks that could overwhelm you. By nurturing your self-discipline, willpower, and hard work, you will find it easier to uphold your commitments. As you honour these personal commitments, you will notice a lovely boost in your confidence and self-esteem.

Elon Musk, currently the wealthiest man in the world, is often cited as an example of exceptional discipline; several factors contribute to this perception. Musk has a strong vision for the future, particularly regarding space exploration (SpaceX), electric vehicles

(Tesla), and sustainable energy. This clarity of goals helps him stay committed and motivated. His passion for technology and innovation drives him to work long hours. He is known for working exceptionally long hours, often 80 to 100 hours a week. This level of commitment can foster a culture of discipline in the teams he leads. Musk sets very high standards for himself and his teams. This expectation can drive a disciplined work environment where excellence is prioritised. He has faced numerous challenges and failures throughout his career but has shown resilience. His ability to adapt and learn from setbacks contributes to his disciplined approach. Musk often holds himself accountable for the success and failures of his ventures, which can cultivate a sense of discipline in his work habits. These factors and his unique personality and experiences contribute to his disciplined approach to work.

One thing all successful people share is a strong sense of discipline. It takes discipline to choose healthy foods, commit to daily workouts, remain persistent, avoid giving up, and have faith in oneself. Without self-discipline, one can crumble under pressure.

Consider success a delightful juice seasoned with self- discipline and hard work. **As the Greek philosopher Aristotle wisely pointed out, the essence of life is about finding happiness through a blend of discipline and hard work.** Always remember that success is within your reach if you stay disciplined and put in the work. So, keep pushing forward and never lose hope. You can achieve anything you set your heart on with determination and self-discipline!

Golden Nuggets

- Discipline means doing what needs to be done and when it needs to be done, even if you don't like it.

- Motivation initiates your journey, while discipline sustains your progress.

- Building and maintaining self-discipline requires a multifaceted approach based on four pillars: goal- oriented, committed, intrinsically motivated, and consistent habits. By focusing on these four pillars, individuals can create a robust framework for enhancing their self-discipline, ultimately leading to personal and professional success.

- While taking shortcuts or opting for quicker solutions may lead to temporary success, those who work diligently and maintain self-discipline tend to achieve more tremendous success in the long run.

- Without discipline, dreams may remain just that— dreams— while discipline transforms them into tangible outcomes through perseverance, focus, and dedication.

- Every goal requires two things: discipline and consistency.

- One thing all successful people share is a strong sense of discipline.

- Success is within your reach if you stay disciplined and put in the work.

Asking for Help is Not a Sign of Weakness

Asking for help is not a sign of weakness; seeking assistance often **'leads to solutions'**. Therefore, it is vital not to hesitate to ask for help. Unfortunately, seeking help is frequently perceived as a sign of weakness. Some view it as an admission of 'incompetence,' but this perspective is misguided. Admitting our struggles or limitations to others can be daunting, as this may challenge our sense of autonomy and competence. On the contrary, it demonstrates strength, not weakness, and can empower you and boost your confidence.

How do you do this? As a first step, **it is crucial to 'recognise when responsibilities become overwhelming'**, whether in personal life, relationships, college, work, or business. Seeking help demonstrates **'understanding one's limitations and showcases strength'**. We can seek support from close family members, friends, neighbours, colleagues, or professionals. By using the collective knowledge, experience, and resources of others, individuals can overcome difficulties, enhance their mental well-being, achieve their goals, and reach their full potential.

I often interact with numerous young adult college students who share their challenges with me. Many experience significant levels of stress, anxiety, and depression that require treatment, rest, or ongoing counselling. Sadly, most hesitate to disclose these struggles to supervisors or line managers. By not sharing their issues, they neglect to prioritise self-care and often conclude that they will be perceived as incompetent. This misconception prevents them from receiving the much-needed support, leading to tragically high levels of distress among students—some even reaching the point of contemplating or attempting to end their lives. Embracing this concept empowers individuals to seek assistance when needed and enhances the overall support system within any community or organisation.

Imagine you are stuck with a particular problem and don't know how to escape it. **It is always a good idea to go to your mentor or a coach and ask for help to get out of the problem.** Instead, if you keep those emotions within yourself, beat yourself up and don't discuss your concerns, then you may get stuck inside and will never be able to come out of the issues. Therefore, asking for help would help you move in a positive direction and improve your emotional well-being.

Many people want to help others when they see someone truly in need. However, each person is certainly responsible for seeking assistance at the appropriate time moment. Have you noticed the bells in large temples and shrines? They typically do not sound unless someone attempts to ring them. Asking for help is similar. We should also 'ring the internal bell' by expressing our thoughts and feelings aloud so others can hear us. Only by doing this can people truly assist us.

Asking for help is not about you becoming dependent on other people, nor does it display your vulnerability. When I was a junior doctor, I always asked for help. I understood my limitations in treating my patients, and whenever I needed assistance, I always looked forward to my consultants' advice. This helped me to solve and manage many clinical medical situations effectively and allowed me to learn from them. This gave me a sense of respect for my seniors and contributed to my professional growth. When faced with challenging situations, seeking assistance brings solutions and enhances personal development and resilience. By asking for help, you tap into the knowledge, skills, and experiences of others, which can provide solutions to the challenges you may face. Reaching out for assistance can strengthen connections with colleagues, friends, or family and encourage a culture of support and collaboration.

Some don't ask for help 'due to their ego'. It is essential to keep your ego aside, not pump it up and bring down the ego bar, which can force people to deny the need to seek help. Human beings are social animals who are dependent on each other. It would be best if you aimed to live and do things independently. However, when you feel that you need help, then you should know when you should need help and ask for it briefly. Sharing the burden can bring relief, making you feel less stressed and more at ease.

Sometimes, people may not help or may be unable to assist you, but you shouldn't develop a negative thinking pattern by generalising that this is true for everyone. If you cannot seek help from one source, don't just give up and make preconceived assumptions about others; **instead, look for the next source of help**. Don't waste your time sitting and feeding your ego. Instead, change your thought process and approach the next person to ask for help if needed.

The notion that asking for help is essential for receiving support is fundamental in both personal and professional contexts. As noted in the Bible, "**Ask, and it will be given to you. Knock, and it will be opened to you.**" This verse underscores the belief that when individuals ask for help, they open the door to solutions and support that may not have been available otherwise. This act is not a sign of weakness; it demonstrates self-awareness and a willingness to engage with others. By acknowledging that we cannot do everything alone, we foster collaboration and strengthen relationships. When you request assistance, you can alleviate the burden of feeling overwhelmed. Sharing responsibilities can lead to more manageable workloads and improved mental well-being.

Asking for help is not a sign of weakness. Many people I encounter often feel compelled to project a positive image and conceal their vulnerabilities. They create a facade to protect themselves, but this can be counterproductive and potentially harmful. True strength lies in being honest about both your strengths and weaknesses, without hiding anything. It is perfectly acceptable to express your vulnerabilities and seek assistance when necessary. Unfortunately, many individuals struggle with negative thoughts, such as fears of being seen as weak by others or worrying that they might be labelled as such. These cognitive distortions can lead them to conceal their struggles rather than seek help. However, by bravely asking for support, individuals can achieve much greater success.

There are various ways to ask for help. You can speak to someone directly, or reach out through writing via platforms like WhatsApp, email, or other social media channels. If you prefer a more casual approach, we can meet for coffee, or you can arrange a formal appointment if necessary. Whether you communicate your need for help verbally or through written messages, it is essential to express yourself comfortably. Seeking help is not a sign of weakness but a testament to humanity and resilience. It can also be a learning opportunity, allowing you to gain new perspectives and insights that enhance your understanding and skills. Let us recognise the strength involved in asking for help and embrace the journey toward self-improvement and empowerment through shared support and collective growth.

Golden Nuggets

- Seeking assistance often leads to better solutions. Asking for help is a proactive step towards finding solutions and achieving tremendous success.

- Seeking help shows an awareness of one's limitations and highlights strength and courage.

- Asking for help is not about becoming dependent on others, nor does it show your vulnerability.

- We must recognise when to seek assistance and have the courage to reach out to others.

- If you are not seeking help from one source, don't give up; look for the next one.

- Requesting assistance is a crucial and essential step that can foster both personal and collective growth.

Conquering Your Fears and Facing them Head-On

There is a famous quote on overcoming fear
**– "The brave man is he who does not feel afraid,
but he who conquers that fear"**

The greatest fears individuals confront are often the fear of failure and rejection. **Worrying about failure and rejection is natural, as this fear represents one of our biggest challenges in life.** In today's world, the fear of failure can hold people back from pursuing their dreams and goals. People frequently hesitate to put in the effort needed to pursue success because they are preoccupied with the possibility of failure and the setbacks that may accompany it. Failure is not a dead end; rather, it is simply part of our pathway to achievement. The fear of failure and the fear of rejection are closely intertwined and often occur together. The fear of failure is intensified by the fear of rejection, which is rooted in concerns about how others perceive us. As the fear of rejection heightens, it becomes a powerful deterrent, preventing many from taking risks or stepping outside their comfort zones. Recognising and addressing these fears is a crucial step towards breaking free from their constraints and pursuing success.

It is crucial to know that rejections and failures present us with fantastic opportunities to learn and grow. They help build our perseverance and resilience, showing us that stepping outside our comfort zones is okay. These experiences motivate us to strive for excellence in everything we do! We all experience these moments at some point, whether it is a job application that didn't go as planned, a relationship that didn't work out, or a project that fell short of expectations. These setbacks can feel discouraging, but they don't define our true potential. In fact, rather than being roadblocks, these experiences can ignite our personal growth and lead us to eventual success. The founders of WhatsApp encountered a hurdle while trying to secure jobs at both Twitter and Facebook, but things didn't go as planned. Instead of dwelling on the setback, they boldly moved forward by starting WhatsApp in the vibrant heart of Silicon Valley, California. What seemed like a challenging moment transformed into a wonderful opportunity, as their decision ultimately led to great success. By 2014, Facebook recognised the potential of WhatsApp and acquired it for an impressive $19 billion! Fast forward to December 2017, and WhatsApp proudly boasted over 1.5 billion active users. This journey beautifully illustrates how challenges can become incredible blessings in disguise. Embrace setbacks as stepping stones to success rather than viewing them as a dead end.

As far as we know, most people in this world have faced failure in various aspects of their lives. During those times, it may feel like the end of the world for them. However, it is important to ground yourself in such situations and remind yourself that it is not the end of the world or your life; the world will not collapse or fall apart. It is essential to remember that everyone experiences failures. These reminders are extremely helpful. The reason people struggle to accept failure is that they have been conditioned to believe it is bad.

Have you ever wondered why people might feel worried about failing and hold back from trying again? One answer could be found in the term **"learned helplessness."** Learned helplessness is a psychological concept developed by the American Psychologist Martin Seligman. It describes a state **'where individuals feel unable to change their circumstances due to exposure to adverse events or previous failures'.** This sense of helplessness can lead to sadness and a lack of motivation. Seligman's early experiments with dogs offered some fascinating insights! In these studies, some dogs discovered that they could escape electric shocks by leaping over a barrier, while others were kept in a harness that prevented them from escaping.

Over time, the dogs that could not escape stopped trying altogether, even when the chance presented itself. This finding revealed that they had "learned to be helpless." Similarly, when people face failures or tough situations, they might begin to feel like their efforts don't really make a difference. This can lead to a sense of powerlessness and a belief that future attempts will be futile. Consequently, this mindset might cause individuals to feel passive or avoidant or to invest less effort in situations where they once felt excited to succeed. Recognising the patterns of thought and behaviour that come with learned helplessness is important. Doing so can help us develop strategies to overcome those feelings of powerlessness and build resilience!

People often feel helpless when faced with setbacks or failures, which leads them to avoid trying new things. Even if they have good ideas or thoughts on moving forward, they quickly revert to past disappointments, allowing negative experiences to overshadow their potential for success. When individuals encounter failure—especially if they have previously experimented with new ideas that failed— they may feel increasingly helpless. This reluctance to try again stems from the belief that new efforts and experiences will ultimately lead to more failures. **Consequently, they become trapped in a vicious cycle of helplessness, hindering their ability to progress.** This sense of helplessness can lead individuals to believe they cannot change their circumstances, ultimately causing them to stop trying altogether. Over time, this mindset can escalate, impacting their ability to succeed across various aspects of their lives.

It is like a creepy mould that starts growing on the surface of a bathroom wall. It can quickly spread to neighbouring areas such as the ceiling, floors, and adjacent walls. This creeping nature of mould can cause damage to structures, making them weak and unsettling. Cultivating feelings of learned helplessness is akin to growing mould inside your mind. It will creep in and destroy your potential and the structure of your mind. Please don't let this happen to you. Feelings of helplessness can emerge early in life and may persist for extended periods, becoming significant barriers to achieving future success. It is crucial to recognise this cycle and take steps to break free, fostering a mindset that embraces resilience and the possibility of change.

Another hurdle to overcome is the fear of others' opinions. People often lose happiness when they worry about what others think or say about them, spiralling into negative thoughts that undermine self-confidence and self-esteem. Questions like "What will people think?" and "How will others react?" can create anxiety about gaining approval and validation. In this cycle of fear, individuals often choose to remain in their current situations to avoid potential disapproval. Consequently, they may forgo opportunities for growth and achievement to maintain the status quo and seek approval. Have you ever taken a moment to observe how plants are watered? Sometimes, they receive fresh, clean water, while at other times they might get some dirty water. Yet, regardless of the quality of their nutrients, these little green wonders keep growing strong! Similarly, negative and judgemental comments from others don't have to hold you back. Just as plants can thrive even in challenging conditions, you too can flourish, regardless of what anyone says. This valuable lesson about resilience teaches us that we can rise above negativity. Learning how to manage negative comments directed at you is crucial, as those words can't genuinely block your path forward! Success is about embracing the freedom to be yourself, without allowing the opinions of others to weigh you down.

> **'The best way to lead a miserable life is to**
> **pay attention to what other people are saying about you'**
> – Paulo Coelho

Often, people are concerned about making mistakes, which can hinder them from embarking on new adventures. Don't worry about making mistakes; we all tend to make them. Making mistakes is part of being human. There is a Korean proverb: '**Even monkeys fall from trees,**' which acknowledges that everyone makes mistakes. What's important is learning from those mistakes and not repeating them, as they can be valuable learning experiences. It is perfectly fine to make mistakes. You may make mistakes and stumble during the process, but don't repeat the same errors; instead, learn from these experiences. Mrs. Sudha Murthy, one of the greatest Indian authors and the founder of the Infosys Foundation, states, "**You will probably make some mistakes. Everyone does. Just don't make the same ones again.**" Sudha Murthy quoted this in her book, An Uncommon Love. It is all right to make mistakes if you learn from them.

'If you make a mistake and do not correct it, this is called a mistake' - Chinese philosopher Confucius. There is no such thing as a successful person who never makes a mistake. Successful people are those who make mistakes and then adjust their plans accordingly. In 1956, engineer Wilson Greatbatch accidentally installed the wrong resistor into a heart rhythm recording device he was building. When powered on, the misplaced resistor caused the device to emit a steady pulse, and Greatbatch realised that his engineering error had effectively created a primitive electronic pacemaker. This mistake prompted him to refine the device, which became the first implantable pacemaker designed to regulate irregular heartbeats. Thanks to Greatbatch's fortunate error, millions now live longer with rhythm-correcting pacemakers that keep their hearts beating steadily. This engineering blunder sparked a lifesaving medical breakthrough.

One simple yet powerful technique to overcome fear is to take a few deep breaths before facing daunting situations. Breathing deeply for a short period can effectively manage overwhelming thoughts of rejection, failure, and the fear of making mistakes. I recall an instance when I instructed one of my clients to inhale and exhale deeply to address these fears. He remarked that as I guided him, he felt as though he was "**inhaling courage and exhaling fear,**" which was indeed helping him. His insight highlighted an important point: deep breathing can be a valuable strategy for those striving to gather the courage to confront their fears.

Golden Nuggets

- Feeling worried about rejection and failure is natural; this fear is one of our biggest challenges in life.

- The fear of failure and rejection can hold people back from chasing their dreams and goals.

- People struggle to accept failure because they have been conditioned to believe that failing is bad.

- Avoid falling into a cycle of learned helplessness that limits your ability to progress. This trap can create the impression that new efforts and experiences will lead to further failures.

- Negative and judgemental comments from others should not hold you back.

- Making mistakes is part of being human. What's important is to learn from those mistakes and not to repeat them, as they can provide valuable learning experiences.

Step Out of Your Comfort Zone

'Comfort is the worst addiction'
– Marcus Aurelius, Former Roman Emperor

Staying within one's comfort zone is a key reason many people experience limited success in their lives. Most individuals prefer to remain in their comfort zone and adhere to a routine. They resist change and are less willing to adapt. They frequently find excuses to avoid change, even when it could be positive, helpful, and beneficial for them.

It is important not to linger in your comfort zone. We don't grow when things are easy. Comfort is like a recreational drug; once you become accustomed to it, it can become addictive, making it difficult to escape. If you want to achieve greatness, you must challenge yourself, step outside your comfort zone, and succeed in unfamiliar areas. It is essential not to remain in your comfort zone. We don't grow when things are simple. Comfort is like a recreational drug; once you become used to it, it can become addictive, making it difficult to escape. If you want to achieve greatness, you must challenge yourself, step outside your comfort zone, and succeed in unfamiliar areas.

People should understand the concepts of both the comfort zone and the growth zone. Within the comfort zone, we often feel safe and in control of our situations. Unfortunately, this zone allows little room for growth and is not conducive to personal development. When you step outside your comfort zone, you encounter challenges that help you acquire new skills. As you expand your comfort zone, you move closer to the true growth zone, where you can set goals, pursue your dreams, and experience genuine growth. Gradually, you begin to realise your aspirations and discover a true purpose in life. Although leaving your comfort zone can initially be difficult, as you start to live your dreams, you will enjoy the journey from the comfort zone to the growth zone.

The famous scientist Albert Einstein once said, **"A ship is always safe at the shore, but that is not what it is built for."**

To become a skilled sailor, one must confront the rough sea. Navigating calm waters will never produce a great sailor. Thus, for significant achievements and personal growth, it is essential to step outside your comfort zone.

Have you heard the famous story about frogs and boiling water? I saw this in a YouTube video titled "RIP Motivational Speech." I appreciate the powerful life lesson this story offers and have realised how important it is to step out of your comfort zone. I want to share it with you so that you can reap the benefits of this lesson.

If you place a frog in boiling water, it will react immediately, jumping out of the pot to save its life. However, if you put the same frog in a pot of room temperature water and gradually heat it, the frog will remain in the pot. It will not attempt to leave or jump out, even as the temperature slowly rises to the boiling point. Ultimately, the frog will boil to death without realising its 'comfort zone has become lethal.' We need to engage in introspection: Do you want to be like the frog that slowly boils to death, or do you prefer to jump out of your comfort zone and navigate life's challenges? Take control of your life. Stepping out of your comfort zone is essential for growth, even though it may involve facing numerous challenges. Be courageous in confronting every obstacle and seize every opportunity for growth and development.

Unfortunately, most people stay in their comfort zones while only a tiny minority venture out. We love to stay within our comfort zones and resist exploring beyond them. We often linger too long in relationships, friendships, jobs, businesses, and communities. Initially, these situations provide comfort, leading us to stay, but they can become unfulfilling or harmful over time. However, we hesitate because we fear the unknown. People often avoid taking risks to leave their comfort zones due to worries about what lies ahead. We grow so accustomed to it that we prefer to stay within our comfort zone even when unhappy. This familiarity and an illusion of comfort can lead to stagnation and lack of growth.

By moving out of your comfort zone into a new area, many people worry about uncertainties in the future. Instead of becoming anxious, take a deep breath and proceed with your next step. **"Uncertainty is the only certainty,"** said mathematician Allen Paul. As mentioned before, this new area will be your growth zone, and your thoughts of uncertainty should not prevent you from moving forward.

You also face a choice between 'comfort and accomplishment.' You can either remain in your comfort zone or step outside to achieve more. While you may choose either path, it is important to note that you cannot have both. If you seek progress, be prepared for discomfort, as growth comes with a cost. Learn to embrace discomfort to make meaningful progress.

I can share my experience of stepping out of my comfort zone and achieving more. I worked in the UK for nearly 14 years, enjoying a successful journey with a stable job, a spacious home, and a thriving teaching business. However, one of my most essential aspirations was to establish a mental health service or hospital in India to serve the Indian community and apply the principles I had learned in the UK. This was a challenging task. I knew I needed to push beyond familiar boundaries to evolve and thrive. After careful consideration, I left my comfort zone and returned to India for a new beginning. This decision was undoubtedly one of the toughest I have ever made, and the fear of an unknown future and uncertainties weighed heavily on me.

As anticipated, transitioning from the UK to India to launch my venture proved immensely challenging and exhausting. However, over time, I adapted to life in India, successfully launching mental health services and introducing new types of care that were previously unavailable through my hospital. This initiative set a new standard for future generations in the mental health field and enabled me to significantly enhance the quality of life for the local community in India. I discovered high levels of fulfilment in both my professional and personal pursuits. This journey has brought me tremendous success and remarkable personal growth. None of this would have been possible had I chosen to remain in my comfort zone in the UK. I have no regrets about embracing change, new experiences, and challenges while embarking on this new chapter of my life. Today, I run my private 200-bed psychiatric hospital in Chennai, which is recognised as one of the best facilities in the area. We offer a variety of innovative mental health services, have treated over 10,000 patients in 10 years, and employ more than 300 people (www.shadithyahospital.com). Undoubtedly, to achieve greatness, one must challenge oneself, step out of their comfort zone, and strive for success beyond familiar boundaries.

Imagine a bird in a cage. While the bird may feel comfortable receiving adequate food, safety, and protection within its confines, it cannot explore the outside world. Although stepping out can be challenging, it is also a thrilling experience. The bird will neverfly high until it leaves the cage. Only by leaving its cage can it soar, explore different directions, witness the real world, gain valuable experiences, and truly cherish life. Similarly, we must consider leaving the cage of our comfort zones. We should strive to fly high towards our goals, accomplishments, and ambitions. We can only achieve these aspirations by venturing out, not remaining confined within our comfort zones.

Life presents us with many challenges, but we must push ourselves out of our comfort zones. This push beyond familiarity is a blessing in disguise, as it compels us to start anew and challenge ourselves in fresh ways.

Golden Nuggets

- Step outside your comfort zone. Discover new areas.

- Stepping outside your comfort zone is vital for growth, even if it means confronting various challenges. If you want to achieve great success, you must challenge yourself, push beyond your comfort zone, and excel beyond your usual limits.

- While leaving your comfort zone can be challenging, as you begin pursuing your dreams, you will come to appreciate the journey from the comfort zone to the growth zone and reap the benefits of this journey.

- If you seek progress, prepare for discomfort. Growth comes at a cost, and you must learn to embrace discomfort to achieve meaningful progress.

- By stepping outside your comfort zone, you can soar towards your goals and aspirations, making them attainable.

Change is Constant and will Happen

'Intelligence is the ability to adapt to change'
– Theoretical Physicist and Cosmologist
Sir Stephen Hawking

Change is undoubtedly the most inevitable aspect of human existence. Adapting to the changes that come our way has been crucial throughout history. Since the beginning of time, embracing change has been vital. Change disrupts our familiar routines and challenges our comfort zones; nonetheless, it offers opportunities for personal growth and self-discovery. **In today's world, change is the only constant.** As the world continues to evolve, we will strive to change alongside it. Embrace change as much as possible. We should learn to adapt to it. This is essential in life, and those who can adapt 'can survive' and continue to grow. Those who fail to adjust to change eventually succumb and will not be able to grow further. Change is inevitable. You need to understand that everything changes—your friends, your body, your circumstances, your living environment, and more.

**"Progress is impossible without change, and those
who cannot change their minds cannot change anything."**
– George Bernard Shaw, Irish writer and
Nobel Prize winner for Literature

Sir Charles Darwin made the extraordinary observation that nature does not care how strong or intelligent the species on this planet are. Still, if you don't adapt to changes according to the needs of time, you will not be able to survive and eventually perish.

**'It is not the strongest of the species that survives nor
the most intelligent that survives. It is the one that
is most adaptable to change**
– Naturalist and Biologist Sir Charles Darwin

Most people are firm, stubborn, and fixed in their belief systems, thought processes, ideologies, and ways of living. Sadly, this fixation can lead to more problems over time. They desire familiarity and comfort, making it difficult for them to change.

Why is it hard to change? This is because our entire brain network is already tuned and wired. When a new change occurs, it requires a **rewiring process** that can be uncomfortable and time-consuming. The new neural pathways take time to form and initially require more effort. Therefore, people often avoid the difficult path of rewiring and hesitate to reset their neural pathways, which leads them to hold onto fixed ideas. Consequently, they become stuck, but this will not help, as change is inevitable. It can initially feel complex and scary. Instead of fearing it, we should view it as a new, adventurous journey and be willing to embrace that journey.

In the words of the Greek philosopher Socrates, *"The secret of change is to focus all your energy, not on fighting the old, but on building the new".*

Imagine you are travelling on a motorway. New, modern roads are being constructed to ease and expedite the journey. Would you take these new roads or prefer the old, scruffy ones? The first time you travel the route can be a novel experience. But once you have done it, you begin to embrace the new paths and abandon the old ones. It may be scary and anxiety-inducing initially, but the outcome will likely be positive and favour your journey. The old roads will gradually fade away and eventually be closed. This is all done to enhance them.

We all desire improvements but resist change. That's not going to work. True transformation is unlikely to occur without accepting and adapting to new changes; therefore, we should embrace these changes.

'The measure of intelligence is the ability to change,'" said Sir Albert Einstein.

Adapting to new changes requires individuals and societies to embrace innovation, flexibility, and a forward-thinking mindset to thrive in our ever-evolving world. While change may evoke feelings of insecurity and uncertainty, it enables individuals to step outside their comfort zones. Failing to do so could hinder our ability to adapt and leave us behind. Although adjusting to new changes can present challenges, taking small steps toward adaptation is essential and can be approached gradually in response to shifting circumstances.

> **'Adapt to the changing times, situations, and opportunities
> at hand. Only those who adapt survive'**
> – Chetan Bhagat, one of the best-selling Indian authors

Let's look at this modern example of how adapting to change is essential. What do you think is the secret behind Apple's success? Between 2000 and 2010, BlackBerry was extremely popular among consumers. However, one significant drawback was its lack of an innovative touchscreen. BlackBerry was not quick enough to transition from physical keyboards to touchscreen options and was slow to adapt to this new requirement. Apple seized this opportunity, identifying a gap in the market and creating a new iPhone design with touchscreen capabilities, effectively eclipsing BlackBerry's physical keyboards. As a result, the smartphone market experienced a major shift, and millions of consumers swiftly migrated from BlackBerry to the iPhone. BlackBerry's slow adaptation led to a significant loss of market share, greatly diminishing its sales and rendering the company largely irrelevant in the mobile phone industry. Ultimately, this shift towards smartphones, exemplified by the iPhone, marked a turning point in the market.

Those who can say, 'it is fine, and we will adjust to such changes,' will help move forward in all aspects of life. We must adapt our personal and professional lives, as well as our relationships, health, business ventures, work, and community. When the environment changes, we should cultivate an adaptable attitude and embrace it as part of our growth. Unfortunately, people often dislike change and fail to realise it is inevitable. If we remain stubborn and stagnant, we risk losing ground and failing to progress.

"Change is hard at first, messy in the middle and gorgeous at the end"
– Mr. Robin Sharma, the author of the book
(The Monk Who Sold the Ferrari)

Consider my medical field, where doctors must learn to use computers for maintaining medical records, utilise software for dictating notes, conduct online consultations for improved patient access, and issue prescriptions online (telemedicine, along with integrating artificial intelligence in healthcare. Over the last 25 years, many changes have occurred. Embracing these changes at various points in time has proven beneficial. Adapting to these technological advancements has been essential for progress and effectiveness in medical practice. Resisting these innovations could have left professionals outdated and unable to practice. This same concept applies to all other fields, where change is constant and should be embraced without resistance. I have accepted this challenge and have been a forerunner in implementing these advancements in my workplace, which has helped me remain a leading practitioner in my field. Although these changes were undoubtedly difficult at first, they eventually facilitated significant progress.

'Be like water, flexible and adaptable to every life's situation'
– Chinese philosopher Laozi

It is important in life to be flexible and adapt to various situations. Consider how water behaves: it can adjust to any vessel, conforming to different shapes and surfaces. Just as water adapts effortlessly, we should strive to be like water— flexible and adaptable in every circumstance. The renowned martial artist Bruce Lee famously advised, "Be water, my friend. If you put water into a cup, it becomes the cup. You put water into a bottle, and it becomes the bottle. You put it in a teapot, it becomes the teapot." What does he mean by this? People should not get trapped in a certain mindset; they should be able to adapt to various situations, grow, and change. Through this, one can adopt the qualities of water and be flexible enough to change.

Some of history's greatest thinkers, including Albert Einstein, Charles Darwin, Socrates, Laozi, George Bernard Shaw, and Stephen Hawking, embraced change and encouraged others to do the same. There is no evidence supporting the idea that anyone should resist change or ignore the insights of these remarkable minds. It is essential to recognise that change is constant, and we must embrace it to achieve growth, enhance our intelligence, reach greater heights, and create significant positive transformations.

Reduce your stress levels by embracing acceptance. In situations where you can't do much, acceptance is the first step toward adapting to change. Acceptance enables us to see the reality of the situation and helps you move forward to adapt and evolve; otherwise, your mind may become paralysed, crippled, and stuck. You must acknowledge the reality of what is happening instead of retreating into a fantasy world, accepting the changes occurring around you in the present moment. That's the only way to find peace and hope. Change is a continuous process that cannot be controlled. **Acceptance and adapting to change are your only viable options.** Doing so can decrease your stress levels and achieve peace of mind. If you can't accept change, you hinder your ability to progress and move to the next level. This is certain. However, those who recognise this truth learn to embrace change, even in discomfort. This acceptance empowers them to level up and continue their journey forward.

'What's dangerous is not to evolve' is a famous quote by Jeff Bezos, founder and CEO of Amazon. This suggests that staying stagnant and failing to adapt to change can result in failures in an ever-evolving world.

Golden Nuggets

- Change is the only constant. We must acknowledge and develop the crucial skill of navigating and embracing change with grace.

- Change has been inevitable since the dawn of time, and it is essential to adapt to it.

- Adapting to change is regarded as a key indicator of true intelligence.

- True transformation is unlikely to happen without accepting and adapting to new circumstances.

- Although adjusting to recent changes can present challenges, it is key to taking small steps toward adaptation. These steps can be taken gradually in response to shifting situations.

- Acceptance is the initial step toward adapting to change.

- Change can be uncomfortable for anyone, but it becomes necessary if you genuinely want to elevate your life.

Work Smart to Become a Better Version of Yourself

**'If you want to live like a king,
first you have to work as a slave'**
– Oscar-winning Music Director A R Rahman

Hard work truly pays off! Why not explore the biographies of real-life heroes and champions from various fields? One inspiring trait they all share is their dedication and strong willingness to work hard. Let's remember that the hard work we invest today shapes the bright progress we'll see tomorrow! Hard work involves the energy and effort you put into getting things done. **It is about dedicating your time and focus, showing your commitment to a project, and embracing a disciplined mindset.** Often, a dash of persistence and resilience is precisely what you need to overcome the challenges and obstacles that life throws your way.

This journey demands determination, discipline, commitment, and continuous effort. While talent and intelligence certainly contribute to your achievements, unwavering dedication to hard work often makes the most significant difference in unlocking your true potential and getting closer to your goals. Challenging work also shows your commitment and helps you tackle challenges. If you are genuinely dedicated to achieving success, combining that determination with a readiness to roll up your sleeves and work hard is essential.

'Hard work takes you to the right destination.'
The path may be difficult, but without effort,
no progress can be made"
– American psychologist William James

Hard work and relentless dedication pay off in the end. Putting in effort is crucial for unlocking your full potential and advancing toward your goals. Most of us know the famous Olympic athlete, Usain Bolt. I admire his well-known saying: **"I trained four years to run nine seconds."** People often expect quick results, but that is not how success works. We must work hard continuously, keep pushing forward, and never give up; these traits help transform dreams into real achievements. At 19, he had no medals to his name. From that humble beginning, he became the fastest man in the world. He beautifully reminds us that greatness is a journey, not something that happens overnight. With hard work and unwavering dedication, we see the rewards that enrich our lives in the end. This enables us to discover our strengths and weaknesses, encourages us to step outside our comfort zones, and serves as an extraordinary catalyst for our personal growth and development. If he had given up early, the world would have missed witnessing his incredible legacy of winning twenty-two Olympic gold medals. **"Dreams are free, but goals have a cost, which is time, effort, sacrifice and sweat",** stated Mr. Usain Bolt, an Olympic gold medalist widely regarded as one of the greatest sprinters of all time.

To reach your goals, you must embrace hard work. Relying on luck can be misleading. In fact, hard work almost always paves the way to success! Remember, there are no elevators to success; taking the stairs through hard work and dedicated effort makes the journey much more fulfilling. It is easy to be tempted by the notion of luck or shortcuts, but those paths often lead to disappointment in the long run. Therefore, let's prepare our minds to work harder. **"Work twice as hard as others,"** stated by the American businessman Mr. Elon Musk.

Are you excited about the journey to becoming an even better version of yourself? Have you come across the concept of smart working?

I recently came across a captivating image on social media that illustrates the classic story of how a crow cleverly drinks water from a pot. In this tale, the crow drops small pebbles into the pot, gradually raising the water level until it can finally quench its thirst. While this story beautifully demonstrates cleverness, a modern crow would likely update its skills and think outside the box. Instead of dropping pebbles, it might simply use a straw to sip more efficiently! In the same way, we must modernise ourselves and continually enhance our skills to thrive in today's world. Holding on to outdated ways of thinking will only slow us down and make it harder to adapt to new challenges.

Hard work doesn't have to mean endless hours that leave you feeling drained; **it is also about working smart, which is even more important.** Hard work and success often go hand in hand, and when you combine hard work with smart work, you set yourself up for even greater achievements! It is not about grinding away for 12 hours a day—it is all about using your mind effectively. Every day, aim to work both harder and smarter on your journey of self-improvement.

Smart working is outcome-oriented, but what does it mean? It emphasises the quality and results of the work produced (outcome-based), and productivity is not measured by hours spent at a desk. Smart working is a modern approach that highlights key aspects of work, such as efficiency, flexibility, proactive planning, and the use of technology, to enhance productivity. While hard work is essential, working smart alongside it is equally important for reaching your fullest potential in today's fast-paced world.

Smart working emphasises flexibility, allowing employees to work from locations beyond the traditional office (remote work) and choose their hours based on personal commitments (flexible hours). It incorporates technology through digital tools like Microsoft Teams, Slack, and cloud computing, enabling file access from any location and facilitating data sharing and seamless collaboration. This approach fosters teamwork among various teams, often enhanced by digital communication tools.

To achieve higher levels of success, we need to learn to '**think outside the box**' as part of smart working. For example, when Infosys, a global software company, was founded, it implemented both onshore and offshore options, introducing a 24-hour shift pattern for the first time. This approach allowed employees in offshore locations to communicate with customers in their own time zones, addressing concerns more effectively. In India, where operations occur onshore, employees could conduct research, programming, and development while their counterparts in America were asleep. This enabled the team in India to resolve issues raised by U.S. employees and provide solutions by the time they logged back in. This 24-hour shift pattern became a significant success for Infosys, primarily due to innovative thinking and smart working principles.

Smart workers prioritise self-development, invest in their core skills, and regularly update their knowledge base. They consistently hone their skills, stay informed, and embrace ongoing professional development to maintain a competitive edge in their journey towards success. While the term "investment" typically refers to creating and safeguarding wealth for the future, it is essential to recognise that financial investments, though significant, are not the most vital investments in life. Instead, allocate time to focus on more important investments, such as enhancing your competence, knowledge, and skills. Continuous learning and updating are crucial for achieving this.

"By not updating, you may miss the opportunity to evolve into an even better version of yourself and feel somewhat outdated".

Once you have updated your knowledge, apply it in your field. **Putting your knowledge into action is essential;** merely acquiring it is not enough. Dedicate at least one hour daily to strengthening your skills and proficiencies through activities such as reading, watching, learning, practising, revising, and updating your skill set. For example, as a successful doctor, I dedicate an hour each day to enhancing my medical knowledge and psychiatric competencies by engaging with resources like books, articles, podcasts, webinars, medical education programmes, consultations with experts, and conferences.

Every individual should prioritise investing time in maintaining and enhancing their core competencies. This commitment helps them strive to be among the top 1% of professionals in their respective fields and achieve higher levels of success. While many people gather knowledge, they sometimes fail to put it into practice. **"There is no excuse for not trying"** – former American President Barack Obama. Competent workers take steps for further action, and that difference in moving forward often sets high achievers apart.

Let me share the Power of Smart Working with my own story.

In the small town of Chennai, Shadithya Hospital, which I own, is recognised as a valuable centre for mental health patients needing care, support, and treatment. As demand grew, my staff and I felt overwhelmed, spending long hours in the hospital at the expense of our health and family time. After a particularly exhausting week, I spoke with my tech-savvy friend Aaron, who suggested, "Have you considered smart working using the latest technology?" Intrigued, I listened as he explained that smart working with the latest technology and software maximises productivity and efficiency for those in the hospital industry while preserving a work-life balance. Inspired, I made changes after realising my staff spent too much time on repetitive tasks. With Aaron's help, I purchased hospital management software that streamlined processes, integrated departments, and improved collaborative communication.

I developed a website with booking options for customers statewide, utilised customised software to maintain electronic patient databases, and implemented AI software (Artificial Intelligence for appointment scheduling. The hospital software systems contributed to optimising operations, enhancing patient safety, improving workflow, and effectively managing resources. This innovation benefited hospital staff, attracted new customers due to its user-friendliness, and enabled the hospital to thrive. Above all, I gained more free time, reconnected with my family, and revived my passion for writing. I have inspired other small to medium-sized hospitals through workshops at the local community centre, sharing my journey and emphasising the importance of working smart. "It's about finding balance," I say. **"When we work smarter, we enjoy our successes without sacrificing health and happiness."** My hospital stands as a testament to smart working due to its embrace of technology and new approaches. Simply putting in the hours is not enough; one must also seek knowledge and apply it effectively.

Did you know that 80 per cent of millionaires and 66 per cent of billionaires in the United States are self-made? They've succeeded through hard work, discipline, commitment, and a strong entrepreneurial spirit. Just like them, you can carve out your path to success! Remember, it is possible to go from having nothing to becoming a millionaire or billionaire. If others can reach this goal, so can you! It is all about having a personal strategic plan and working smart. If anyone asked me about my greatest strength, I would say I can work harder and smarter. Working smart is absolutely essential, especially when you are passionate about achieving success.

Golden Nuggets

- Hard work includes the effort, energy, and time you put into achieving your goals and dreams.

- Talent and intelligence are wonderful, but your relentless determination to put in effort makes all the difference!

- Hard work helps us uncover our strengths and weaknesses and acts as an exceptional catalyst for our personal growth and development.

- Hard work and success often go hand in hand; when you combine diligence with smart strategies, you prepare yourself for even greater achievements!

- Smart working emphasises the quality and results of the work produced (outcome-based); productivity is not measured by hours spent at a desk.

- Smart working represents a modern approach that emphasises key aspects of work, such as efficiency, flexibility, proactive planning, and the use of technology, to enhance productivity.

- Part of smart work involves continually enhancing your skills to remain relevant and regularly update yourself with continuous learning.

- To achieve higher levels of success, we need to learn how to think outside the box as part of smart working.

Failure is the First Step Towards Success and Serves as a Stepping Stone

Diverse perspectives exist on the concept of success. Success varies from one individual to another and is shaped by personal goals, circumstances, and viewpoints. Success is a relative concept; let's reflect on its relativity. It **involves subjective interpretation, often defined by individual aspirations and value systems.** What one person considers a significant achievement may not resonate the same way for another. Let's explore the varying perceptions of success among individuals preparing for a competitive examination. For 'high achievers' who aim for excellence, attaining over 90% and being selected signifies success. They may have set high-performance goals due to their academic ambitions or future career aspirations. Conversely, for 'cautious achievers,' simply participating in the exam represents a major milestone. This group may have overcome significant obstacles, such as anxiety and personal circumstances, to arrive at the examination hall and take the test. Some individuals who are 'learning participants' might view the exam as a practice opportunity, like a mock exam, focusing on learning and experience rather than grades. Their goal is to gain insights that will prepare them for future success. This subjective nature illustrates that there is no universal standard for success.

Success is a relative concept influenced by individual values, perceptions, and experiences. Recognising this variability allows us to appreciate both our own journeys and those of others. There is no universal standard for success, as it involves subjective interpretation."

'Success is stumbling from failure to failure with no loss of enthusiasm'
– Sir Winston Churchill

Have you heard about some incredible journeys from failure to remarkable success?

Sir Albert Einstein, celebrated as one of the most renowned scientists of the century, faced a tough start – he could not speak until he was nearly four years old! His teachers doubted his potential, but he went on to become one of the greatest scientists of all time.

Steve Jobs, the visionary behind Apple Inc., was ousted from the company at just 30 years old. Although this was challenging, he didn't allow that setback to define him. He returned to Apple and played a key role in transforming it into one of the world's leading corporations. Oprah Winfrey, regarded as one of the greatest television anchors of all time, was once told she wasn't suited for TV. However, she didn't back down; instead, she made an inspiring comeback and became a prominent figure in the industry. Jack Ma, a Chinese businessman and philanthropist, was rejected by KFC when he applied for a job, while twenty-three other applicants were hired. Six candidates were interviewed for his military position, and all but him received offers. But look at him now – he is a billionaire and a successful entrepreneur. J.K. Rowling, the creator of the Harry Potter series, faced multiple rejections from publishers before eventually finding one for her first book. Today, she is recognised as one of the best-selling authors of all time. Let's not forget the Beatles! This legendary band faced rejection from recording companies that deemed their sound unappealing and believed they wouldn't succeed. However, they didn't give up; they persevered and eventually became one of the most successful bands in history. Just because you experience a setback doesn't mean you should stop trying. Remember, failure is not the end of the road.

It is worth noting that many successful individuals have encountered significant failures and rejections on their paths to success. The stories of renowned figures testify to the transformative power of failure and rejection. These individuals faced numerous setbacks and obstacles but persevered in the face of adversity, ultimately achieving remarkable success in their respective fields. Consider what might have happened if these individuals had allowed their failures to discourage them.

Everyone makes mistakes and may ultimately face failures. Sir Albert Einstein once stated **"Anyone who has never made a mistake has never tried anything new"**. This underscores that all human beings are prone to errors, and those who engage more actively in their pursuits are likely to make more mistakes. On one occasion, he wrote the multiplication table for nine on the board, starting from 9×1 to 9×9, and he wrote them all correctly. However, when he reached 9×10, he mistakenly wrote ninety-one instead of ninety. The entire class laughed and pointed out his error. He then remarked that despite having made nine correct calculations, no one noticed them; instead, they fixated on his one mistake and laughed at it. This phenomenon mirrors real-life: People may overlook our successes but are quick to highlight our failures. Failure is part of the journey toward success, and we all must confront it. Understanding this is crucial, as it allows us to learn and grow from our experiences. Einstein's experience in the classroom serves as a metaphor for life: despite a series of accomplishments (the correct multiplication facts, it is often the one mistake and failures that captures attention. This perspective emphasises that making mistakes is a natural part of any endeavour, especially in the pursuit of knowledge and progress. Everyone's journey involves ups and downs, and recognising that failures are not the end but rather a part of the growth process can be empowering.

One of the most fulfilling aspects of these setbacks is the opportunity for reflection and self-improvement. Setbacks offer a perfect moment to reassess our strategies and behaviours, helping us identify areas for growth and development. This kind of reflection often yields valuable insights and lessons that we can carry into future endeavours, ultimately enhancing our chances of success.

'If you are walking down the right path and are willing to keep walking, eventually you will make progress,' said former American president Mr. Barack Obama. So, don't let a negative mindset hinder your progress. Instead, keep moving forward to achieve advancements. If you are not progressing, slow down, every small step toward success matters. Martin Luther King Jr. stated, **"If you can't fly, then run. If you can't run, then walk. If you can't walk, then crawl, but whatever you do, you have to keep moving."**

Do not give up. Keep trying. Perseverance pays off eventually. For instance, when we learn to speak as children, we struggle to find the right words, often stumbling and stuttering. Did we give up? No, we persisted and ultimately learned to speak fluently. Similarly, all challenges present difficulties and obstacles. Failure is not the end of our journeys; instead, it is a vital stepping stone to success. Every stumble or setback is an opportunity to learn and grow. By persevering through challenges, you can achieve success in your goals.

"Fall seven times, Stand up eight"
– Japanese proverb encouraging to keep trying

You may encounter multiple failures, but that's part of the journey. Even if you stumble, it is essential to rise, dust yourself off, analyse why you fell, and keep moving forward. With persistence, your efforts will eventually pay off. Thomas Alva Edison, the renowned inventor of the lightbulb, faced over a thousand attempts before achieving it, but he did not give up and ultimately succeeded.

"It is not bad to fail. After all, everybody is human. We always say it is better to fail early and to learn from our failures. Perseverance and a never give up attitude are very important. You have to keep going at it, and as long as you are unwilling to give up, you have that internal conviction and perseverance; it always helps," - Mr Mukesh Ambani, Indian billionaire and businessman, stated in one of the interviews about success and failures.

When people experience failure, they often forget everything they have achieved. Consider the flip side of the coin and remind yourself of your accomplishments in various aspects of life. Compiling a list of successes, memorable events, and achievements is useful. During challenging times, it is crucial to revisit this list and remind yourself that your life encompasses much more than the failure you are currently facing. Strive to focus on the brighter side during moments of failure.

It is okay to express your feelings about your failures, including sadness and regret. It is perfectly fine. You can also cry over your failures, which can be therapeutic for many people. However, one should not dwell in the river of self- pity and must strive to reach the shores. **Focus on the areas where you have succeeded.** You may face failures in one area, but there are aspects in which you have excelled. For instance, you may encounter challenges in your marital relationship, but this setback should not bring you down. You can still be a loving son or daughter to your parents, a caring mother or father to your children, a supportive sibling to your brothers and sisters, and an overall wonderful person. Therefore, try to focus on the other aspects you have succeeded in. It is important to reflect on the areas where you have thrived. You still have a healthy body, a stable job, strong relationships with your family, a quality education, and a beautiful home to live in. You may have excelled academically and established a solid professional life. Thus, be grateful for what you have and avoid dwelling in self- pity for what you have lost.

True success comes from dedicated effort, and hard work often demands sacrifices. We should reflect on what we are willing to give up achieving our goals. Without making sacrifices, attaining success becomes significantly more difficult. Ask yourself if you are ready to sacrifice for your desires. If you are, undertake your journey with determination and a resilient heart. Patience is vital for success. Rushing and losing patience heighten the chances of setbacks. Success often demands time, and those who stay patient and diligent will ultimately prevail. In contrast, the impatient may give up or attain only partial success.

Consistency is essential for achieving your goals. Many individuals begin their journey motivated but struggle to maintain consistency, ultimately failing to follow through until they reach their desired success. Consistency is the key. Success comes from actions taken consistently, not sporadically. It arises not from what you do occasionally, but from what you do regularly. It is all about the commitment to keep making progress! Consistency truly makes all the difference; it can significantly change your life in incredible ways! Ensure your thoughts, feelings, and actions consistently align with your goals.

" To be successful at anything, you don't have to be special"
– Tom Brady, a seven-time Super Bowl champion.
Be consistent and willing to work for it

Many people believe that others achieve success solely due to inherited genes. While genes do not dictate destiny, they can highlight areas of opportunity. **It is essential to recognise that although genes may indicate natural skills, they do not control fate.** Instead, they suggest potential avenues for development. Although genetics can provide insights, your destiny is ultimately shaped by the effort, hard work, consistency, and perseverance you invest. Identifying areas where you are naturally predisposed and feel passionate is crucial. You can shape your own path and destiny by aligning your efforts and skills with these interests. There is a fantastic quote by Indian cricketer Rohit Sharma: '**Hard work beats talent when talent doesn't work hard."** Having natural talent and inheriting exceptional genes is a gift, but it is the hard work, consistency, and perseverance that refine it to reach its full potential.

You don't need to push yourself to take a step forward every single day; moments of reflection can be just as rewarding—and sometimes, stepping back can lead to success. Consider the game of tug of war. In that game, participants often need to pull back to gain an advantage and win. Similarly, in many aspects of life, taking a moment to step back and collect your thoughts is crucial for achieving success. Look at the world of real estate—buying and selling can be constant, but sometimes, individuals need to hold back or wait a bit before making their next move. In the stock market, traders and investors don't always keep pouring in money; often, they take a breather or even withdraw funds. This doesn't mean they've failed; it is actually a smart part of their strategy to protect their investments and ultimately succeed.

"Success isn't just about always moving forward. Sometimes, taking a step back or enjoying a little pause can lead to amazing victories!"

Life can be viewed as a continuous series of "exams," where each experience presents an opportunity to learn and grow. It is essential to embrace both successes and failures as integral components of this process. Each "exam" in life teaches valuable lessons, and the continuous effort to engage, learn, and evolve genuinely defines our journey toward success. Like academic examinations, life's challenges and milestones are assessed differently based on individual perspectives and contexts. Regardless of how success is defined, the importance of persistence and resilience remains constant. Adopting the mindset of "continuing to tackle the next exam in life" fosters growth and development.

Remember, success is indeed possible with dedication and self-discipline. Investing effort can lead to remarkable outcomes. As you learn and grow, you will acquire the skills and knowledge necessary to thrive in your field. Challenges may arise along the way, but your perseverance and hard work will surely pay off in the end. **Everyone encounters failures in life; it is a universal truth!** Whatever game you choose to play, there will be moments of loss, but that's all part of the journey. Life is like a rollercoaster, filled with thrilling ups and downs, and every twist makes the ride worthwhile!

Golden Nuggets

- Success is a relative concept shaped by individual values, perceptions, and experiences. There is no universal standard for success; it involves subjective interpretation.

- When people face setbacks, they often overlook their past achievements. Creating a list of successes, memorable life events, and accomplishments can be helpful when seeking the brighter side.

- True success arises from dedicated effort, and hard work frequently necessitates sacrifices.

- Patience is essential for success. Rushing and lacking patience increase the likelihood of failure.

- Consistency is essential for achieving your goals. Ensure your thoughts, feelings, and actions consistently align with your objectives.

- Never give up; keep trying. Ultimately, perseverance pays off.

- You might make mistakes and stumble, but don't repeat those errors; learn from the experience.

- It is essential to understand that while genes may suggest natural talents, they do not determine your destiny.

- Success is not solely about constant progress. Sometimes, stepping back or enjoying a momentary pause can result in remarkable victories.

ME Time: The Most Valuable Gift You can Give Yourself

Taking "ME time" is one of the most valuable gifts you can give yourself. **It is a dedicated moment just for you!** This time is all about self-care, and it is not selfish; it is a vital practice for your overall well-being. Taking time for yourself involves recharging your body, caring for your mind, and nurturing your spirit. You deserve to set aside at least one hour daily to nurture yourself and refresh your spirit. **"ME time" is essential for finding balance in your life—it helps you connect deeply with yourself.** By prioritising "ME time," you can focus on what matters most to you and let go of distractions. This special time for yourself also opens the door to creative thinking and sparks innovative ideas.

When I suggest it to people, I immediately receive responses like, 'I don't have the time for that.' and 'I wish I had the time.' Many individuals feel overwhelmed by work and family commitments, making it difficult to carve out some "ME time." However, the real challenge often lies not in having enough time but in managing time effectively. **Remember, you are the most important person in your life!** So, take a moment to create a cosy space for yourself, prioritise your well-being, and let go of any excuses that might hold you back. After all, if you don't take care of yourself, who will? What's the point of living, working, and investing energy in other pursuits if you can't find time for your well-being? To truly live fully and joyfully, embracing and treating yourself with love through ME time is essential.

Prioritise yourself and dedicate at least 60 minutes daily to practising "ME time." You can spend as much time as you wish on your ME time, but 60 minutes, or an hour, is the minimum. Many individuals do not know how to prioritise their own health and well-being. A famous quote states: '**Self-care is the first step to health care.**' This involves offering love, respect, and protection for yourself every day. Self-care is the ability of individuals to promote and maintain their health while preventing disease. Always remember that self-care is not selfish. The initial step in practising self-care is making time for yourself. Although it may be demanding and challenging in this fast-paced world with busy schedules, it is important to invest time in yourself and prioritise your health— physical, emotional, mental, and spiritual. Establishing boundaries between yourself and others is also essential, and this can be achieved through "ME time."

Consider reducing your television time since many people spend a significant portion of it watching soap operas, sports, or series. Cut down on TV time by one hour each day. Additionally, limit your screen and phone time to free up even more hours. Research shows that people in the U.S. spend nearly three and a half hours daily on their phones or screens. While staying connected to technology is essential, you can often limit this to about one hour a day. The goal is to decrease social media usage by one hour each day. By reducing time spent on TV and social media, you can reclaim at least two hours each day, totalling 60 hours a month. This minor adjustment can provide you with around two extra hours of personal time! You can spend this extra time on activities that promote your well-being and personal growth, which I wholeheartedly recommend!

Additionally, aim to minimise the time spent managing emails by keeping them concise. When someone calls, shorten the telephone conversation by conveying essential information through messages instead. These actions could help you save about 30 minutes daily, totalling approximately 15 hours each month.

Implementing these simple strategies could save you up to 75 hours each month. This gives me a minimum of 2½ hours daily (150 minutes) for my ME time. This valuable period of 75 hours can be allocated for my ME time, creativity, enjoyment, hobbies, interests, and learning new things. Reflect on your situation and think of strategies to reduce time in other areas. Stop making excuses about not having enough time and focus on using your time wisely.

To make the most of your "me time," consider the following simple practices to start with:

Rejuvenating Your Body: Spend about 30 to 45 minutes on physical activities. Engage in light stretching exercises to relax tired muscles, take a 20- to 30-minute walk or jog, or practice yoga. Conclude with five minutes of deep breathing to connect with your body further.

Nurturing Your Mind: Dedicate time to enhance your mental well-being. Read a chapter from a book, listen to an insightful podcast, or watch an inspiring video. This is a wonderful opportunity to learn from great minds and stimulate your brain. Consider journaling your thoughts to express them on paper.

Connecting with Your Soul: Dedicate five to fifteen minutes to meditation. Close your eyes and focus on your breath. Start with simple meditation techniques and gradually progress to more complex practices. This will help you connect deeply with your soul.

As you develop your "ME time" strategy, **consider incorporating a joyful activity into your day!** This is my favourite part; I truly believe everyone can benefit from it. I call these "pleasurable or enjoyable activities" that bring happiness and joy into our daily lives. Try to engage in at least one pleasurable activity each day for at least 30 minutes. These activities should be things you genuinely enjoy and look forward to—they're your picks, not someone else's suggestions, including those from professionals. So, why not compile a list of at least ten meaningful activities that bring us joy and keep it on your desk? This list can encompass anything you love to do! Make a habit of engaging in one of these activities each day for at least 30 minutes; it will enhance your enjoyment of life; help elevate our moods and improve our well-being. It is so helpful to have a list of enjoyable activities to turn to during those more challenging moments when you might feel down. Remember, you are working hard and honestly deserve to find happiness throughout your day. So, don't feel guilty about prioritising your well-being!

Here are some fun ideas: listen to music, have a phone chat, watch a funny video or comedy, take a leisurely walk, dive into a good book or magazine, play with your pet, enjoy a relaxing bath, share a meal with a friend, do some stretching exercises, play a musical instrument, dance a little, watch one of your favourite shows or a good movie, browse through old photos, soak up some sun, go shopping, or enjoy some board games. The possibilities are endless, and the goal is to have fun! Also, try to mix it up a bit—avoid doing the same activity every day, as variety can be wonderfully refreshing for your mind, body, and soul! **Remember, variety is key.** Different activities can bring a refreshing spark to your mind, body, and soul.

Spending about 1-2 hours daily on "ME time" can significantly transform your feelings. Embrace self-love as much as possible. Doing so, you will begin to achieve a fulfilling and balanced life. **Incorporating "ME time" into your daily routine will cultivate wellness within yourself**. Only when you reach this kind of wellness can you share it with those around you. If you are not well, it becomes challenging to extend that positivity to others; however, when you prioritise your well-being, you can positively influence your family, friends, and the wider community.

Whenever I share my experiences of embracing "ME time" and making space for myself each day, I often hear people express their curiosity about how it is possible with such a busy practice schedule. I want to assure you that it is genuinely achievable! I have developed a strong self-awareness and understood that my main goal is to nurture my body, mind, and spirit. By dedicating ME time to yo urself, yo u are in vesting in yourself and nurturing your joy and happiness!

Schedule regular time for enjoyable activities in your calendar. Prioritising yourself by setting boundaries, graciously saying no to other commitments, and reserving time in your schedule are necessary steps for nurturing yourself. It is essential to avoid letting guilt weigh you down or giving in to negativity or self-criticism. Instead, let's practice self-compassion and take a moment to soothe ourselves—it is a tremendous step toward finding happiness and nurturing our souls. Remember the most essential point: Your well-being should be your top priority and a central focus in your daily agenda.

Golden Nuggets

- "ME time" is a period for self-care; it is not an act of selfishness, but rather an essential practice.

- ME Time is for revitalising your body, nurturing your mind, and connecting with your soul.

- Embrace self-love as much as you can. By incorporating "ME time" daily, you will cultivate wellness within yourself; it is one way to invest in yourself and nurture your joy and happiness.

- Spend at least one hour each day practising "ME time." Concentrate on your well-being and eliminate any excuses that may hinder you.

- To free up more time for yourself, limit television viewing, reduce social media use, keep emails brief, and avoid lengthy phone calls.

- Participating in a pleasurable activity daily is one of the most effective ways to improve one's mood and elevate one's spirits.

- Strive to gather a few enjoyable activities and keep them on your desk. Having a selection of activities to choose from can be extremely helpful when you feel down.

- It is essential to prioritise yourself by setting boundaries, gracefully saying no, and reserving time in your calendar for pleasurable activities.

Organise Your Space and Declutter Your Surroundings

"Declutter your mind, declutter your body, and declutter your environment."

All three are equally essential to a chieve more health, happiness, and peace.

Decluttering your environment by removing unwanted items that no longer serve a purpose is just as important as decluttering our minds by eliminating negative thoughts and by shedding unhealthy eating habits. **Maintaining a clean and tidy home and workspace allows you to experience increased energy, foster a positive spirit, and boost satisfaction.** Engaging in regular physical activity enhances physical health, while deep breathing and meditation promote mental well-being. Additionally, regularly tidying up your room, wardrobe, and living space is essential for maintaining a conducive environment. Focusing solely on your mind and body is not enough; it is also crucial to pay attention to your environment. Maintaining a fit body, a stress-free mind, and a clean living space is essential. Just as keeping your mind organised—free of excessive baggage and painful memories—is vital, so too is ensuring your environment is tidy, free of trash, and devoid of outdated items.

Be mindful of your surroundings and what you have around you. **Surround your environment with positive vibrations,** as everything around you vibrates and allows energy to flow through your spaces.

If you are unsure where to start, I recommend tackling clutter gradually. Begin in one specific area each week and dedicate 2 to 3 hours to decluttering—begin with your living room, then move to the kitchen, children's room, study room, and storage. By the end of four weeks, you will have organised at least four areas of your living space, significantly reducing clutter. Developing a monthly routine for cleaning your living space is essential to reduce stress and create a more relaxing environment for you and your family. Once you have completed this initial decluttering, **prepare a monthly schedule to allocate 2 to 3 hours for tidying up all spaces.** Making this a regular practice will help decluttering become a habit, and you will begin implementing these strategies over time. I usually set a specific day each week or a particular date in a month for this task to ensure my living space remains tidy and organised.

Many people don't know how to declutter their living spaces and prevent the accumulation of unnecessary items. I recently found a helpful article suggesting a simple practice: '**Whenever you purchase an item for your home, make it a habit to give away one item.**' Be sure to discard one item whenever you bring in a new one. This approach helps maintain balance and prevents clutter from building up. If you believe the item is in good condition, you can donate it to a charity shop when acquiring something new. Countless individuals would benefit from your generosity, and by donating, you will create a lighter atmosphere in your space, leading to a happier mindset. By doing so, you hit two targets with one stone: a decluttered home and personal satisfaction. Isn't this a great idea? I encourage you to give it a try.

Many people hold onto old clothing, hoping to use it someday, resulting in vast collections of clothes in their wardrobes that they have not worn in years. If you have not worn a clothing item for over a year, there's little chance you will wear it in the future. Therefore, if the items are in good condition, consider donating them to charity. If the clothes cannot be worn, it is best to dispose of them. People often develop unhealthy attachments to clothing, children's items, and other old belongings. Although having sentimental attachments is normal, these items can occupy valuable space and often serve as reminders of the past. It is beneficial to let go of these attachments and declutter your space. While keeping a few pieces for sentimental reasons is acceptable, maintaining a decluttered wardrobe and living space is essential.

You can follow the 'one-item-per-day' rule: get rid of one item each day. This will eliminate thirty items in a month and 365 items in a year. If you have items in cupboards, wardrobes, or rooms that you don't use, it is time to let them go. These unnecessary items can drain your energy. Take this opportunity to clear them out for something new.

First, list the items you no longer want or are unlikely to use. Be specific about these items to ensure their complete removal. Next, list any items you have purchased that are sitting unused in drawers, cupboards, or wardrobes. For example, picture frames that need to be hung, lamps that require installation, or garden pots waiting to be placed. Evaluate these items and consider how to utilise them. Additionally, check if anything can be recycled. Attempting to recycle items can give you a sense of optimism about saving the planet.

Ensure your living spaces are visually pleasant. They should appear organised and tidy, resonate with lovely music, have a pleasing scent, and feel inviting. In short, they should look, sound, and smell nice. Consider using beautiful paintings to brighten the rooms. Add appealing wall art, posters, and attractive pieces of furniture. Good lighting from windows and spacious arrangements with less clutter are vital for creating a positive atmosphere. Consider using room sprays, fragrances, or scented candles to maintain a delightful aroma in your rooms. Ensure that the space sounds pleasant with soothing background music and minimal chatter. An organised home creates openness and freedom to move around. This will boost your energy levels and significantly improve your mood. It can bring you serenity and inner peace.

Ensure that your storage space is easily accessible and label items that you want to keep long-term. Some people have a separate storage space, while others use part of the garage. Regularly clear out unused items in your storage space – if you have not used something in a couple of years in your storage, there's a high probability you might never use it. In such cases, it is best to discard those items. If possible, consider recycling to help protect the environment.

Try this simple strategy of taking photos before and after decluttering to compare them. It will help motivate you to do more. Choose one area, like your wardrobe, and take photographs first. Then, start decluttering, remove the items in the picture, and take a photo after clearing the area. Once you see how good it looks after decluttering, it will inspire you to tackle other areas of the house.

Throwing out the clutter certainly helps to clear our minds.

Let's now move on to our working space. Your working space should be regarded as a sacred shrine. Decluttering and creating a practical working space are as important as your living space. Your workspace should be more organised and create a positive atmosphere to enhance your productivity. '**If you spend one minute organising things, you save at least one hour**," an anonymous person quoted.

I have created a fantastic office space that many people appreciate when visiting. My arrangements work to my advantage, and both visitors and customers always want to return. I want to share some of the things I have done that others can replicate and adopt the principles and customise it for their own office space in any field.

First, ensure you have a "**suitable desk**" of the right height. This helps you feel confident and maintain professionalism while interacting with customers and colleagues. Additionally, I have invested in "**ergonomic chairs and tables/desks**" that prevent back pain, shoulder, and wrist injuries and provide adequate support for my elbows. Since I spend many hours seated daily, I must take precautions to protect my back, spine, and other joints using the right chair.

Moreover, I use a **"compact laptop"** that saves space but is equipped with all the necessary tools and software for my work. Most of my tasks are completed on the laptop, which allows me to save my job immediately. While it is generally rare for doctors to use computers in their practice, I started incorporating them early in my career. This has helped me avoid excessive paperwork and keep all the information readily accessible.

I have a **"good window"** in my workspace allowing occasional views outside. This helps alleviate eye strain and prevent damage. The office is well-ventilated and maintains a comfortable temperature—not too hot or cold. My office features a collection of antique items and posters that enhance the beauty of the space, along with lovely indoor plants that bring joy to both me and my customers. I also use a fragrance diffuser to keep the room pleasantly aromatic and often play soft background music. Positive distractions can also soothe the mind, such as listening to calming music, enjoying pleasant aromas from perfumes or air fresheners, and applying soothing hand creams.

During breaks, I have a small area designated for stretching and light exercises in my office. I personalise my workspace with cherished items like family photos and artwork created by my children, which keeps me motivated and connected to the purpose of my work.

Finally, I ensure that all essential items are **"within arm's reach"** so that I can easily access important files and stationery, enhancing my work efficiency. I also use noise-cancelling headphones when I want to disconnect from the outside world and focus while completing my paperwork. They help me concentrate on my work without distractions.

Tidy your table by keeping only essential items. Avoid allowing paperwork to accumulate, as it can signify procrastination and a backlog of tasks needing attention. This clutter can be overwhelming, so strive to maintain minimal paperwork on your table. In today's digital age, managing documents electronically is easy. Consider scanning your papers, creating specific folders labelled with appropriate names, and organising these digital files for easy retrieval later. Storing documents on cloud- based servers allows access from any location, even when you are physically away from home or the office. Once you have done this, you can safely discard the physical paperwork, and the original physical copies can be shredded for proper disposal. This process can help tidy up your study room and table.

When I finish my work each day, I ensure that all the paperwork on my desk is cleared away and looks neat. You can have a workspace either at home, as many people do, or in your designated office area. These simple environmental adjustments bring me immense satisfaction, mental peace, and happiness. Decluttering your environment should be regarded with the same importance as decluttering your body and mind. Finally, take proactive steps to create an office environment conducive to success and serenity.

People often ask me about the existence of heaven, God, and holy shrines. I have simple answers for them: my home, shared with my wife, children, and family, is my version of heaven. My work represents my God; my workspace serves as my temple and holy shrine. Transform your workplace into a shrine and strive to maintain it. This space should inspire, encourage, and help you move forward despite any challenges that arise.

Golden Nuggets

- Regularly declutter your space by removing unwanted items and aim for a clean living environment.

- Whenever you buy something for your home, make it a habit to donate one item. When you bring something in, take one out to minimise clutter.

- Consider removing an item each day if possible. Avoid developing unhealthy attachments to your possessions.

- Make sure your living spaces are visually appealing, generate a pleasant scent, and provide a tranquil atmosphere with little noise.

- Creating a monthly cleaning routine for your living space and making it a consistent practice will help turn decluttering into a habit.

- Transform your workspace by decluttering.

- Your workspace should foster a positive atmosphere to enhance your productivity.

- Aim to keep paperwork minimal on your desk.

- Make sure to clear your desk or worktable every day.

Associate Yourself with the Right People in Your Life

**'Life is never going to be easy,
but it makes it easier if you have the right people in your life.'**
– Former Miss World Priyanka Chopra

It is essential to choose our friendships and relationships wisely by surrounding ourselves with positive influences. **Surround yourself with individuals who make you feel comfortable, uplift you, and prioritise healthy connections.** Positive relationships foster a nurturing environment for our personal growth and well-being. By cultivating a safe network of people who encourage and empower us, we enhance our confidence and navigate life's challenges with greater ease and optimism. Connecting with the right kind of people is fantastic, as the company we keep plays a significant role in our growth.

Develop the skill of networking with others. Networking entails maintaining healthy connections with a diverse range of individuals and expanding your network. Ensure you interact with people in various settings, including your workplace, home, schools, colleges, neighbourhoods, gyms, common areas, and the broader community. Learn to initiate conversations and actively participate in activities. Additionally, focus on engaging with others and creating a positive impression during these interactions, demonstrating genuine curiosity about their lives. Be sincerely interested in others. **Master the art of socialising with people**. Once you begin socialising, you may encounter individuals who inspire positivity in you; surrounding yourself with such people can uplift your mood and diminish negativity. It is necessary to step outside, meet others, and allow their connections to elevate your spirit. Celebrating life also involves nurturing meaningful relationships. Human connection adds richness and depth to our lives, providing support, companionship, and love. By fostering strong, healthy relationships with family, friends, and the community, we can discover joy, belonging, and a sense of purpose that enhances our celebration of life.

Associating with people who share similar interests, and ideally those who are more accomplished than you, can help guide you in a positive direction. Surrounding yourself with more successful individuals can be a powerful catalyst for your growth. Their experiences, insights, and achievements can inspire you to aim higher and challenge yourself. When evaluating your life and career trajectory, it becomes increasingly clear that the people you associate with greatly influence your progress and development. The company you keep is not just a matter of social preference; it can significantly affect your mindset, opportunities, and overall direction.

Therefore, it is crucial to intentionally select those you surround yourself with. You foster an environment conducive to motivation an d su ccess by al igning wi th in dividuals with similar interests, values, and aspirations.

Mr Elon Musk, a billionaire and one of the world's wealthiest individuals, stated, **"Build a circle of friends who like to talk about investments, business ideas, and personal growth instead of gossiping about other people."** Good conversation, connections, and social relationships can recharge your mental batteries. People can also help recharge each other through their vibes.

Distancing ourselves from negative individuals and disengaging from harmful energies is important. Learning to avoid negativity is an essential skill for achieving well-being and happiness. Associating with the wrong crowd can lead to challenges we'd rather avoid. Just as milk stored in clean containers stays fresh, our lives flourish when we engage with positive influences who share our interests. It is all about nurturing the joyful connections that help us shine brighter!

Positive individuals exude good vibes and consistently foster a comfortable environment. When you are with them, you typically feel safe and happy. In contrast, negative individuals can be challenging to deal with; they often bring negative vibes and emotions such as anger, irritability, resentment, disappointment, mistrust, and sadness. The label you assign to someone as positive or negative often depends on your perspective and life experiences, which may differ from those of others. For instance, a person you perceive as negative might be viewed differently by different people. Identify those people who make you uncomfortable and distress you.

In society, there are always individuals who can create negative feelings and circumstances for you. I want to use an analogy comparing this modern world to a dense forest from a few thousand years ago. Initially, the world resembled a thick forest, but over time, it has evolved into villages, townships, and modern cities. In a dense forest, we may encounter a variety of animals: some are adorable and safe, some are neutral and do not cause any problems. At the same time, a few are dangerous and can affect your safety and survival. Likewise, navigating the modern world involves encountering positive, neutral, and negative individuals. Overall, choose the kind of people with whom you want to associate. If you wish to maintain a sense of comfort and happiness, avoiding negativity and negative individuals is crucial.

Negative or toxic individuals can take various forms, such as chronic complainers and pessimists. Interacting with them can leave us feeling exhausted, demotivated, and emotionally drained. Their toxic energy can hinder our personal growth and happiness. Therefore, establishing clear boundaries with such individuals is essential, as is firmly asserting our needs. Setting boundaries is not a selfish act but rather an act of self- preservation and self-care. By establishing healthy boundaries, we signal to others that our well-being is a priority and that we cannot tolerate behaviours that compromise our mental health. This may involve limiting contact with negative individuals or even choosing to distance ourselves from toxic relationships entirely. Moreover, avoiding those who drain our energy helps us preserve our mental well-being.

"It's far better to stay alone than to be in bad company", said former President of the United States, George Washington.

Some individuals can be quite negative, often appearing self-centred and focused solely on their own needs, and they are frequently described as narcissistic. Instead of trying to change others, **focus on accepting them while prioritising your self-protection to avoid harm**. The harsh reality is that such negative people and external circumstances are unlikely to change significantly, as they often lie beyond our control. While some may sincerely attempt to change, it does not happen frequently, leading to more disappointments. Repeated exposure to negative behaviour can result in increased pain, frustration and negativity in your life. People who tend to create negativity will likely continue to do so. The best solution is to distance yourself from them. Instead, prioritise developing your internal state of mind and reactions to such negativity. A common saying is that '**you do not need to drink the whole sea to realise it is salty'.** Therefore, you do not have to stay around them continuously to recognise that negative feelings are unlikely to change.

At times, when dealing with toxic people, you may encounter situations where you cannot completely avoid them and must maintain contact, such as with family members or work colleagues. They may emit negative energy and say things that are off-putting. **Learn to stay detached from such individuals if you must interact with them for any reason.** Once the necessary interaction is done, keep your distance from them entirely. For example, if you find yourself needing to interact with colleagues or individuals who bring negativity, such as when sharing an office space, it is beneficial to discuss only essential matters while maintaining some detachment. Don't amplify their presence or give excessive attention to those who cause us more pain. Dim your light and refrain from sharing your opinions and contributions with them. The toxicity may be temporary, but the energy lost can be significant—be aware of these individuals and try not to focus too much on those who seek to derail you. Instead, strive to be more thoughtful and mindful. Please pay more attention to those who help us unlock our potential.

The best way to handle someone who has hurt you with their words or actions is to refrain from reacting and adopt a nonchalant attitude. Avoid immediate responses; instead, create the impression that you don't care about the situation. Ask yourself, "Am I truly bothered by this?" and reinforce the notion by telling yourself, "I don't care." **By staying calm and composed and not reacting to hurtful actions, you can have a much more significant impact on the other person than you might expect.** Retaliating or responding with hateful messages or actions only perpetuates negativity. When you remain unaffected, the other person is often more impacted by your indifference. You are more likely to influence the other person's emotions by not caring and remaining unbothered. We must learn this valuable skill; others' actions and words should not affect us, allowing us to maintain emotional detachment. Demonstrating such detachment is also a sign of maturity.

Some individuals may verbally assert that they don't care; however, their actions might tell a different story, revealing their vulnerabilities. It is crucial to tell yourself that you don't care and to act consistently to demonstrate this to others. Although challenging, this mindset can be nurtured over time with practice. When you react to others' provocations, you give them power and allow them to control your emotions. It is crucial to resist this temptation. Instead, take control of your feelings by refraining from reacting and staying strong.

It is important to practice compassion towards individuals exhibiting negative behaviour, recognising that their actions reflect their own issues and weaknesses without allowing them to become victims. Responding with negativity only perpetuates a harmful cycle; therefore, learning to remain calm and non-reactive is crucial, albeit challenging. Sometimes, people worry about toxic individuals and want to resolve their issues, which can work against them. You don't have to spend your time and energy convincing them or helping them solve a problem; furthermore, you may become exhausted.

They should learn to address these issues themselves. They may carry considerable baggage of unresolved problems that can be offloaded onto you, and you are not responsible for it. Therefore, try to avoid them and ensure you don't spend too much time dealing with or fixing their problems. Beautiful things tend to happen when you distance yourself from negativity.

"Do not let the behaviour of others destroy your inner peace"
– Tibet's spiritual Leader Dalai Lama

Let's steer clear of individuals who bring us down – they can be like toxins to our spirit. Avoid endless conflicts, as they often drain our energy without resolution. Remember, it is not worth trying to please those who fail to appreciate your worth. By distancing ourselves from these harmful elements, we pave the way for a healthier, happier life. Doing this is truly an act of self-care, and you deserve all the goodness it brings! **Sometimes, maintaining distance can be a helpful solution.** You no longer react and argue but withdraw from these people who create negativity. We can forgive people, but that doesn't mean we accept their behaviour or trust them again. We must forgive them for our own good so we can let go and move on with our new lives.

'The people you choose to be around can greatly influence your growth, success, and overall experience, so be mindful of whom you surround yourself with.'
– Facebook founder Mark Zuckerberg

In essence, associating with the right people is not merely a matter of companionship; it is a strategic decision that can propel you towards your goals. The relationships you forge can help you move forward in harmony with their ambitions and commitments, thus amplifying your own potential for success. This path of surrounding yourself with inspiring and driven individuals will pave the way for continuous learning and growth, ultimately leading to a fulfilling and accomplished life journey.

'Associate with people who are likely to improve you' – Ancient Roman philosopher Seneca.

Golden Nuggets

- It is essential to consider whom you associate with, as the company you keep can greatly influence your life journey.

- The company you keep is not just a matter of social preference; it can profoundly influence your mindset, opportunities, and overall direction. Surrounding ourselves with positive-minded individuals can lead to greater success and happiness.

- Avoiding negativity is crucial for your well-being. Reduce the time spent on negative influences and concentrate more on those who offer you positive vibes and energy.

- Avoiding those who drain our energy helps us preserve our mental well-being.

- Individuals who tend to foster negativity are likely to continue doing so.

- Maintaining a certain level of detachment is helpful when interacting with individuals, especially when avoiding them altogether is impossible.

- Setting boundaries with people who bring negativity is not selfish; it is a vital act of self-preservation and self-care.

- It is essential to be compassionate towards individuals who exhibit negative behaviour, recognise that their actions reflect their own issues and weaknesses, and avoid spending excessive time dealing with or fixing their problems.

- The best way to handle someone who has hurt you with their words or actions is to avoid reacting and adopt a calm attitude.

- Responding with negativity only perpetuates a harmful cycle; therefore, it is essential, though challenging, to learn to stay calm and non-reactive.

The Voice of the Soul is Silence

Many people frequently inquire about how to connect with our soul and communicate with it. **The answer lies in silence, the true voice of the soul.** Engaging in silence is an art that fosters a deeper connection with your soul. Silence offers numerous benefits, including the gift of inner peace. In moments of silence, you can hear the rhythm of your breath and feel the stillness of your soul. This connection to your soul can only be achieved through silence, making it essential for attaining inner peace.

Finding a bit of silence can lead to incredible insights when you are facing challenges and feeling uncertain about your next steps. Taking about 10 to 15 minutes for calm reflection can help unlock meaningful answers by the end of that peaceful time. **'The answers you seek are written in the silence.'** In these quiet moments, your inner voice may begin to shine through, offering the gentle wisdom you've been seeking. This inner voice can become a trusted guide, sharing helpful insights and solutions. Embracing silence as a regular practice is beneficial, allowing your inner voice to grow stronger and more supportive over time. Ultimately, this practice can enhance your confidence in decision-making and is essential for exploring your identity and boosting your self-awareness.

As Confucius wisely stated, **"Silence is a true friend who never betrays."**

Silence helps to conserve energy and foster mental clarity. Our minds are often crowded with thoughts, and it is essential to practice silence to minimise this clutter and reduce the mental burden.

Moreover, talking and chatting can lead to fatigue for both our minds and bodies. Learn to speak precisely and communicate only what is necessary. This discipline requires you to express what is essential and conserve your energy by not talking more than you must. '**Measured, precise speech is a sign of clear thought and a serene mind**,' says Robin Sharma in his book, Who Will Cry When You Die.

Embracing silence greatly enhances our focus and concentration, particularly in bustling environments like the office with colleagues or at home among family. While external noise can often distract us, we have the capability to remain focused and boost our productivity by incorporating moments of silence into our day. **When we combine silence with solitude, the benefits become even more remarkable!** It nurtures our creativity, as a calm mind is far better at generating exciting and innovative ideas. By practising silence and solitude, you can truly unlock a treasure trove of creative potential.

As Meister Eckhart famously said, "**Nothing in all creation is so like God as silence.**"

When you practise silence, your mind becomes calmer. With a relaxed, quiet, and peaceful mind, you are in a much better position to make thoughtful decisions. Conversely, when a restless mind and agitation take over, it is easier to make unwise choices that may not serve you well.

'If you seek to elevate and upgrade your life, consider practising silence.'

You can start with just 15 to 30 minutes each day, gradually extending your practice to an hour as you discover all the wonderful benefits. I have seen many individuals fall in love with the beauty of silence, extending their practice to two hours or even choosing not to speak for four to six hours! The best part? There are no strict rules—it is entirely up to you! Taking time for silence and solitude can truly help you connect with your inner self, paving the way for greater peace and happiness.

In Hindu philosophy, there is a beautiful concept called "**Mouna,**" **which means silence.** This silence speaks volumes, representing peace of mind and a deep sense of inner calm. Buddhist monks have embraced silence as a key approach to nurturing their willpower and inner strength, viewing it as a vital part of their discipline. Many esteemed figures, such as Gandhi and Buddha, have championed silence to strengthen their connection with the soul. It is lovely to see silence gaining recognition as a meaningful spiritual practice today.

I have had the pleasure of chatting with some clients who dream of escaping to the woods or forests for moments of peace. Some love to sit quietly by a flowing stream, soaking in tranquillity, while others prefer the breathtaking view from mountaintops as they savour the beauty of the sunset. These cherished experiences often stem from our deep-rooted desire for inner peace, gently beckoning to us. It is heartening to see that the practice of silence is becoming increasingly popular. Many people are choosing to retreat into silence for days or even weeks, allowing themselves to truly embrace stillness and surrender. Engaging in practices like meditation and mindfulness can be wonderful ways to connect with one's soul and find deeper peace and happiness. However, I have noticed that some people find meditation a bit challenging or may not fully understand mindfulness. In these instances, **embracing silence can be a much simpler and profoundly rewarding path to take.**

Anyone seeking greater inner peace and happiness must practice the art of silence. **Embracing silence can establish a foundation for deeper practices like meditation and mindfulness, paving the way for a more fulfilling and tranquil life.** Spending 30 minutes daily in solitude and silence is usually advisable and viewed as an excellent habit to nurture our souls. Commit to a vow of silence for half an hour a day.

"Silence is an ocean. Speech is a river. When the ocean is searching for you, don't walk into the river. Listen to the ocean." quote by Rumi, a Persian poet and Islamic scholar. This meaningful quote suggests that there is a depth and stillness in silence (the ocean) that can be more powerful than the constant movement and noise of speech (the river). It encourages us to seek out peace and tranquillity and appreciate the quiet, profound aspects of our life instead of becoming absorbed in the incessant chatter of everyday life.

Golden Nuggets

- Silence can provide inner peace and enhance your connection with your soul.

- Silence can yield valuable solutions when you are faced with problems. Spending about 10 to 15 minutes in calm reflection can help unlock meaningful answers by the end of that peaceful time.

- Silence helps our inner voice grow louder and more helpful over time. It can enhance your confidence in decision-making.

- Silence fosters creativity and boosts focus and concentration.

- Combining silence with solitude makes the benefits even more remarkable.

- Silence and solitude will help you grow. If you want to elevate and enhance your life, consider practising silence.

- Embracing silence can establish the foundation for deeper practices such as meditation and mindfulness.

Meditate to Harmonise the Mind and Body

**'In moments of madness, meditation has helped
me find moments of serenity, and I would like to think
that it would help provide young people a quiet
haven in a not-so-quiet world'**
– Singer and songwriter Sir Paul McCartney

Meditation is an ancient practice that dates back thousands of years. Various cultures have embraced it for mind-body harmony. Initially, people were unaware of its true value, but modern research has expanded our understanding of how meditation works, and its benefits are backed up by scientific evidence.

The true purpose of meditation practice is to 'improve focus and prevent the mind from wandering.' Meditation helps to create **'singular thoughts.'** When you observe a person meditating, you may not notice much happening beyond their breathing or the repetition of a particular sound, phrase, or mantra. However, significant brain activity can now be studied using advanced instruments such as EEG (Electroencephalogram) to detect electrical activity in the brain and functional MRI scans, which can identify changes in various parts of the brain during meditation.

Research has shown that meditation can positively impact the brain and mind. In an Indian study, **92% of meditation users reported stress reduction.** In terms of mental health, meditation is effective in reducing symptoms of anxiety, depression, pain, and traumatic memories while decreasing the frequency of negative recollections from the past. It also has benefits, including reduced stress levels and improved sleep quality. Additionally, it helps improve thinking and concentration abilities. Over the long-term, it can enhance problem-solving skills and give individuals the mental strength to overcome emotional challenges. On a physical level, meditation can lower blood pressure and strengthen heart function.

It is crucial to engage with your mind and work on gaining control over it; otherwise, your mind may dominate you. Meditation plays a significant role in achieving this mental discipline. It can help eliminate distracting thoughts and extract valuable ideas from your mind.

Significant changes have been observed in individuals who are long-term meditators.

Meditation helps reshape your brain and forms new neural pathways. Brain studies have shown that regularly meditating individuals exhibit changes in specific brain areas that are larger or thicker than expected. This indicates that **neurons in the brain are forming stronger connections through meditation**. These findings relate to regions involved in thinking, concentration, emotional processing, problem- solving, and sensory control. We can create new neural pathways by training and retraining our minds through techniques like meditation. Practising meditation in the longer term can strengthen these new circuits. This phenomenon is known as **neuroplasticity, which refers to the brain's potential for mental change through training.**

Meditation helps maintain "**grey matter density**" in our brain, which is responsible for memory, speech, emotions, decision-making, self-control, movements, and sensory perception such as seeing and hearing. Ageing reduces grey matter density; however, for long-term meditation practitioners, grey matter remains intact.

Long-term meditation reduces the **activation of the amygdala,** a pea-sized organ responsible for emotional processing, including fear. Increased activity in the amygdala results in heightened emotional arousal, stimulating the emotional centres of the brain. When we experience strong emotions, we often become less rational, making decisions based on feelings rather than effectively utilising the rational part of our brain. With reduced amygdala activation, long-term meditators can manage situations calmly instead of succumbing to a fight-or-flight response.

Regarding the benefits of meditation, when Gautama Buddha was asked, "What have you gained from meditation?" he replied, "Nothing." However, let me share what I have lost: anger, anxiety, depression, insecurity, and the fear of old age and death.

Many people mistakenly believe that meditation is a religious practice, but this perception is inaccurate. There are both religious and non-religious (secular) forms of meditation. The non-religious method is often referred to as guided meditation, which is frequently practised in counselling and group sessions.

There are different types of meditation, and there is no one specific way to meditate. However, it is helpful to have a basic understanding of the common types. Find a method that suits you best and commit to practising it consistently.

Body-Centred Meditation: One of the most popular practices is body-centred meditation, commonly referred to as body scanning. In this process, you gently concentrate on the physical sensations you can experience throughout your body.

Emotion-Centred Meditation: Next, we will explore emotion-centred meditation, which focuses on a specific emotion. For instance, you might reflect on situations or people that bring you joy or contemplate how to be kind and grateful to others.

Mantra Meditation: Another common type of meditation is mantra meditation, in which you repeatedly recite a specific mantra, word, or phrase either aloud or silently in your mind. You focus on this phrase or sound for a defined period. This practice is prevalent in many religions, including Buddhism and Hinduism.

Movement Meditation: The fourth type is movement meditation, which involves focusing on your breath and the rhythm of inhaling and exhaling.

Mindfulness Meditation: Mindfulness meditation is a relatively recent and increasingly popular form of meditation. This practice involves staying aware and fully conscious of what is happening now rather than allowing your mind to wander or worrying about the past or future. I have discussed this in detail in the chapter on mindfulness. Meditation serves as a tool for developing a consistent mindfulness practice.

Visual-Based Meditation: Visual-based meditation is a type of meditation frequently practised in group settings. It involves focusing on something visible, either through observation or by visualising a mental image, to enhance concentration. One of the most common practices in South Asian countries is gazing at a flame, candle, diva, or light source for extended periods. It is believed that this stimulates the third eye or the pineal gland. Long-term practice can improve alertness, intuition, creativity, and sleep patterns.

The key to effective meditation is a long-term commitment and regular, disciplined practice. Consistent and extended practice is essential to reap the benefits of meditation. I have noticed that many individuals who are just beginning their meditation journey tend to give up easily, often claiming it is unhelpful. Without establishing a proper daily practice discipline for a significant duration, experiencing the full advantages of meditation can be challenging. Many clients have mentioned that they do not have time to meditate in the mornings. However, meditation can be practised at any time of day; it is important to choose a time that works best for you. While most people prefer to meditate in the morning or at night before bed, it is perfectly acceptable to practice at any time.

> **'My life is better when I get still regularly.**
> **Call it meditation or call it quiet time - doesn't matter.**
> **The benefits are the same.'**
> – American host and television producer, Oprah Winfrey

Practising meditation can last anywhere from just one minute to ten minutes, an hour, or even several hours, depending on individual needs and time availability. The duration is not the most critical factor; instead, you should aim to set aside a specific time for meditation and integrate it into your routine. This can be the most challenging aspect, as many people struggle to find time for it. To gain the most remarkable benefits, dedicate time to your practice and strive to meditate in a quiet and calm environment. Get comfortable while meditating, and don't worry excessively about posture. Assume a relaxed position without putting undue pressure on your muscles, bones, and joints. Numerous videos, podcasts, and teaching materials are now available online, but if you need guidance, consider seeking help from an expert in meditation. Joining meditation groups can also be beneficial, as participants can motivate each other to maintain consistency.

The true purpose of meditation practice is **to prevent the mind from wandering.**

Recent research utilising EEG technology indicates that long-term meditators experience greater focus and less mind wandering during meditation than those who do not. The standard brain frequencies identified in long-term meditators, as recorded by EEGs, consist of **"relaxed theta and alpha waves"**. Regular meditation practice can increase the prevalence of these two waves. What does this imply for the average person? The key takeaway is that both theta and alpha waves are essential frequencies that can promote a sense of calmness and enhance creativity and problem-solving abilities over time when one engages in consistent meditation. As alpha frequencies take precedence in the brain, the benefits become pronounced, including improved mood, enhanced memory functions, and better learning skills. There is a rise in the activity of the parasympathetic nervous system, which is a network of nerves that relaxes the body. It helps **slow down breathing and heart rate**. Over time, practising meditation serves as a mediator that connects and strengthens the mind-body connection, allowing both aspects to communicate effectively and achieve a state of equilibrium.

How to do a simple meditation: Find a quiet place or room with minimal lighting. Play some calming music and then close your eyes. Focus solely on your breathing. Inhale through your nose for 3 seconds and exhale through your mouth for 3 seconds. Continue this for at least 5 minutes. Avoid thinking about anything other than your breath. Try not to let distracting thoughts disturb your focus during these 5 minutes of meditation, as this greatly helps in calming your mind.

During meditation, try to relax your mind and avoid drifting into negative thoughts or feelings that may upset or anger you. It can be challenging to sit and meditate at first, as other thoughts may distract you. However, don't worry—keep trying. The power of meditation emerges through consistent practice. Aim to practice daily for several weeks to months to realise its benefits. Begin with one minute of meditation and gradually increase the duration. Strive to reach nearly 10 minutes of daily meditation within a few weeks. You can extend this time, even up to 60 minutes, but five minutes is the minimum. To gain the most remarkable benefits, spend time on your practice and aim to meditate in a peaceful and tranquil environment.

Golden Nuggets

- The true purpose of meditation practice is to improve focus and prevent the mind from wandering.

- Meditation promotes positive transformations in both the body and mind, establishing a strong connection between the two.

- Meditation plays a vital role in developing the mental discipline necessary to control a wandering mind. It can help eliminate distractions and draw out valuable ideas from within.

- Practising meditation over the long-term can strengthen neural circuits in the brain, increase grey matter density, reduce activation of the amygdala, and enhance the network of nerve fibres associated with relaxation.

- The standard brain frequencies found in long-term meditators include relaxed theta and alpha waves, which promote calmness, enhance creativity, and improve memory, learning, and problem-solving skills over time.

- The key to effective meditation is a long-term commitment along with regular, disciplined practice.

Nothing Compares to Maintaining a Daily Reading Routine

"The more you read, the more things you will know.
The more that you learn, the more places you will go"
– Dr. Seuss, American children's author

Research indicates that 85% of millionaires and billionaires in the US today are first-generation, self-made individuals, while only about 15% inherited their wealth. When interviewed about one of the secrets behind their success, many first-generation self-made millionaires provide a simple answer: they read one book each week, primarily focusing on self-help and other knowledge-rich literature rather than merely fiction. While fiction has its merits, self-help books offer invaluable ideas

and perspectives. The insights gained from a well-structured book can be worth millions of dollars, helping you achieve your goals.

Often, a single powerful idea can significantly impact your journey to success. This idea may arise from self-help books or other literature filled with knowledge. There's a popular saying: "**One good idea is worth $1 million**." Regular reading can help you uncover these transformative insights and ideas.

Sadly, many people claim they don't have time to read. However, it is essential to **identify pockets of free time** in your daily routine—such as during your morning and evening commutes, breaks at work, or while waiting for meetings to start. Make the most of every opportunity to read. Additionally, always carry a book with you.

This way, you can take advantage of unexpected downtime and seize chances to enrich your knowledge.

Many successful individuals have cultivated a reading habit in their bedtime routines. Even if you read just a few pages before falling asleep, the key is to incorporate reading regularly into your daily life. I recommend setting aside specific time blocks in your schedule for reading—just as you would for other essential activities. Nowadays, even if you don't have physical books, you can enjoy audiobooks while engaging in activities like working out, walking, exercising, or cooking.

"Spending time each day reading and gaining knowledge is extremely beneficial. Dedicating just half an hour daily to reading can unlock a world of knowledge and imagination, profoundly transforming your mind"

Reading can also strengthen your relationships by offering opportunities to spend time with family and children, turning shared reading into a bonding experience. I have always enjoyed reading books to my children, Shakthi and Adithya.

Many people in book clubs form strong friendships and meaningful connections.

There are lots of advantages in reading books regularly.

Regular reading engages brain regions associated with comprehension and vocabulary, ultimately enhancing communication skills. **Reading can spark creativity, provide fresh ideas, and stimulate new thought processes.** As individuals read more books, they often become **better problem solvers**. Engaging with a book is a calming activity that helps you relax and unwind, improving sleep quality and onset.

Reading a good book is often regarded as a **stress reliever**. Many find it an excellent way to unwind and temporarily escape daily problems. Replace the habit of watching TV with reading a good book; a strong piece of advice is to swap screen time for reading before bed. Prioritise reading over binge-watching shows or scrolling through social media. This simple change can enhance your knowledge and provide you with greater peace of mind.

"Reading good books is like engaging in conversation with the most cultivated minds of past centuries who composed them, or rather, taking part in a well-conducted dialogue in which such minds reveal to us only the best of their thoughts."
– French Philosopher and Scientist René Descartes.
In simple terms, reading good books is like having a conversation with the greatest minds of the past centuries

Studies suggest that reading sharpens memory and cognitive function. By reading regularly, you keep your mind active and engaged. Reading protects cognitive function in later life. In the long-term, frequent reading activities are associated with a reduced risk of cognitive decline (memory and learning for older adults at all levels of education. It has also been shown to slow the progression of cognitive decline, even in individuals with cognitive impairment and early dementia. Maintaining focus and concentration for extended periods can be challenging in a world full of distractions. However, regular reading helps one regain control and enhances one's ability to concentrate. This advice is especially valuable for teenagers and young adults who face attention challenges.

**"The man who doesn't read has no advantage
over the man who can't read."**
– American writer and humourist Mark Twain

If you are unsure where to start, consider following the **10-minute rule.** For instance, you might keep a book beside your bed and dedicate 10 minutes to reading before sleep. Gradually increase your reading time over time to 15, then 20, and eventually to 30 minutes or more if you can. Keeping the book close to your bed and consistently following this routine will help you extend your reading time. By placing the book within reach, you create visual reminders to read before bedtime, helping you develop this beneficial habit.

I often read for at least an hour before drifting off to sleep. Much of the knowledge I have gained, and the insights involved in writing this book stem from my bedtime reading. The ideas and insights I have acquired through this practice have been instrumental in my journey to success. Therefore, I urge you to make reading a regular habit and enjoy its long-term benefits.

What are you waiting for? Numerous resources are available to help you discover which books are worth reading and to find valuable recommendations and excellent reads for self- improvement. Compile a monthly list of suggested books and dedicate at least 30 minutes each night to reading. This routine will enrich your knowledge and spark brilliant ideas, leading to greater success and happiness in life. Read great books to educate yourself. Choose quality books for self-education. **"There is more treasure in books than in all the pirate's loot on treasure Island"-** Walt Disney

Some people prefer reading on screens using their mobile phones, tablets, or iPads. Research shows that we learn more from reading on paper than from screens. We process printed words more deeply than digital content, especially when the material is informational rather than purely narrative. A study published in the Review of Educational Research indicates that reading print can enhance comprehension skills by six to eight times more than reading digital text. This research analysed over two dozen studies on reading comprehension published between 2000 and 2022, involving nearly half a million participants.

Have you heard of the term **"digital dementia"**? German neuroscientist Dr. Manfred Spitzer popularised a term that describes cognitive decline, impaired thinking, difficulties concentrating, learning challenges, and memory issues resulting from excessive smartphone, tablet, and computer usage. Young adults who overuse internet and Wi-Fi devices may exhibit diminished attention spans and memory retention, mirroring signs of dementia. Excessivetechnology use can trigger dementia- like changes and lead to cognitive decline. Many individuals scroll through social media at night, delaying sleep onset. Screen time stimulates the brain, complicating sleep initiation, resulting in late bedtimes and reduced productivity. To improve sleep quality, it is advisable to avoid using mobile phones or other gadgets before bedtime. Instead, I recommend establishing a positive habit: creating a bedtime routine of reading books free from gadgets. Consider engaging in alternative activities such as reading a book. With regular practice, you can fall asleep in about 30 minutes. Digital dependency is a modern hazard; we should learn to unplug to thrive. Prioritising reading over screen time enriches our knowledge and creativity while fostering a deeper connection with ourselves and the world around us. This shift can lead to more meaningful leisure activities and a greater appreciation for the written word. Replace it with a beneficial habit like bedtime reading, which enhances your knowledge and promotes sleep. By consciously reducing our digital screen time and replacing it with reading good books, we can cultivate a more enriching and fulfilling experience.

In essence **reading books offer a unique opportunity for intellectual engagement**, allowing us to explore new ideas and perspectives. Reading stimulates our imagination, enhances our vocabulary, and improves our critical thinking skills. Unlike the often passive consumption of digital media, reading encourages active participation and reflection. Moreover, setting aside time for a good book can serve as a form of relaxation and mindfulness, helping to reduce stress and enhance mental well-being

Golden Nuggets

- Read a book every week, focusing mainly on self-help and other knowledge-rich literature instead of just fiction.

- Reading helps generate great ideas, and one powerful idea can significantly change your journey to success.

- As individuals read more books, it can stimulate new thought processes, and they often become better problem solvers.

- Reading sharpens memory and cognitive function. By reading regularly, you keep your mind active and slow down the progression of cognitive decline in older adults.

- We engage more deeply with printed words than with digital content, particularly when the material is informational rather than purely narrative.

- Seize every opportunity to read by carrying a book to take advantage of unexpected downtime and enrich your knowledge.

- Substitute nighttime smartphone or gadget use with a productive habit, such as reading before bed, which enhances knowledge and promotes better sleep.

- Explore quality books for your education. Select excellent reads for self-improvement

Allowing Yourself Breaks is Fundamental for a Healthy Lifestyle

**"There is virtue in work and virtue in rest.
Use both and overlook neither."**
– Alan Cohen, popular author and life coach

Regular intervals of rest are crucial for maintaining well- being. Like most electronic devices that rely on batteries, our bodies and minds operate in a similar way and require regular recharging to energise us. **Taking adequate breaks allows us to recharge effectively.** They cannot function at their best without proper rest and replenishment.

Incorporating breaks into your routine promotes better health. **Prioritising self-care and rest is crucial for maintaining your well-being**. Recognising when your mind and body need recharging is incredibly important! Once you become aware of this, it is essential to address it; neglecting it can significantly impact your health. To check if you feel fully charged, take a moment to reflect on your mood and overall state. Give yourself a score from 0 to 10, where zero is the lowest and ten is the highest. If you score three or lower, it is a sign that your mental and physical batteries might be running low, indicating that it is time to pause and take the necessary steps.

The common misconception is that our brains can handle endless tasks without breaks. However, recent research shows that this is not the case at all! **Our brains truly require breaks throughout the day.** Taking short, frequent breaks can work wonders for your mind. These breaks refresh your mind, providing clarity and insights into specific problems. By resting during breaks, the prefrontal cortex (the front part of the brain), responsible for planning, problem-solving, and productivity, enters a restful state, allowing clearer thinking. A rested prefrontal cortex can enhance cognitive function and decision-making abilities. New ideas may emerge from the subconscious, making problem-solving easier. Therefore, avoid working continuously and take regular breaks from work. **Regular downtime is mandatory for our brains to feel rejuvenated.**

During breaks:

- Stay hydrated by drinking water.

- Stretch your legs to avoid stiffness.

- Choose healthy snacks like nuts, seeds, and fresh fruits to enhance energy levels.

- Engage in light exercise and stretching.

- Improve blood circulation by taking a walk.

- To calm your mind, enjoy peaceful silence, practice deep breathing exercises, or meditate for a few minutes.

These small actions can recharge your brain and enhance your overall cognitive function. "**Almost everything will work again if you unplug it for a few minutes, including you,**" said American novelist and writer Anne Lamott. Isn't this a valuable hack to follow?

The brain is like a **charged battery:** it must be recharged regularly to remain alert and active. The brain typically focuses for 25 minutes when you study or work effectively. Remember, approximately 80% of energy is spent on mental activities rather than physical ones. However, like phone batteries that take a few minutes to recharge, the brain requires a few minutes. Therefore, you should take a five-minute break. After this five- minute recharge, you can return to your studies or work for another half an hour, allowing for a break every half an hour to recharge for five minutes before returning.

Regular downtime is essential for rejuvenation and clarity.

Rest if you feel unwell. If you are sick, don't feel obligated to continue. A short break for a few days will help your body heal more quickly.

On hectic days, consider adjusting your pace and reducing the intensity of your activities. For instance, when you are tired, you might opt for lighter workouts at the gym instead of your usual routine or choose simpler tasks at work rather than more complex ones. If you are feeling down, you could spend less time on social media. This approach helps conserve energy and prevents you from quickly depleting your reserves. By shifting your focus away from high-energy tasks, you can better maintain your overall well-being and save those tasks for when you feel refreshed. In the past, many people believed they had to push through their challenges, regardless of how drained they felt. This mindset can cause more harm than good.

Have you heard the term **'traffic control' of the mind**? After every hour of work, take a one-minute pause for meditation, deep breathing, stretching or positive affirmations to slow down your mind and prepare for the next hour. This practice helps maintain a high vibration even while you are in action. Practice traffic control of the mind to help monitor your thoughts. When we work continuously, our minds can become flooded with a myriad of thoughts and ideas, pulling us in various directions. This mental overflow can create chaos, akin to traffic jams, and sometimes even lead to "accidents" in our thinking. Just like roads require traffic control mechanisms to prevent accidents, our minds need a similar system. Visualise how unmanaged thoughts can lead to chaos and decreased productivity, much like a traffic jam. To facilitate this mental traffic control, it is essential to incorporate regular breaks throughout the day. During these breaks, we can pause to manage the flow of our thoughts and clear mental clutter. Engaging in a mindful traffic control process during break times allows us to reset and prepare for the next "journey" of focused work. By taking these moments to breathe, reflect, and organise our thoughts, we can enhance our productivity and maintain a clearer, more focused mind for the challenges ahead. The analogy of traffic control mechanisms is particularly insightful and helps us understand the importance of taking regular breaks during work. I encourage readers to consider the benefits of incorporating breaks into their work routine.

We also need to take a break every few days. A weekend break is essential for reducing stress. If you work for five days, take a two-day break. Go on a holiday for at least a week every few months to recharge your energy levels. Taking holidays periodically offers numerous benefits for physical, mental, and emotional well-being. A break from daily monotonous routines and responsibilities can significantly lower stress levels, allowing individuals to recharge and return with a fresh perspective. Moreover, holidays provide an opportunity to spend quality time with family and friends, which can strengthen relationships. Regular breaks can enhance overall productivity, as individuals often feel more motivated and focused when they return from a holiday. Stepping away from familiar environments can also stimulate creativity and inspire new ideas when individuals come back to their daily lives. Incorporating regular holidays into one's schedule can lead to a happier, healthier, and more fulfilling life while maintaining a healthy work-life balance, ensuring that work doesn't consume all of one's time and energy.

Many people believe that relaxation is a luxury, but that is not true. **Adequate rest and feeling relaxed are necessities, not luxuries**. When people feel stressed, they often ask me what therapy they can pursue. My simple answer is that taking a break from routine is the best form of treatment. It is okay to take a break.

If we neglect to rest, we won't be able to recharge, which can lead to a decline in our energy levels, burnout and eventually your body will take rest for you but it probably won't be at a convenient time . To avoid this outcome, it is crucial to prioritise taking regular breaks in all circumstances to recharge our body and mental batteries and sustain our productivity.

**"If you don't have time for a break,
you definitely need a break"**

– Dominique Anderson

Golden Nuggets

- Adequate break time allows our bodies and minds to recharge effectively. Without proper rest, they cannot perform at their best.

- Resting during breaks enables the prefrontal cortex—the brain's front portion responsible for planning, problem-solving, and productivity—to achieve a state of relaxation, thereby promoting clearer thinking.

- Taking breaks rejuvenates your mind, enhances clarity, and provides insights into problems.

- Regular breaks can prevent mental fatigue, making you less vulnerable to distractions.

- Incorporating regular breaks into one's schedule can lead to a happier and more fulfilling life while fostering a healthy lifestyle.

- Taking adequate rest and feeling relaxed are necessities, not luxuries.

- Incorporate short breaks into your schedule to rest, recharge, and optimise your productivity.

Sleep Like a Baby and Slumber Peacefully

You must have heard phrases like "Rest like a log," "Sleep like a rock," "Snooze without a care," "Drift into a deep sleep," and "Have a restful night's sleep." All of these phrases convey the idea of sleeping well or peacefully, similar to 'sleep like a baby'.

Why is it important to get enough sleep?

Most guidelines recommend aiming for at least eight hours of sleep. Sleep helps maintain energy and is essential for proper bodily functions and brain health. Keeping your mind calm and clear, resting and sleeping helps to energise it. One way to achieve this is by waking up after a good, restful, and peaceful night's sleep, which leaves you feeling refreshed the next day. Both sleep quality and quantity are important; inadequate sleep can hinder concentration, memory, and overall performance. Like all great adventures, the journey toward better mental health requires sufficient sleep.

Think of the brain as a car that requires petrol, diesel, or another form of fuel. It consumes a considerable amount of oxygen and glucose from the body, both of which are crucial for proper brain function. However, after working continuously for 8 to 10 hours, your brain gradually depletes its fuel reserves. To replenish this energy, adequate sleep is essential. **Aim for 8 to 9 hours of sleep each night to refuel your brain and prevent exhaustion.** Just as you refill your car, you must recharge your brain through proper sleep. You have to spend money to fuel your car, but you don't have to spend any money to fuel your brain. However, you must allocate adequate time for it, which is sleeping for 8 hours.

New brain pathways and connections form during sleep, enhancing thinking, memory, and concentration. Your brain may be strained if you don't sleep well each day. Sleep deprivation can lead to mental exhaustion, cognitive fog, and difficulties in making even simple decisions. When you sleep, your body temperature drops, and brain and muscle activity diminish, allowing you to experience greater rest. **Our vital organs also engage in self-repair during deep sleep.** Insufficient sleep can disrupt metabolic functions, leading to various health issues such as diabetes, hypertension, fatty liver, stroke, and dementia. The body performs maintenance during sleep, regulating hormones and producing proteins. This process restores energy resources, repairs cell tissues, and boosts the immune system. At night, cortisol levels, often known as the stress hormone, decrease. As bedtime approaches, cortisol production diminishes; however, inadequate sleep can elevate stress hormone levels.

Maintaining a consistent circadian rhythm by waking up and going to bed at the same time each day is essential. When darkness falls, certain hormones activate in our brains, reducing alertness levels, making us feel more relaxed, and aiding in sleep. Melatonin is secreted at night, and its production increases, helping the body prepare for rest. Its circulating levels follow a precise circadian rhythm, being high at night and low during the day (Cardinali and Pévet, 1998.

If you don't get enough sleep—defined as 7 to 8 hours a night—it is linked to the greater accumulation of harmful fat mass, also known as visceral fat, around vital organs such as the liver, heart, and lungs. This can potentially result in serious metabolic health complications. **"Not getting the appropriate amount of sleep, which is 7 to 8 hours a night, is associated with a greater visceral fat mass,"** says Cardiologist Sherrie Khadanga from the University of Vermont Medical Centre in South Burlington. Other studies replicate similar findings. Inadequate sleep can cause fat to be diverted to vital organs in the body, such as the heart and liver. Insufficient sleep can elevate the circulation of appetite-stimulating hormones throughout the body. Poor sleep activates brain regions that trigger cravings for and promote the consumption of junk food.

Sleep duration is not fixed for everyone; it varies from person to person. However, it is crucial to **maintain a consistent routine**, going to sleep and waking up at the same time each day. For instance, you might go to bed at 10:00 pm and wake up at 6:00 am.

It is advisable to keep phones, laptops, iPads, and other gadgets out of the bedroom before sleep. Out of sight is out of mind. This way, you can avoid the visual cues that tempt you to check electronic devices. This issue has a scientific basis; nighttime phone use exposes the brain to bright light, tricking it into believing it is daytime and hindering the transition to sleep. The blue light (photons emitted by phones and gadgets also suppresses melatonin production, further obstructing sleep and morning alertness. When you use gadgets and look at bright lights, the brain produces certain neurochemicals and releases daytime hormones, which can make you feel more alert and make it difficult to sleep. As a result, more thoughts may arise due to your brain being active, leading to overthinking and disturbances in falling asleep. The bright light at night can confuse our brains; therefore, sleeping in a dark environment with the lights off is vital. If you have visual cues and triggers nearby, you may find yourself watching your phone or other gadgets, negatively impacting your sleep. During your sleep time, ensure that your phones and devices are kept out of reach, and try placing them on a charger at a distance you can't reach from the bed or in another room where they are entirely out of reach. Avoid overstimulating yourself by playing video games or watching horror movies. Train yourself to fall asleep in bed rather than staying awake, and ensure your bed is associated with sleep. Completely detach yourself from the digital world. A helpful mantra to remember is, **'Practice digital detox one hour before sleep.'**

Have you heard of the modern term "revenge bedtime procrastination"?

Revenge bedtime procrastination occurs when individuals stay up late to enjoy time alone instead of going to bed. This concept originated in China. It involves delaying sleep at night by engaging in activities like excessive social media use and binge- watching television. This behaviour is often seen as a response to stress and can arise from a lack of free time during the day. People intentionally stay up late to reclaim their personal time after a long, stressful day, sacrificing sleep to enjoy some "me time." Those experiencing significant stress, feelings of burnout, or a busy schedule may partake in this psychological phenomenon, staying awake to decompress after a challenging day. For example, an individual might work for 9 to 12 hours and find it difficult to engage in social media or relax during the day. As a result, they may develop a screen addiction at night, justifying it as revenge bedtime procrastination. Later bedtimes can lead to sleep deprivation, adversely affecting mental and physical well-being.

The best way to combat insomnia is to prioritise sleep, establish a proper bedtime, maintain routines, limit social media use, and reduce screen time before bed by turning off devices at least an hour before bed. **Establishing a relaxing nightly routine can aid in preparing for sleep**. Our body, mind, and brain require preparation before bedtime, and these preparation rituals are known as pre-sleep routines. These routines involve engaging in calming and enjoyable activities for at least a few minutes before sleep. Commonly, individuals take a soothing bath, listen to music, or read a book. Such activities also assist your brain in transitioning into sleep mode, with this shift occurring over the next few minutes to an hour. Don't jump onto your bed expecting to fall asleep immediately; this typically doesn't occur. Taking a lukewarm shower before bedtime activates the parasympathetic nervous system, which is responsible for the relaxation response. This process lowers blood pressure and heart rate while slowing your breathing, creating a sense of calm. Isn't it wonderful? As a result, you feel more relaxed before sleep and can enhance the quality of your rest.

If you have been awake for more than half an hour, get up and do something relaxing until you feel sleepy. You can listen to soothing music or relaxation audios, read a book, or engage in another activity. **Don't let yourself worry about things in bed —write them down before going to sleep (Journaling) and remind yourself to deal with them tomorrow.** You really cannot sort out anything in the middle of the night, so rather than thinking about situations you can't change then, it is better to resolve to face them the next day and focus on enjoying the present moment to help you return to sleep.

Journaling reduces emotional burdens and creates mental space. We sleep with fewer clothes on our bodies to feel physically lighter. Journaling lightens your mind, just like shedding physical weight. By jotting down a list of tasks to accomplish the next day, you can feel emotionally lighter and avoid overthinking. This practice allows you to sleep without emotional overload, enabling you to address these thoughts tomorrow. Additionally, using an alarm clock to wake up is a helpful strategy. Avoid sleeping during the day and limit excessive daytime napping. Some people prefer taking power naps of 10 to 15 minutes during their break, which is fine. However, these naps should not be extended, as sleeping for prolonged periods during the day is not advisable.

Establish a morning routine and wake up at the same time each day. Upon waking, try to get some sunlight. This will help you achieve the necessary vitamin D levels, which is vital for your body's absorption of calcium and phosphate. Vitamin D supports the health of bones, teeth, and muscles and is essential for the immune, nervous, and musculoskeletal systems. A vitamin D deficiency can lead to symptoms such as excessive fatigue, muscle weakness, body aches, bone pain, and mood changes.

Golden Nuggets

- Most guidelines recommend aiming for at least eight hours of sleep.

- Our vital organs engage in self-repair during deep sleep and the body conducts maintenance work by regulating hormones and producing proteins. This process replenishes energy reserves, repairs cellular tissue, and strengthens the immune system.

- Adequate sleep improves one's thinking abilities, decision-making capacity, concentration, memory and brain efficiency.

- Our body, mind and brain need some preparation before sleep, and these activities are known as pre-sleep routines.

- Gadgets and electronic devices, including phones, should be kept out of the bedroom before bedtime or further beyond reach from your bed. Practice the good habit of ensuring a digital detox one hour before sleep.

- Don't let worry consume you in bed. Instead, write your thoughts down before sleeping (journaling) and remind yourself to address them tomorrow.

Physical Exercise is Significant for Optimal Health

To achieve true success and happiness, prioritising fitness and health is essential.

Life can present many challenges related to money, work, or relationships. However, everything else seems to fade into the background when faced with a health issue. Your health becomes the main priority; suddenly, it feels like the only problem that truly matters. It is essential to take care of your body by prioritising both fitness and health; they are treasures that should never be taken for granted. Physical activity is absolutely necessary for well-being.

Although I may not be a fitness expert or a dietitian, as a doctor and someone who has been going to the gym regularly for more than 20 years, I am eager to share some insights on the importance of maintaining our health and fitness. After all, without good health, true success and happiness can often feel out of reach, even when we excel in other areas of life. This chapter offers foundational thoughts on fitness, exercise, and physical activities. Various research studies and evidence-based practices support the insights you will discover here.

Many people consider fitness to be just about exercise, but that's not accurate. **The term fitness encompasses both exercise and diet.** Diet combined with exercise equals fitness. Many individuals are unaware of this and believe that fitness solely involves physical exercise. Two essential elements of fitness are engaging in exercise or physical activities and enjoying a healthy, balanced diet in moderation. **It is crucial to make fitness our top priority!** Exercise energises our bodies and minds, while nutritious food serves as fuel for our well-being. It paves the way to look great, feel fantastic, and function at our best.

Fitness requires your attention nearly every day. Although being fit, becoming fit, and maintaining fitness are not easy tasks, they are achievable goals. Regular physical activity is a form of self-care. Aim to exercise regularly, ideally on most days of the week. Exercise is an excellent way to burn off unwanted calories, helping you maintain a healthy weight while boosting your energy levels. It motivates you to stay active, builds your muscles, and improves your overall tone, making you appear and feel fit! By increasing blood flow throughout your body, exercise improves your cardiovascular health, providing you with an extra boost of energy. It is also beneficial for keeping your joints loose and supple, helping to prevent discomfort such as joint pain and arthritis.

Health experts recommend at least 30 minutes of moderate exercise five days a week, totalling 150 minutes weekly. You can divide this into 30 minutes per day or create your own plan based on your schedule. You can take one or two rest days in between to allow your muscles to recover, which helps reboot your body. According to the Centres for Disease Control and Prevention (CDC), adults should engage in moderate-intensity aerobic activity, such as brisk walking, for at least **150 minutes per week.** The optimal amount of physical activity to enhance cardiovascular health is four to five times a week, consistently throughout a lifetime (Cooper Clinic).

The connection between physical activities and health has been established, and exercise should be viewed as a cost- effective form of medication universally prescribed as a first- line treatment for almost every chronic disease.

**'Those who do not find time for exercise have
to find time for illness'**
– Edward Smith Stanley, Ex-Prime Minister of the UK

Please don't say you have 'no time to exercise'. You are solely responsible for your body, and you should take care of it. Nobody can do it for you. Try to spend an hour every day doing some form of physical exercise to stay healthy. You can do it, and it is an easily achievable goal!

According to the Harvard Alumni study, **for every hour you exercise, you can extend your lifespan by two hours. This finding is truly remarkable.** Therefore, committing to regular exercise is essential for increasing your chances of living longer. Incorporating exercise into your routine becomes a fundamental principle for enhancing longevity.

The Journal of Ageing Research published a literature review highlighting that most authoritative studies indicate that physically active individuals who maintain consistency can expect to live up to **7 years longer** than those who are sedentary. "**Your body is the temple of your identity**", so it is our primary responsibility to take care of it.

Regular exercise is essential for our brain function and mental health. Research from the University of British Columbia indicates that just thirty minutes of vigorous exercise daily can enhance performance in attention, problem-solving, and memory tests. Regular exercise stimulates the production of new brain cells in the hippocampus, increasing both its size and the number of hippocampal cells, which can improve memory and learning abilities.

Additionally, exercise releases neurotransmitters such as endorphins, dopamine, and serotonin. Dopamine is linked to pleasure, mood elevation, motivation, and happiness, while serotonin serves as a mood regulator. Endorphins contribute to feelings of happiness and well-being. Elevated dopamine and serotonin levels can help sustain motivation and propel individuals towards achieving their life goals. Exercise also has a remarkable effect on your happiness! It releases feel-good chemicals like endorphins and oxytocin in your brain, uplifting your mood and boosting your confidence. It dispels negative energy and offers wonderful relief from stress, helping to reduce anxiety and leaving you feeling more relaxed. Many find that exercise helps them sleep better at night, making those restful hours even more restorative. Furthermore, regular activity enhances your concentration and memory, making it easier to learn new things!

There is a famous quote: **'Exercise is the most underused antidepressant drug.'**

When exercising, make sure to allocate time for both aerobic and anaerobic activities.

Aerobic exercises can encompass a variety of activities, including brisk walking, jogging, running, cycling, rowing, climbing, swimming, and dancing, which can elevate your heart rate. Ensure your heart rate increases but remains within a safe range to avoid health disturbances. Choose activities you enjoy, from indoor treadmill walking, outdoor walking, gym workouts like cross trainers and high-intensity training. People prefer to do group activities with others, which motivates them to watch others do it. Therefore, they try to do activities like dancing Zumba, Taichi Pilates, etc. based on your preferences and convenience. If you are not a gym person, play your favourite games like badminton, volleyball, tennis, table tennis, etc. By incorporating these exercises into your routine, you can spend quality time focusing on your physical well-being. The Department of Health and Human Services recommends at least 150 minutes of moderate aerobic weekly exercise.

Many trainers recommend that incorporating both anaerobic and aerobic sessions into workouts can be beneficial. Additionally, it is helpful to stretch both before starting and at the end of the session to relax your muscles. If your goal is to build strength or muscle mass, starting with anaerobic exercises, such as weightlifting or high- intensity interval training is generally suggested. This gives you maximum energy and strength for these demanding activities, leading to better performance and results. If your goal is to improve cardiovascular endurance or lose weight, starting with aerobic exercises (like walking, running, cycling, or swimming) can be beneficial, especially if your primary aim is to burn calories or enhance endurance. Doing aerobic exercise first can help warm you up and elevate your heart rate. A balanced approach might be best. You could alternate between starting with aerobic and anaerobic exercises in different workouts to ensure you address all aspects of fitness. Ultimately, the best approach is the one that aligns with your specific goals and preferences.

Walking is a great form of exercise that helps you lose weight. When you walk briskly and take 5,000 to 10,000 steps a day, you also burn more calories. If you would like to adopt a more structured approach, step-counting apps and fitness apps can help motivate you. There are no specific guidelines for the number of steps, but the actual count really depends on your age, body mass index (BMI), and other health factors. "Start with 3,000 steps a day. Set small, realistic goals, such as adding an extra 500 steps a day, and build from there. It is considered one of the best exercises for maintaining cardiovascular fitness and lowering blood pressure. Additionally, walking benefits your mental health and serves as an effective mood booster. You can also burn fat and shed pounds by incline walking at a moderate speed on a treadmill for 30 minutes a day. Studies have shown that regular walking can lead to a longer lifespan, potentially adding up to eleven additional years to your life. Consistent walking routines decrease the risk of type 2 diabetes, heart diseases, and cancer.

Incorporate anaerobic exercises, including weightlifting and high-intensity workouts targeting large muscle groups such as the legs, glutes, back, abdomen, chest, biceps, triceps, deltoids, and latissimus dorsi. If you don't have equipment at home, consider simple bodyweight exercises like sit-ups, push- ups, pull-ups, squats, jumping jacks, lunges, squat variations, bench presses, and deadlifts. You can also integrate regular bodyweight exercises that don't require extensive equipment.

While these exercises may appear straightforward, focusing on proper techniques to prevent injuries is essential, and there are plenty of instructional videos online to guide you in teaching the correct methods. **Proper breathing technique is essential to maximise the benefits of physical activity and workouts.** Instructors commonly advise inhaling during the eccentric phase of a movement and exhaling during the concentric phase. This means that you should inhale or breathe in while lowering the weight, (towards gravity) allowing your body to take in air that will fuel your power output. Conversely, you should exhale or breathe out as you lift the weight, (away from gravity) as this requires more energy. For example, during push-ups, you inhale as you lower your body and exhale while pushing back up, since the latter requires more significant effort. Following proper breathing techniques can reduce fatigue and ensure your muscles receive an adequate oxygen supply.

Before and after exercising, perform stretching exercises to relax your muscles. Most muscles go into contraction mode following your exercises, and stretches help to relax them. There are plenty of videos available to learn stretching exercises, and yoga is one among those to stretch your body in a good way. Yoga is also beneficial for stretching and can be practised moderately.

'For me, exercise is more than just physical - it's therapeutic' - Former American First Lady Michelle Obama

Incorporate regular physical movement into your daily routine to prioritise staying active instead of leading a sedentary lifestyle by lounging on the couch. Engaging in physical activities throughout the day is essential for maintaining overall health. Moving more not only enhances blood circulation but also boosts energy levels. If space is limited, such as in a small apartment, consider integrating regular exercises and simple stretching routines into your daily life. **Sitting is often compared to modern smoking.** Individuals who spend prolonged hours seated in offices should try to take regular breaks and engage in stretching or simple exercises whenever possible in their workspace.

Regular exercise helps preserve muscle mass after the age of forty. Keeping muscle mass as we age is essential for maintaining agility. Therefore, prioritising protein intake and adhering to a consistent resistance training programme is vital. It is necessary to work out regularly. Regular exercise offers protection against cancer. When you exercise, you release natural killer cells. These cells also target tumour cells in the body, fragmenting and releasing them into the bloodstream.

Lack of exercise leads to the accumulation of visceral body fat mass (dangerous fat mass) and metabolic complications that affect the liver, heart, and lungs. For example, dangerous fat mass accumulation can affect the liver, causing fatty liver, which can lead to liver enlargement, followed by shrinkage and eventually liver failure.

The rule is straightforward: If you want to live longer, exercise daily and stay active. Obesity and a lack of exercise can significantly lead to various diseases, increasing the risk of mortality from multiple conditions. However, incorporating daily exercise into your routine aids your body in warding off various health conditions, such as diabetes, hypertension, high cholesterol, heart diseases, strokes, dementia and even some types of cancer. We all have a choice: to exercise or not. Being active can lead to transformative health benefits and a more fulfilling life. Incorporating proper techniques and controlled breathing into your fitness routine is essential for maximising the benefits of your workouts while minimising therisk of injury.

In the next chapter, I discuss diet and healthy eating, which are part of fitness.

Golden Nuggets

- Two essential elements of fitness are engaging in regular exercise or physical activities and maintaining a healthy, balanced diet in moderation.

- Strive to exercise regularly, ideally on most days of the week. Staying active each day will contribute to a longer life.

- Health experts suggest 150 minutes of moderate exercise each week, at least 30 minutes on five days.

- Engaging in physical activity four to five times a week throughout one's life is essential for maintaining optimal fitness and well-being.

- When exercising, allocate time for both aerobic and anaerobic activities. Stretching is helpful for relaxing muscles.

- Movement is crucial for health.

- Walking is an excellent form of exercise that aids in weight loss, is regarded as one of the best activities for maintaining cardiovascular fitness and benefits mental health.

- Regular exercise helps preserve muscle mass after the age of forty. Maintaining muscle mass as we age is essential for overall health agility.

Eating Healthy Food in Moderation is the Key

There is a helpful quote: **"You are what you eat."**

My friend Charlie went for a health check-up and came to me with his results for supportive counselling since I am his only doctor friend. He was upset that his cholesterol was high, particularly the bad cholesterol, and some of his liver tests were abnormal. His scan revealed a fatty liver. His doctor advised him to exercise regularly and eat healthier foods. He felt disheartened because he goes to the gym three times a week and still has a fatty liver. While discussing this with him, he realised he was active but was overeating and consuming many unhealthy foods. He is not alone; many of my clients and others experience similar results. Many people I know go to the gym and exercise to stay fit. However, when they have health check-ups, they may discover imbalanced sugar levels, high cholesterol, and deficiencies in vitamins and iron. This often occurs because they don't eat healthily. The key point is that fitness involves both exercise and diet, not exercise alone. **Eating healthy foods in moderation is as vital as doing regular workouts at the gym.** Fitness is like a coin with two sides: exercise and healthy eating. We discussed exercise in the last chapter. This chapter will explore the other side of the coin more deeply.

Food fuels the body. The dietary requirement for men is 3,000 kilocalories per day, while for women, it is 2,500 kilocalories. If you lead a sedentary lifestyle and exercise very little, approximately 2,000 calories should suffice. Remember this mantra: "Eat in moderation while prioritising healthy food choices".

Both the quality and quantity of the food we consume matter. Select healthy foods and eat in moderation, avoiding excess relative to weight and age. This approach is also a component of mindful eating, which was discussed in the chapter on mindfulness.

Choose healthy food options. It is essential to see food as nourishment for the body rather than just a source of pleasure or comfort. People engage in comfort eating, leading to a gain in weight and fat accumulation in the body. 'Food is the most abused anxiety drug. 'Many people, due to ignorance, tend to overeat from stress, anxiety, boredom, or cravings, which can develop into a form of addiction.

Our diets are generally recommended to include more fruits, vegetables, proteins, fibre, and natural foods as the main components. Vegetables and fruits are rich in fibre, which contributes to satiety. They provide a sense of fullness, meaning you don't tend to get hungry again soon after eating them.

Vegetables should primarily be consumed in steamed forms and not combined with unhealthy items. Vegetables provide the body with necessary fibre and nutrients. However, when vegetables are mixed with oil or deep-fried, they lose their nutritional value and become unhealthy. It is best to consume them in their raw or steamed forms. **Fruits should be consumed as fresh fruits or juices but not mixed with sugars.** Fresh fruits or fresh fruit juices are the ideal choice rather than mixing them with sugar, salt, flavourful ingredients, or adding colouring agents. Sugary drinks should also be avoided, as they can cause sugar spikes and crashes, which are detrimental to the body.

Protein sources include lean chicken, eggs, legumes, and pulses. After exercise, we need to consume more protein to build muscle, and increased muscle mass helps stabilise the various joints in our body. A higher protein intake is essential for maintaining muscle mass for those who exercise regularly.

Soluble fibre can be found in oats, barley, peas, beans, apples, carrots and citrus fruits like oranges and lemons. It slows digestion and can help reduce cholesterol and blood sugar levels. Additionally, consuming proteins and fibre can slow digestion, reducing the likelihood of frequent hunger pangs.

Conversely, limiting carbohydrates, fats, sugars, and salt is essential. Carbohydrates, sugars, and fats are digested quickly, leading to a rapid return to hunger. Junk food, unhealthy takeout, and processed or ultra-processed items are not advisable. Regularly consuming fried foods is dangerous. **"If you eat fried foods, you are dying"** because eating them daily can shorten your life. Sugary foods are often high in calories and can cause rapid spikes in blood sugar. However, they are also digested quickly, leading to faster feelings of hunger. It is best to limit their intake. **Avoid processed and highly refined foods such as pasta, white bread, and sugary cereals, as these typically contain high amounts of carbohydrates and saturated fats.** Sweets, savoury snacks, chips, chocolates, cakes, biscuits and ice cream are easily accessible, so it is advisable to resist these temptations. Enjoying these treats occasionally is reasonable, but try to limit consumption more frequently. Minimise the temptation to eat unhealthy foods and strive for balance in your diet.

Brian Tracy suggests avoiding three 'white poisons', (as mentioned in his book): **sugar, salt, and white flour.** Reducing sugars of all forms and sugar-rich products in our daily lives can significantly help with weight loss. Reducing salt intake is also crucial. Consuming more than necessary is easy with the excessive addition of salt in various foods. When the body retains excess salt, fluid retention can occur. **Limiting salt intake and ensuring adequate hydration by drinking 8 to 10 cups of water daily can help flush out excess fluids, making you feel lighte**r. You need water to burn fat, dehydration disrupts the body's ability to break down fat and convert it into fuel. It is also important to avoid white flour, as it lacks essential nutrients. Pastries, pasta, rice, bread, and rolls made from white flour are essentially nutrient-deficient, high-calorie foods. Therefore, opt for whole-grain alternatives for better nutritional value.

Eat slowly and mindfully. It takes about 15 to 20 minutes for your brain to register feelings of fullness. By eating slowly, you allow your brain to signal when you are satisfied, which reduces the chances of overeating. Strive to consume around 80% of your perceived capacity and stop when you feel full to prevent overindulgence. Research shows that people who eat quickly are four times more likely to develop metabolic syndrome, which affects vital organs such as the liver, heart, kidneys, brain, and lungs, compared to those who are slow eaters. Therefore, it is not just the amount that matters; it is also about how you eat. Slow and mindful eating promotes a healthy body and helps protect against metabolic syndrome, which includes issues like abdominal fat, fatty liver, insulin resistance, and various diseases. **Practice mindful eating by gradually incorporating nutritious foods into your diet**. Take time to plan your meals and set aside dedicated time for eating. Remember to eat slowly and chew your food thoroughly before swallowing. In addition, to relishing the taste, smell, and texture of food, also spend some time planning your meal as part of a mindful eating strategy.

Additional Hacks for Developing Healthy Eating Habits

- Choose smaller plates to avoid overeating and better manage portion sizes.

- When planning your meal, prioritise vegetables, fruits, lean proteins, and finally carbohydrates and fats. Aim for at least 50% of your meal to include fruits, vegetables, and lean proteins for a well-balanced diet.

- Hydrate properly by drinking a small glass of water before your meal, another during the meal, and a final glass afterwards. Adequate hydration aids digestion and promotes a sense of fullness throughout the meal. Aim for plenty of water—at least 8 to 10 cups daily, each measuring 150-200 ml. Drinking plenty of water throughout the day is crucial, as dehydration can negatively impact brain function, leading to problems with attention and memory.

- **Enjoy a variety of foods in moderation and savour them.** Consume healthy foods mindfully, avoiding excessive amounts of any single item. You don't have to eliminate anything unless required by specific diets for diabetes, high blood pressure, high cholesterol, kidney disease etc . Embrace portion control and savour each bite. Instead of restricting certain foods, concentrate on consuming everything in moderation to maintain a balanced and healthy lifestyle.

- Maintain your energy levels by eating regularly, with small and frequent meals, while minimising snacks between meals. Aim for 4 to 6 small meals each day. Choosing frequent small meals can help regulate appetite and metabolism, providing a steady source of energy.

- **Most dietitians recommend eating a lighter meal before going to bed.** Choose lighter, healthier meal options instead of heavier ones, and ideally, eat your last meal at least three to four hours before bedtime to prevent digestive discomfort.

- Unhealthy snacking can result in weight gain and decreased cognitive function. When choosing healthy snacks, prioritise fresh fruits and vegetables, seeds, and nuts over fruit juices with added sugars.

There is a saying, **"You cannot outrun a bad diet."** Eating healthy and nutritious food is essential for ensuring good nutrition, as healthy food provides energy for the body.

One key to longevity is eating in moderation—consuming slightly less than what is truly required—while also increasing your physical activity through regular exercise. Eating in moderation helps you avoid excessive fullness or discomfort. I like this simple quote: **'Zip your lips and move your hips,'** which sums up everything. There is a saying that too much of anything is good for nothing, and this statement underscores the importance of moderation. Eating in moderation is essential; consuming too much can disrupt the balance in our lives. Without balance, we may struggle to achieve our fitness goals. Therefore, practising moderation in eating is crucial. This key advice is something everyone should strive to follow.

Maintaining a balanced diet is a rewarding journey that requires self-discipline and the ability to resist tempting treats. It can be challenging to decline biscuits, chocolates, ice cream, fries, and similar snacks—especially since they often beckon from our fridges! Resisting these cravings resembles the effort needed to complete a workout at the gym. By embracing exercise and mindful eating, you prioritise your long-term well- being over short-term indulgences. However, with time and perseverance, you will begin to savour the sweet rewards of success. Once you experience this achievement, you will find that this positive trait can permeate other areas of your life, allowing you to focus on what truly matters while enjoying a sense of balance.

Golden Nuggets

- Two essential elements of fitness are engaging in regular exercise or physical activities and maintaining a healthy, balanced diet in moderation.

- In terms of diet, it is generally recommended to include more fruits, vegetables, proteins, fibre, and natural foods as their main components.

- Both vegetables and fruits promote a sense of satiety, meaning you will feel full for longer periods.

- It is essential to limit carbohydrates, fats, sugars, and salt. Reduce the temptation to indulge in unhealthy foods and strive for balance in your diet.

- Reducing carbohydrate intake and steering clear of processed and junk foods is wise, as these can lead to mental fog.

- Sugary drinks should also be avoided as they can lead to sugar spikes and crashes that are harmful to the body.

- Unhealthy snacking can result in weight gain and reduced cognitive function.

- Drinking plenty of water throughout the day is essential, as dehydration can negatively affect brain function, leading to issues with attention and memory.

- One key to longevity is to eat in moderation—consuming just a bit less than necessary—while increasing physical activity through regular exercise.

- By embracing exercise and mindful eating, you prioritise your long-term well-being over short-term pleasures for immediate gratification.

Identifying Stress and Understanding Stress Response

'Every day brings a choice -
To practice stress or to practice peace'
— Dr Joan Borysenko,
distinguished pioneer in integrative medicine

Stress is a reaction of the mind and body to overload, disrupting the system's balance and inducing emotional and mental strain. There are two types of stress: good stress and bad stress. We all require a certain amount of good stress (also called eustress to enhance performance and boost productivity. Being completely stress-free is unrealistic and not a part of life. Instead of trying to eliminate all stress, it is essential to learn how to harness good stress to enhance productivity. However, it is equally important to manage negative stress (distress. Chronic negative stress can lead to burnout and significantly impact our mental and physical health. When people struggle to cope with negative stress, they may resort to harmful behaviours such as smoking, excessive alcohol consumption, recreational drug use, overeating unhealthy foods, and spending countless hours scrolling through social media. Understanding the distinction between good and bad stress, along with managing both effectively, is crucial for maintaining overall well-being.

Self-improvement always begins with self-awareness. Recognising the types of stress and their symptoms is essential.

There are four primary types of stress that must be recognised and identified. **The first type is major crises and catastrophes**, which occur entirely beyond our control. Examples include natural disasters, floods, droughts, major accidents, and fires. **The second important type involves significant life events**. This category encompasses experiences such as major separations, loss, death, job loss, illness, divorce, relocating, and retirement.

The third category includes daily hassles, commonly referred to as micro-stressors. These consist of difficulties meeting important deadlines, challenges in decision-making, strained relationships, and conflicts with colleagues. Daily hassles significantly contribute to the stress we encounter in life. Often, combining these micro-stressors intensifies the pressure on our minds, resulting in increased stress levels and, ultimately, mental fatigue. **The final type involves ambient stressors**, such as traffic, noise, various forms of pollution, and other environmental factors. Understanding these stressors and their impact on our overall stress levels is essential.

Beyond external factors, stress can also arise from negative cognitions or thoughts that lead to overthinking. The heaviest burden we bear is our negative thoughts, which can increase our stress levels. This type of negative thinking may result in cognitive errors (thinking e rrors, w hich I h ave previously discussed in earlier chapters.

Everyone should be able to recognise the symptoms of stress. I distributed a questionnaire in a recent workshop with 100 participants to help them identify these symptoms. I found that only 10% of the attendees could recognise the symptoms of stress; the others thought these symptoms were normal.

Stress symptoms can be categorised into four types: emotional, cognitive, physical and behavioural.

1. **Emotional Symptoms**: These include feelings of anger, irritability, anxious thoughts, excessive worry, negative thoughts, and fear. When these emotional symptoms persist, they can undermine confidence and potentially result in depression.

2. **Cognitive Symptoms**: Individuals may struggle to concentrate on their work and may have difficulty making both important

and trivial decisions. Additionally, repetitive or circular thoughts can exacerbate confusion.

3. **Physical Symptoms:** Physical manifestations of stress may include excessive sweating, tremors, dry mouth, increased heart rate, chest tightness, and difficulty breathing. Chronic stress can also result in persistent aches and pains, muscle tension, and headaches that do not respond to pain relief medications.

4. **Behavioural Symptoms:** Stress can also lead to changes in behaviour, such as overeating or undereating, sleeping too much or too little, and excessive consumption of coffee, tea, or alcohol. Additionally, smoking and using recreational drugs to relax may increase. Some individuals may isolate themselves, neglect their responsibilities, and develop procrastination habits. Moreover, nervous habits like nail-biting and pacing may become more noticeable.

If these symptoms are left untreated, they can escalate into anxiety and depression, potentially developing into anxiety disorders and depressive disorders that require professional intervention. Therefore, recognising symptoms of stress early allows us to take steps, develop strategies to manage them, and ultimately enhance our mental well-being.

When we become stressed, **our bodies enter a fight- or-flight response** that releases various chemicals, hormones, and neurotransmitters. This normal reaction to a perceived threat impacts our survival. In ancient times, when humans lived in forests, they faced numerous dangers and had to either confront (fight) or flee from them (flight). During this response, individuals experience increased heart rate, excessive sweating, shakiness, anxiety, fearful thoughts, and elevated blood glucose levels. While the fight-or-flight response can be beneficial in emergencies, modern life exposes people to frequent stressors. This leads individuals to enter fight-or-flight mode more often and for longer durations.

Such chronic activation causes the release of various chemicals that can harm the body. For example, the hormones adrenaline and noradrenaline increase heart rate and blood pressure, which can last longer and can be raised frequently. Blood sugar levels remain elevated as the liver releases stored glucose into the bloodstream. The adrenal glands, situated atop the kidneys, produce cortisol, a crucial stress hormone that elevates blood glucose levels while inhibiting non-essential functions such as digestion and immune responses. Chronic stress results in prolonged high levels of cortisol, which can suppress the immune system and make the body more vulnerable to various illnesses.

Cortisol can also enhance appetite, leading to weight gain and heightening cravings for sweet, salty, and fatty foods. Prolonged stress results in the persistent release of cortisol, which can impact the quality of our sleep. Due to fluctuations in levels of neurotransmitters such as serotonin, dopamine, and GABA, persistent stress can lead to mood changes and anxiety.

While some of these physiological changes are vital for immediate survival, they can have detrimental long-term health effects if the stress response is activated frequently or persists for extended periods. This can lead to cardiovascular problems affecting the heart, metabolic disorders like diabetes, weight gain, and mental health issues such as anxiety and depression.

Therefore, **it is crucial to learn stress management strategies** to minimise the effects of the fight-or-flight response and help maintain a more relaxed state rather than being constantly on alert. The next chapter will discuss this topic further.

Golden Nuggets

- Stress is a response of the mind and body to overload. It disrupts the system's balance and induces emotional and mental strain.

- There are four primary types of stress that must be recognised: major crises and catastrophes, significant life events, daily hassles (commonly referred to as micro- stressors), and ambient stressors.

- Daily hassles play a significant role in the stress we face

- in life.

- Understanding these stressors and their effects on our overall stress levels is crucial.

- Everyone should be aware of the symptoms of stress.

- Stress symptoms can be categorised into four types: emotional, cognitive, physical, and behavioural.

- When we become stressed, our bodies enter a fight-or-flight response, releasing various chemicals, hormones, and neurotransmitters.

- While some physiological changes during the stress response are vital for immediate survival, if the stress response is activated frequently or persists for extended periods, it can have detrimental long-term health effects.

Strategies for Managing Stress and Achieving Wellness

**"Stress Management is not an Event,
it is a Life-Long Process"**
– Beverly Buermann King, Wellness strategist

People often ask me how to remove stress from their lives. While nobody can eliminate stress, we can strive to minimise it and take measures to lessen its impact on our physical, mental, and overall functioning. These are simple to follow yet effective.

- Ensure adequate sleep for at least 8 hours (covered in the previous chapters).

- Rest and take regular breaks during work. Weekend breaks and regular holidays are important (they were covered in the previous chapters).

- Proper "ME time" daily is crucial (as discussed in previous chapters). Our well-being should be our priority.

- Incorporate mindfulness into all daily activities (discussed in previous chapters).

- Time Management: Effectively Manage Your Time. Prioritise your tasks and tackle the most important ones first.(discussed in previous chapters).

- Adapting to change helps to make progress (as discussed in the previous chapters).

- **Stress Diary**. Keeping a stress diary is an effective stress management tool, as it helps you become more aware of the situations that cause you stress. Record the date, time, and place of each stressful episode, along with what you were doing, who you were with, and how you felt physically and emotionally. Assign each stressful episode a stress rating on a scale of 1 to 10, and use the diary to understand your stress triggers and your effectiveness in stressful situations. This will enable you to avoid stress-inducing scenarios and develop better coping mechanisms.

- **Try relaxation tools like deep breathing, meditation, and yoga which are helpful.** Deep breathing: Take a moment to breathe. Inhale for 3-4 seconds through your nose, hold your breath for 1-2 seconds, and exhale through your mouth for 3-4 seconds. Focus solely on your breathing, as this helps distract you from the situation. Taking a few deep breaths can be very helpful for effectively facing most stressful situations and can provide immediate relief, so be sure to practice it regularly. You connect with the present moment when you quietly observe your breath. Our breath exists in the present; by observing it, you align yourself with now. While we often spend significant time beautifying the external world, we may overlook the importance of nurturing our internal world. Mindful breathing enhances breath awareness. By focusing on your inhales and exhales, you anchor your mind and prevent it from jumping from one thought to another, as if experiencing a 'monkey mind.' Establishing a regular breathing routine can be incredibly beneficial for organising your thoughts, reducing stress, and promoting relaxation.

- Consider purchasing and **using a stress ball**; it encourages you to squeeze and release, leaving you feeling less tense than when you started. Learning how to relax when facing stressful situations and to remain calm and composed is crucial. When you become excessively stressed, even minor problems can feel overwhelming. You have even more reasons to be ineffective when you are stressed and tense. Therefore, take the time to help your body relax in your tasks. By maintaining a relaxed mindset, you can navigate challenges more effectively. This approach is vital as it prevents you from feeling overwhelmed and allows you to emerge from difficulties successfully.

- **Engage in enjoyable activities daily** to reduce stress. Participating in at least one pleasurable activity daily can lift your spirits! Engaging in activities that bring you intrinsic pleasure is a beautiful way to boost your mood and reduce your stress (I have discussed it in ME time).

- **Establish a Routine**—Having a Structured Day with designated times for sleep, work, travel, rest, family, and social activities is essential. Avoid significantly disturbing this schedule, as maintaining equilibrium and stability for both body and mind is crucial. When your body and mind are in harmony, all chemicals and hormones can function effectively together. A disciplined routine and regular daily activities are vital for stabilising your biological clock and sustaining balance in both your mind and body.

- **Stay organised**—It is essential to stay organised. Many micro-stressors, such as meeting deadlines, achieving small targets, daily hassles, and challenges in simple decision-making discussed in previous chapters, can be managed effectively if you remain organised. You can maintain a balanced workflow by setting aside dedicated blocks of time for focused work, breaks, and personal activities. Many individuals waste time looking for their phones, glasses, keys, or even essential files and folders on their computers; all of these are micro-stressors that trigger the stress response. Being organised can save a significant amount of time, whereas disorganisation can prolong the completion of your tasks and drain your energy as you search for misplaced items.

- **Establishing healthy boundaries in your life is vital.** Sometimes, this involves politely and gently saying no to requests or obligations that you can't commit to. If someone asks you to take on additional commitments beyond your current schedule, remind yourself that your time is valuable, too! Your personal time truly matters! Learning to say no can feel intimidating at first, but it is a skill that yields benefits in the long run. A practical tip is to block off time on your calendar just for yourself. There is no need to provide detailed explanations—let them know you have other commitments. Your priorities deserve that special attention! Remember, by setting boundaries, gracefully saying no, and reserving time on your calendar, you are taking necessary steps to nurture yourself. People often experience stress because they struggle to decline such demands. It is crucial not to take on additional projects, especially when overwhelmed, as this can increase stress. There's a saying: **"Don't bite off more than you can chew."** Unfortunately, many individuals fall into the trap of accepting tasks from others to please them, even when they are already struggling. In doing so, they often sacrifice their happiness and well-being. As motivational speaker Josh Billings wisely stated, **"Half of the troubles of this life can be traced to saying 'yes' too quickly and not saying 'no' soon enough."** Therefore, it is essential to think carefully before agreeing to new commitments. If necessary, don't hesitate to decline; prioritising your peace and happiness is essential. I aim to emphasise the importance of assertiveness in declining requests. Learn to say no with confidence. Some people resort to lying instead of providing a clear response—try to avoid that. Don't feel obligated to make excuses or explain yourself extensively if you cannot fulfil a request; a simple "no" suffices. If you want to be more polite, you can offer to help later.

- **Learning to delegate tasks to others is an invaluable skill to develop!** It doesn't matter how many resources you have; if you don't know how to use them, they will never be enough. Delegating the right tasks to the right person and utilizing existing resources can help reduce stress levels significantly. I often assign responsibilities to various helpful individuals, including my spouse, children, household helpers, handymen, assistants, and anyone else who can contribute. Before I delegate a task, I always consider whether the person can successfully take it on. If everything aligns, I happily entrust the assignment to them instead of shouldering it alone. This strategy not only lightens my workload and helps me avoid procrastination but also empowers others by giving them meaningful responsibilities. Thus, honing the skill of task delegation is truly essential! Identify which tasks you need to complete personally, and which can be delegated to others. Some tasks can be entirely removed from your list through delegation. Learning to delegate and seek assistance is beneficial. For instance, despite my interest in gardening, I delegate tasks like garden maintenance and watering my plants to a professional gardener. By entrusting these recurring tasks, I save a significant amount of time. Similarly, I have someone responsible for cleaning my cars weekly and a helper who irons my shirts. I also have an assistant who types my letters, including medical certificates and patient summary letters. All these small additional helpers allow me to focus on more important tasks and responsibilities.

- **Talking about and sharing your problems** can reduce stress levels. Spend time with others and discuss how you feel. Share your thoughts and feelings with those who are close to you. Allow your family and friends to help; they may offer the companionship, affection, encouragement, and support you need. Discussing and sharing your problems is indeed a vital aspect of emotional health and well-being. Expressing your feelings can provide immediate relief; while bottling up emotions often leads to increased stress and anxiety. Engaging in conversation helps release pent-up emotions, making it easier to cope. Moreover, sharing your problems can help you feel validated. When others acknowledge your feelings and experiences, it reinforces the idea that what you are going through is real and important. When you share your problems with others, you gain new perspectives. Your close friends, family, or professionals may offer insights or solutions that you had not considered, helping you see your situation in a different light. Discussing your struggles can also strengthen relationships by fostering intimacy and trust. It reminds us that we are not alone in our emotional experiences. Talking about your problems can lead to receiving support from others, whether it is emotional support, practical advice, or simply companionship. Having someone to lean on can make a significant difference, and you won't feel alone or isolated. Sometimes, discussing problems with others can lead to collaborative problem-solving. They may help you brainstorm solutions or strategies to cope with your issues, making challenges feel more manageable. Ultimately, talking and sharing your problems is not just beneficial; it is essential for maintaining mental and emotional health. Reaching out is more helpful than facing challenges alone, and it significantly aids in coping with stressful situations.

Ensure you experience stress only when necessary, particularly regarding the most critical aspects of your life. Avoid worrying about trivial matters and strive to release everything else. Once you learn to let go of less significant issues, your overall stress will diminish, allowing you to enjoy life more. On the other hand, major unexpected catastrophes and natural disasters can happen to anyone in this world. If they occur, see if you can do something about it. If you can't, then you just must wait and watch. In such situations, you can divert your mind or try to stay detached from the unpleasant circumstances. These are the only options to cope with it. Getting stressed about it repeatedly will not make you feel any better.

"Worrying is like paying a debt you don't owe" – American writer and humourist Mark Twain. Worrying often consumes our mental and emotional energy, much like paying a debt we do not owe. Worrying and overthinking can lead to significant levels of stress and anxiety, negatively impacting our mental well-being. By recognising unfounded worries and by breaking the habit of overthinking, we can free ourselves and embrace a more peaceful, present-minded existence.

- **Keep smiling and laughing;** it is essential to smile, and doing so also fosters self-improvement. Your self- confidence, combined with a smile, creates a positive aura that attracts others. Similarly, laughing is equally important. Laugh often, as it helps relieve stress. While laughing, you exhale deeply, which calms the mind and reduces stress. My wife Mythili enjoys watching comedies for 20 to 30 minutes each night and laughs heartily. I have adopted this habit as well. Aim to laugh daily, whether by watching or reading something that brings joy.

  Stay confident and positive. The most beautiful thing you can wear is confidence. Confidence is a powerful tool that can transform our self-perception and how others perceive us. It acts like a magnetic force, attracting people and creating opportunities that might have otherwise gone unnoticed. When we carry ourselves with confidence, we project an aura of positivity and self-assuredness that inspires trust and admiration. By wearing confidence like a beautiful garment, we not only enrich our own lives but also uplift those around us, encouraging them to embrace their strengths and shine brightly.

- "Life presents problems one after another, much like waves crashing endlessly on the shore. By learning to manage stress, relax, and go with the flow, you can navigate these difficulties and confront the waves without succumbing to them. If you resist and battle against these problems without a clear strategy, you risk being overwhelmed and eventually drowning." As I mentioned in the book's first chapter, problems are a part of life. In the 2nd last chapter, I emphasised that stress is an integral part of our lives. We should learn to identify and effectively tackle stressors by using effective stress management strategies.

Golden Nuggets

- You cannot eliminate stress, but you should aim to reduce its impact on your life and well-being.

- Maintaining a stress diary is an effective tool for managing stress. It increases one's awareness of the situations that trigger anxiety and stress.

- Consider using beneficial relaxation tools such as deep breathing, meditation, and yoga. Learn to help your body relax during any task, ensuring you remain calm and composed.

- Creating a breathing routine can help clear your thoughts, alleviate stress, and foster a sense of relaxation.

- Participate in enjoyable activities each day to alleviate stress. Engaging in at least one pleasurable activity daily can significantly uplift your mood.

- Establish a routine and maintain a structured day. Avoid significantly disrupting this schedule, as upholding stability for both body and mind is crucial.

- Decline requests or obligations that you cannot commit to. Many individuals experience stress because they struggle to say no when faced with such demands.

- Delegating tasks effectively is a valuable skill that facilitates assigning responsibilities to capable individuals.

Moderation in All Things and Maintaining a Balanced Approach

"Never get so busy making a living that you forget to make a life"
– Dolly Parton, American pop singer and philanthropist

A healthy work-life balance establishes an equilibrium between personal and professional responsibilities. It involves positively managing your time, energy, and focus, allowing you to perform well at work and in your personal life. In the current landscape, a balanced approach to work and life has become more essential than ever. A healthy work-life balance also contributes to a healthy lifestyle, enhances productivity, and improves individual well-being. When someone is said to have a healthy work-life balance, they have successfully allocated equal time to both personal and professional activities without feeling overwhelmed, stressed, or overburdened. Gaining knowledge is essential for achieving this equilibrium between personal and professional lives.

Proper planning and a precise daily schedule that includes work, leisure activities, fitness, family time, and social engagements is essential. At work, establish firm boundaries and strive to start and finish on time. Utilise technology through various programmes and applications that block distracting websites during the workday and restrict access to work-related tools after hours. Create a designated quiet space for work; a calm environment with minimal disruptions can enhance your team's productivity. You may excuse yourself from specific meetings and opt to attend some via phone or video calls instead of going in person.

At home, your personal time and family should be your priority. Maintain these boundaries by turning off work-related devices, office files, and documents, while also avoiding engaging in post-work tasks. Communicate that you will not be available for work-related meetings or responsibilities after hours. Consider using separate devices, such as a different phone or laptop for work, to ensure complete disengagement during non-working hours. Additionally, working from home a few days a week can reduce commuting time. To save time, consider doing personal shopping more frequently online. Ensure that you take regular time off from work and use your leave effectively, including sick leave and personal leave. Plan regular holidays and take proper breaks to recharge. Regularly reassess your work to identify moments of accomplishment and satisfaction. All these simple strategies can help maintain a healthy work-life balance.

Mastering the art of balance in life is essential for leading a happy and successful life. Finding balance involves nurturing the many wonderful aspects of life, such as work, relationships, health, and leisure, ensuring that each receives the love and attention it deserves. Please take a moment to reflect on what truly matters to you and gently dedicate your time and energy to where it is needed most. To achieve this, let's examine different types of time and see how we can incorporate them into your daily balance sheet. We all have 24 hours; divide them into three components of eight hours, and let's make full use of that time while reviewing the balance sheet regularly.

The first component of 8 hours of our balance sheet

Work Time refers to the primary period dedicated to productivity, encompassing the hours spent working, studying, or engaging in productive activities. This work time is not limited to those who work outside the home; it also includes homemakers who manage a household, perform housework, and care for children, rather than being employed outside. Goal-seeking time emphasises priorities and achievements, which are essential for advancing one's goals and fostering accomplishments in life.

The second component of 8 hours on our balance sheet

Sleeping time is the time for rest. Adequate sleep provides essential mental and physical recuperation and should never be compromised. The mind and body require sufficient rest and sleep each day to rejuvenate for the next.

The third component of 8 hours on our balance sheet

Creativity Time involves learning new things, generating innovative ideas, and exploring various activities. It is essential for personal development, self-improvement, and nurturing creativity.

Relaxing time includes leisure and enjoyable activities that bring pleasure.

Family Time is exclusively reserved for close family members, including partners, spouses, children, siblings, parents, and other relatives. It brings genuine joy and happiness and yields greater rewards for the family.

Socialising time involves conversing and meeting people in person or through social media. Humans are inherently social beings, and dedicating time to connect with others benefits emotional well-being.

Look at your life's balance sheet and make the best use of 24 hours a day.

Have you heard of the 8+8+8 rule? (Adapted from Elevate Your Life. Distribute your 24 hours into three eight-hour segments to make a good balance sheet of your life.

- 8 hours should be spent on hard work (work time, goal-seeking).
- 8 hours should be spent on good sleep and rest (sleeping time).

- 8 hours should be spent on your personal activities, such as creativity, relaxation, and socialising with family and friends. This includes spending quality time with loved ones, nurturing relationships, engaging in enjoyable activities, pursuing physical activities, enjoying leisure pursuits, exploring hobbies, learning new things, and discovering new interests.

Just remember, your balance sheet can adapt as life unfolds! Work deadlines and family needs might shift your priorities, and it is completely normal if the time you allocate to each component varies a bit. That's all part of the journey!

Doing everything in moderation can help achieve balance in life and enhance the art of living. Practice moderation, and you will be in good shape. For example, life revolves around balancing what we eat, what we say, what we read, how we distract ourselves, how much we work, how we spend our money, and how we manage our relationships. Don't overthink, don't stress too much, and don't overeat. Moderation is key. A Mongolian saying states, **"The first glass is for the guest, the second for enjoyment, and the third for chaos**," underscoring the importance of moderation.

People often ask questions such as how much to eat, how much to exercise, how much time to spend on my phone, how much leisure time is appropriate, how much money to spend, how much sleep I need, how much rest is necessary, and how much time to dedicate to relationships. There is no specific answer to these questions. **It is all about finding the right balance in whatever you do.** If you maintain that balance and equilibrium, you can enjoy life's journey and master this art. Practising the principle of moderation invites us to embrace the wonderful value of balance in our lives. It gently encourages us to be thoughtful about what we consume, the activities we engage in, and the choices we make, highlighting the significance of quality over quantity. For example, by embracing moderation in eating habits, instead of following strict diets, you can enjoy a delightful variety of nutrients while savouring balanced meals. This approach allows you the freedom to indulge every now and then, without guilt creeping in. Similarly, embracing moderation in the use of screen time and adopting a mindful approach to digital media helps create a healthy balance between screen time and the meaningful, real-life interactions that bring us joy. The same principle applies to all other areas and habits too. Practising moderation boosts our physical and mental health and helps reduce the risk of burnout, stress, and lifestyle-related issues. Enjoying things in moderation often leads to greater satisfaction and appreciation for experiences rather than taking them for granted.

> **"Life is really simple,**
> **but we insist on making it complicated."**
> – Chinese philosopher Confucius

To maintain simplicity, we should aim for balance in all areas of life. We must learn to balance our health, family, friendships, relationships, business, career, personal growth, enjoyment, recreation, and physical environment. This is one of the most challenging skills to develop, but once learned and practised, it allows us to navigate life effectively and achieve remarkable success and happiness. Unfortunately, few people truly master this art; some discover it much later in life when it is too late. It should be cultivated from a young age and nurtured as we move through different phases of life.

Remember that happiness comes from within! Take a moment to savour every beautiful moment that life offers and make the most of it. **Success is a subjective interpretation and varies from person to person.** It is important to celebrate those small wins along the way and not focus solely on the big milestones. **Enjoy life!**

Golden Nuggets

- A healthy work-life balance establishes an equilibrium between personal and professional responsibilities.

- Distribute your 24 hours into three eight-hour segments to create a balanced overview of your life.

- Please keep your life simple. Practice moderation, and you will be in good shape.

- Moderation is the key. It is all about finding the right balance in everything you do.

- Practising moderation and mastering the art of balance are essential principles that foster well-being, sustainability, and fulfilment in various aspects of life.

References

Books

- Get Organised: Do more in less time- Clara Conlon
- 30 days; Change your habits change your life- Marc Reklau
- S.U.M.O-Shut up, move on- Paul Mc Gee.
- The art of happiness-Dalai Lama
- The Golden rules of success-Napoleon Hill.
- Looking at life differently- Swami Sukhabodhananda.
- The Power of Self-discipline- Brain Tracy
- 21 Ways of being happy by Shama Patel.
- How to talk to anybody, anytime, anywhere- Chris Widener
- Atomic Habits- James Claire
- 11 rules of life-Chetan Bhagat
- Habits of a happy brain- Loreta Grazano Brunning.
- The Power- Rhonda Bryne
- Chanakya in you-Radhakrishnan Pillai
- Think like a monk- Jay Shetty
- Ikigai- Hector Gracia and Francesc Miralles
- Change your thinking with CBT- Sarah Edelman
- Mindfulness on the run- Chantal Hofstee
- Cognitive behavioural therapy- Aaron Beck

- Master your Mind, The Mental health Guide, Neel Burton
- Feeling Good Handbook, D Burns 1989, Morrow: New York.
- Who will cry when you die- Robin Sharma
- Practical Meditation-Sterling ethos
- How to stop worrying and start living- Dale Carnegie
- The Art of happiness- Dalai Lama and Howard c Cutler
- The Rules of life-Richard Templar
- Life's amazing secrets- Gaur Gopal Das
- Before the Coffee Gets Cold- 2015 novel by ToshiKazu Kawaguchi
- Finding Work-life Balance- Christine Carter
- Mindfulness and mindset podcast- Alok Taunk
- It all adds up: designing your game plan for financial success" by Devon Kennard.

References

- Cardinali DP, Pévet P. Basic aspects of melatonin action. Sleep Med Rev. 1998 Aug;2(3):175-90. doi: 10.1016/ s1087-0792(98)90020-x. PMID: 15310500.

- Do New Forms of Reading Pay Off? A Meta-Analysis on the Relationship Between Leisure Digital Reading Habits and Text Comprehension. Review of Educational Research, 0(0). https://doi.org/10.3102/00346543231216463) Ref; Altamura, L., Vargas, C., & Salmerón, L. (2023).

- Chang YH, Wu IC, Hsiung CA. Reading activity prevents long-term decline in cognitive function in older people: evidence from a 14-year longitudinal study. Int Psychogeriatr. 2021 Jan;33(1):63-74. doi: 10.1017/ S1041610220000812. Epub 2020 Jun 5. PMID: 32498728; PMCID: PMC8482376.

- Altamura, L., Vargas, C., & Salmerón, L. (2023). Do New Forms of Reading Pay Off? A Meta-Analysis on the

- Relationship Between Leisure Digital Reading Habits and Text Comprehension. Review of Educational Research, 0(0). https://doi.org/10.3102/00346543231216463)

- Julio Rodriguez-Larios, Eduardo A. Bracho Montes de Oca, Kaat Alaerts, The EEG spectral properties of meditation and mind wandering differ between experienced meditators and novices,

- https://psychcentral.com/health/meditation-brain- waves

- Tang R, Friston KJ, Tang YY. Brief Mindfulness Meditation Induces Gray Matter Changes in a Brain Hub. Neural Plast. 2020 Nov 16;2020:8830005. doi: 10.1155/2020/8830005. PMID: 33299395; PMCID: PMC7704181.

- Lahtinen, O., Salmivalli, C. The relationship between mindfulness meditation and well-being during 8 weeks of ecological momentary assessment. *Mindfulness* 11,

- 255–263 (2020).

- Dobrakowski P, Blaszkiewicz M, Skalski S. Changes in the Electrical Activity of the Brain in the Alpha and Theta Bands during Prayer and Meditation. Int J Environ Res Public Health. 2020 Dec 21;17(24):9567. doi: 10.3390/ ijerph17249567. PMID: 33371283; PMCID: PMC7766487.

- Fogg, B.J. (2019). *Tiny Habits: The Small Changes That Change Everything.* Houghton Mifflin Harcourt.

Websites

- https://www.hrkatha.com/research/92-indian-professionals-feel-meditation-can-reduce-stress-study/

- https://news.harvard.edu/gazette/story/2018/04/harvard-researchers-study-how-mindfulness-may-change-the-brain-in-depressed-patients/

- https://www.technogym.com/hk/newsroom/every-hour-exercise-three-hours-life/#:~:text=The%20Harvard%20

Alumni%20Study%20suggests,2%20whole%20years%20of%20life.

- https://www.health.harvard.edu/blog/regular-exercise-changes-brain-improve-memory-thinking-skills-201404097110

- https://datareportal.com/reports/digital-2024-deep-dive-the-time-we-spend-on-social-media

- https://addyo.substack.com/p/it-takes-23-mins-to-recover-after

- https://mindfulpractices.us/2020/06/16/prioritizing-your-life-rocks-pebbles-sand/

- https://www.youtube.com/watch?v=4HMsk_0AG8w

- https://medium.com/we-talk-it/apply-the-8-8-8-rule-for-living-a-balanced-life-df62426752b7

- https://www.christinecarter.com/2017/01/positive-and-negative-emotions/

- https://jareddees.com/fish-story-soul/

About Me

- Dr M. Sree Prathap is a Senior Consultant Psychiatrist and the Founder and Chairman of Shadithya Hospital, a tertiary care facility specialising in psychiatric care. This 200-bed hospital is based in Chennai, India (www. shadithyahospital.com). He provides care and treatment for individuals with severe mental health issues, addictions, and dementia and has treated more than 10,000 patients so far.

- He is a successful entrepreneur who has been running a revision course for the MRCPsych in the UK for 20 years. He is the Founder and Director of the SPMM course for the MRCPsych in the UK (http://spmmcourse.com).

- His special interest is raising public and professional awareness of mental health. For the last five years, he has run a famous YouTube channel called "Psychiatrist Prathap" and posted many educational videos on wellness on his Instagram.

- He is a gold medallist in psychiatry and received the Pfizer award for the best outgoing student in his final year at medical college.

Contact me on

drsreeprathap@hotmail.com

drsreeprathap@gmail.com

Instagram - dr. sreeprathap_psychiatrist

YouTube -
www.youtube.com/@psychiatristprathap6489

Facebook -
https://www.facebook.com/sreeprathap.mohanamurthy

LinkedIn -
www.linkedin.com/in/sree-prathap-mohana-murthy-62834415

Quora -
https://www.quora.com/profile/Sree-Prathap-Mohana-Murthy
Twitter/X-@Sreprathap

website ID -
www.psychiatristprathap.com